Islam, Justice, and Democracy

In the series
Religious Engagement in Democratic Politics,
edited by Paul A. Djupe

ALSO IN THIS SERIES:

Luis Felipe Mantilla, *How Political Parties Mobilize Religion: Lessons from Mexico and Turkey*

Jeremiah J. Castle, *Rock of Ages: Subcultural Religious Identity and Public Opinion among Young Evangelicals*

Brian R. Calfano and Nazita Lajevardi, ed., *Understanding Muslim Political Life in America: Contested Citizenship in the Twenty-First Century*

Jeanine Kraybill, *One Faith, Two Authorities: Tension between Female Religious and Male Clergy in the American Catholic Church*

Paul A. Djupe and Ryan L. Claassen, ed., *The Evangelical Crackup? The Future of the Evangelical-Republican Coalition*

Islam, Justice, and Democracy

SABRI CIFTCI

TEMPLE UNIVERSITY PRESS
Philadelphia • Rome • Tokyo

TEMPLE UNIVERSITY PRESS
Philadelphia, Pennsylvania 19122
tupress.temple.edu

Copyright © 2022 by Temple University—Of The Commonwealth System of Higher Education
All rights reserved
Published 2022

Library of Congress Cataloging-in-Publication Data

Names: Çiftçi, Sabri, author.
Title: Islam, justice, and democracy / Sabri Ciftci.
Other titles: Religious engagement in democratic politics.
Description: Philadelphia : Temple University Press, 2022. | Series: Religious engagement in democratic politics | Includes bibliographical references and index. | Summary: "Explores Islam and democracy through historical and empirical treatments of Muslim political attitudes and conceptions of justice, focusing on Muslim agency and placing values at the center of its inquiry"— Provided by publisher.
Identifiers: LCCN 2021015324 (print) | LCCN 2021015325 (ebook) | ISBN 9781439921494 (cloth) | ISBN 9781439921500 (paperback) | ISBN 9781439921517 (pdf)
Subjects: LCSH: Islam and justice. | Islam and politics. | Justice—Religious aspects—Islam.
Classification: LCC BP173.43 .C54 2022 (print) | LCC BP173.43 (ebook) | DDC 297.2/72—dc23
LC record available at https://lccn.loc.gov/2021015324
LC ebook record available at https://lccn.loc.gov/2021015325

Printed in the United States of America

9 8 7 6 5 4 3 2 1

For Semra

and

Bahadır, Yusuf, İbrahim, and Yiğithan

Contents

	List of Illustrations	ix
	Acknowledgments	xi
1	Introduction	1
2	Islam and Democracy: A Never-Ending Debate	15
3	Historical and Conceptual Foundations of Justice Discourses in Islam	30
4	Islamist Justice Theory	46
5	Between Order and Freedom: Islamism and Justice Discourses	67
6	New Islamist Movements, Justice, and Democracy	91
7	Distributive Preferences, Individualism, and Support for Democracy	105
8	Constitutionalist Movements, Arab Spring, and Justice	129
9	Conclusion	151
	Appendix A	161
	Appendix B	179
	Notes	181
	Bibliography	201
	Index	215

Illustrations

Figures

1.1	Trajectories of Islamic justice discourses and Muslim political preferences	8
5.1	Evolution of justice discourses in Islamist journals (1960–2010)	80
7.1	Religiosity and support for democracy: Mediating mechanisms	111
7.2	Support for democracy and authoritarianism in the Muslim world	114
7.3	Religiosity in the Muslim world	115
7.4	Distributive preferences and individualistic orientations in the Muslim world	117
7.5	Religiosity and religious outlooks in the Muslim world	125
8.1	Perceptions of political injustice in the Arab world	139
8.2	Perceptions of social injustice in the Arab world	140
8.3	Protest participation in the Arab world	143
8.4	Religion, perceptions of injustice, and protest behavior	147
8.5	Determinants of protest participation	148

Tables

5.1	Prevalence of Islamic Justice Discourses in Turkish Islamist Journals (1960–2010)	79
7.1	Seemingly Unrelated Regression Estimates of Justice Values and Support for Democracy	119

7.2	Direct and Indirect Effects of Religiosity on Support for Democracy	120
7.3	Seemingly Unrelated Regression Estimates of Justice Values and Support for Procedural Democracy and Authoritarianism	122
7.4	Seemingly Unrelated Regression Estimates of Religious Outlooks, Justice Orientations, and Support for Democracy	127
8.1	Most Important Challenges Facing the Nation	138
8.2	Logistic Regression Estimates of Protest Participation in the Arab World	145
A5.1	List of Journals Archived in İLEM (1960–2010)	161
A6.1	Characteristics of the Interviewees	162
A7.1	Fixed Effects for Table 7.1	163
A7.2	Full Results for Table 7.3 (Model 1)	165
A7.3	Full Results for Table 7.3 (Model 2)	167
A7.4	Full Estimation Results for Table 7.4 (Model 1)	170
A7.5	Full Estimation Results for Table 7.4 (Model 2)	171
A8.1	Survey Indicators of Political and Social Justice	173
A8.2	Descriptive Statistics of the Variables in the Models	174
A8.3	Fixed Effects for Table 8.2	175
A8.4	Interaction Effects (Logistic Regression)	176
A8.5	Logistic Regression Estimates for Protest Participation (Egypt and Tunisia)	177

Acknowledgments

I started working on this book in 2013, the year marking the return of authoritarian systems and conflict to the Middle East after two years of protests and regime transitions. The Arab Spring took many by surprise. More recently, protests erupted in Sudan and Algeria with similar demands of justice and democracy. Much has been said about these waves of mass mobilization and their causes and consequences. However, scholars and pundits did not offer much about the culture of these protests, especially about the values and attitudes of ordinary men and women risking their lives chanting for freedom and justice in the Arab squares. As a student of Islam and democracy, I am truly fascinated by the discourses of rebellion and liberation. The Arab Spring presented an opportunity to examine these discourses in action. In my initial research, I learned that social justice was the most significant element in protesters' chants. Therefore, I wanted to understand how Islamic conceptions of justice shape perceptions of ordinary men and women taking to the streets. This was no easy task as I quickly realized that there are deep historical and philosophical roots of conceptions of justice shaping individual attitudes and orientations. Islamic justice discourses may support rival claims about legitimate political orders, sometimes democratic and sometimes authoritarian. I wanted to understand how Islam shapes people's conceptions of justice and how these conceptions affect their views of democracy and authoritarianism. I wrote this book to provide new insights about justice and democracy from the perspective of devout Muslim men and women.

This book is indebted to many people who have motivated and supported me during its development and writing stages. I presented early drafts of this project in the 2014 and 2017 Annual Meetings of the American Political Science Association (APSA). On both occasions, I got constructive feedback from my colleagues, who encouraged me to study this subject. One useful suggestion concerned the need to get into the field to understand how religious people interpret their faith principles to inform their values and perceptions about justice and democracy. A seed grant from the Center for the Study of Religion and Society at the University of Notre Dame, Global Religion Research Initiative (GRRI), helped me get on the field and conduct interviews in İstanbul, Turkey. I am grateful for this funding and, especially, the support provided by Christian Smith, professor of sociology and director of GRRI at Notre Dame (Award #BG5225). I would also like to thank the University Research Compliance Office staff at Kansas State University (KSU) who reviewed and approved the field research proposal (IRB approval #8776).

My field research would not have been successful without the support of many people. To start with, I would like to thank Halil İbrahim Yenigün, who has inspired me with his commitment to Islamic social justice and also introduced me to the members of new Islamic movements. My friends at Islamic Think House (İDE, İstanbul Düşünce Evi) and various social justice organizations in İstanbul were very helpful in the success of the field research. They challenged me intellectually with their intriguing ideas about Islam and justice. I especially thank Yusuf Enes Sezgin, Ammar Kılıç, Kadir Bal, and many others for their valuable comments and support in the fieldwork stage. These individuals helped me understand the true meaning of social justice and benevolence from an Islamic perspective. I am indebted to over two dozen individuals who talked to me for hours to share their understanding of Islam, justice, and politics. Attending the Ramadan dinners in Istanbul's Tarlabaşı neighborhood was an eye-opener for me. It helped me develop an appreciation of how devotion and charity are related. Especially, the social activist Mehmet Abi left a deep impression on me by demonstrating what true benevolence looks like in practice. As part of field research, I also used the library of *İlmi Etüdler Derneği* (İLEM) housing the archives of Islamist journals. I am grateful to İLEM for opening this archive to the researchers. I especially thank Muhammed Yasir Bodur, for his valuable research assistance and for spending hours in İLEM libraries in completing the archival text collection. Muhammed Yasir is also a social activist who provided many insights about Islamic justice conceptions while working as a research assistant for me.

I would also like to thank several colleagues who engaged with me regularly throughout my career and during the writing stage of this book. Thank you, Mark Tessler, for inspiring me to study the attitudes of ordinary Muslim men and women and for your continued support of my research. I am grateful to Amaney Jamal for inviting me to present one of the first drafts of this book in the After the Uprisings conference in Bobst Center for Peace and Justice at Princeton University and Michael Robbins for a second invitation to American University in Beirut to attend the Social Justice in the Arab World conference. I am also grateful for the comments provided by Michael Platow, the president of the International Society for Justice Research (ISJR) during the 2018 ISJR meeting in Atlanta, Georgia. The participants in two APSA meetings also provided helpful comments, including Ariel Ahram at the 2017 meeting. My colleague John Warner helped me understand the Western justice theory and patiently responded to my emails about reading recommendations. I especially want to express my gratitude to Michael Wuthrich and Ammar Shamaileh for encouraging me throughout the process, reading drafts of different chapters, and providing valuable feedback about these chapters. Finally, I thank Dale L. Smith who has been a lifelong mentor and has always shown deep interest in my work.

I would like to extend my special thanks to Temple University Press for agreeing to publish this book. Paul Djupe, the editor for the series *Religious Engagement in Democratic Politics*, has been very enthusiastic about this project from the beginning. He took the time to read different chapters and provided valuable feedback that significantly improved the book. Aaron M. Javsicas, editor in chief at Temple, made this process look extremely easy. He guided me throughout the process and accommodated my needs. I cannot thank Paul and Aaron enough for their encouragement and support. The press and production staff also deserve special thanks for their help in the editing and production stages. I am also indebted to Hassan Massoudy, a great calligrapher of our times who graciously agreed to provide a fantastic piece of his art for the cover image of this book.

I would also like to thank KSU and my colleagues in the Political Science Department. I could not work in a more positive and supportive environment, and I appreciate all the accommodation provided by KSU throughout my career. I am also grateful to John and Karen Hofmeister for supporting my research through a large endowment for the study of the Middle East at KSU, the Michael W. Suleiman Chair in Arab and Arab-American Studies.

My extended family also deserves recognition. First and foremost, I extend my thanks to my parents, Zehra and Cuma Çiftçi who supported me over the years and taught me to be just in my dealings. My brothers and sisters and my wife's family were among the main sources of motivation for me to study Islam, justice, and democracy. I would especially like to recognize my nephew Ali, my sister Songül, my brother-in-law Tahsin, and my sister-in-law Semiha for being friends and keeping me company during my stays in Istanbul.

Finally, I bestow special thanks to my wife and the love of my life, Semra, and my four sons. They are my source of inspiration every day. I cannot thank Semra enough for making so many sacrifices and showing love and patience throughout my professional career and when I was writing this book. My four sons, Bahadır, Yusuf, İbrahim, and Yiğithan, always reminded me of beautiful things outside of academia. Their questions about when I would finish my book, and their wonderful existence, have been a great motivation for me. Despite having zero interest in the subject, they patiently listened to my ideas and read some sections in the process. This book would not have been possible without the warmth and support of my family.

Islam, Justice, and Democracy

1

Introduction

> The heaven and the earth have been founded on justice.
> (A proverb or a hadith.)

This book is about Muslims and democracy. It is not the first volume to study this subject, but it is original in two ways. First, it focuses on Muslim agency and proposes that we study "Muslims and democracy" rather than "Islam and democracy." Numerous explanations for the lack of democracy in Muslim-majority societies focus on institutional, cultural, economic, or historical factors. While the macrostructural approach provides deep insights about Islam and democracy, studying the microcognitive dimension of Muslim support for democracy will expand our understanding beyond structural factors. Second, this book employs a novel perspective in studying Muslim political attitudes toward democracy by focusing on one of the principal values of the Islamic faith, namely justice (*al-'adl*). In Islam, justice is not merely one of the values; it is *the value* that permeates all aspects of life. This book examines this central notion as a religious value related to Muslim political preferences and behaviors. As such, this study is a scholarly attempt to explain how ordinary Muslims use the conceptions of divine justice to make sense of real-world problems, mainly those encountered in the realm of politics.

There are vastly different perspectives on Islam and democracy, and any attempt to infer a common position from this vast field seems futile. Religious scholars, pundits, academics, politicians, and ordinary people all have their views about why and to what extent Islam is friendly or hostile to democracy. However, we can bring some order to this complex field by separating an infamous perspective that sees an irreconcilable contradiction between principles of Islamic faith and democracy from other approaches that view the issue as a matter of complete, partial, or conditional agreement between the two concepts.[1] For the proponents of the first view, also known as the *essentialist* approach, Islam and democracy cannot coexist because Islam serves as a comprehensive blueprint for life, leaving no room for human legislation, secular institutions, and democratic participation.[2] In the opposite camp are scholars who either redeploy classical Islamic concepts or rely on flexible interpretations of the scripture to introduce a native Islamic democratic theory.[3] At the moment, we can somehow confidently argue that scholars have largely discredited the essentialist view, yet it continues to motivate the theoretical and empirical studies about the subject.[4]

The popular sentiment on the ground presents a different reality than the disagreement among scholars in the intellectual field. When Mohamed Bouazizi set himself on fire on December 17, 2010, to protest a repressive regime with zero respect for his dignity, he sparked a massive movement against the Arab region's dictators. The Arab Spring took many by surprise as a solid confirmation of people's desire for democracy and justice in the Middle East. Arab Spring was not the first instance of prodemocracy popular mobilization, and it will not be the last. Since the nineteenth century, people across the Muslim world have participated in large-scale protests demanding constitutional governments, independence, democracy, and justice. The protests rocking the Arab streets and squares were the latest incarnations of the desire for democracy held by ordinary Muslim women and men. Contrary to the lack of consensus among scholars and pundits about the exact nature of the relationship between Islam and democracy, there appears to be widespread support for democracy among ordinary people.

So far, the scholarly debate about Islam and democracy has focused on the principles of faith to make a case for democratic government in Islam. In this debate, primarily neglected are ordinary Muslims' attitudes and behaviors as principal democratization agents.[5] While it is essential to explain the theoretical and conceptual foundations of democracy in Islam, the thoughts and actions of Muslim agency about the normative principles of faith should also matter. It is crucial to explore how individuals interpret values stemming from their faith and use them to inform their political preferences. This book adds to the vast scholarship on the subject by combining this empirical perspective with several theoretical accounts on the subject.[6]

The recent scholarship provides the needed theoretical background for examining the association between religious values and democracy. This scholarship argues that religious values can engender democratic attitudes in Muslim-majority societies where faith remains a potent force.[7] The proponents of this research program favor either a theological approach utilizing elements of doctrine, law, or scripture or religious mobilization by the elites or masses to explain the Islamic roots of democracy. Khaled Abou El Fadl,[8] for example, argues that Islamic values of mercy and justice are the foundations of democratic ideals. In *The Caliphate of Man*, Andrew March[9] contends that in Islamic political theology, God's sovereignty on earth rests on the entire Muslim community (*umma*). This idea stems from the principle that God has appointed man as his vicegerent (*khalifa*). The universal theory of the caliphate, according to March,[10] necessitates the idea of popular sovereignty as a founding principle of government. Abdullahi Ahmed An-Náim[11] argues that democratic government will be acceptable to Muslims insofar as the renegotiation of sharia is possible and civic reasoning and participation allow pious Muslims to influence public policy according to their beliefs. In a critical essay, Ahmed Khanani[12] contends that Islamists substantiate democracy by linking it to religious concepts such as dignity (*karama*), as seen in the Arab uprisings. For Nader Hashemi,[13] liberal democracy can be implemented in the Muslim world only when an indigenous secular order is established due to Islamist mobilization. Finally, Jeremy Menchik[14] argues that historical and political conditions, in conjunction with faith principles, bring about tolerant attitudes in Indonesian religious organizations. In turn, this tolerance engenders favorable views of a specific type of democracy involving the acceptance of communal rights within a legal pluralist framework. The prevailing wisdom following this new genre of scholarship is that Islam can nurture the seeds of democratic government. This conclusion is based on novel interpretations of scripture or the prevalence of religiously inspired participatory and contentious political acts by those who hold religious worldviews.

While agreeing with the central premises of this research program, *Islam, Justice, and Democracy* differs from it on two fronts. First, it argues that the principles of any faith do not necessarily engender political outlooks in only one direction. Like any religion or ideology, Islamic values may engender democratic or authoritarian preferences. This book does not make a claim about the one-way causal effect linking principles of Islamic faith to a regime type. Regime transitions and survival are complex phenomena and individual political preferences about these phenomena will be nuanced. They will be informed by a multitude of factors and may evolve in different directions. Nevertheless, this book argues that Islam will have a significant standing among these factors, which can engender democratic attitudes. Second, it attacks the puzzle about Islam and democracy from a different perspective. Its main contention is that justice is the most significant value in Islam's ethicopolitical system. Therefore, the conception of justice will play a significant role in shaping Muslim political attitudes, whether authoritarian or democratic. This book provides a novel account of attitudinal linkages between different conceptions of Islamic justice and political preferences.

The scholarship cited above recognizes the significance of conceptions of justice in Islamic political theory, but it does not provide a systematic treatment of this notion in relation to democracy, save El Fadl's[15] masterful essay on Islamic foundations of democracy. El Fadl delivers a jurisprudential treatment of the interplay of justice and democracy but does not provide an empirical account of Muslim political preferences. The current volume explores the origins and the legacies of Islamic justice discourses to explain contemporary political preferences, especially those related to democracy. It provides a systematic treatment of associations between conceptions of justice and their attitudinal implications in Muslim political practice.[16] Therefore, it aims to close the gap between theoretical studies[17] focusing on the reinterpretation of doctrine, scripture, and Islamic law and praxis-oriented scholarship focusing on Muslim agency and mobilization.[18] This book demonstrates how theological, historical, and ideological underpinnings of a central Islamic value relate to Muslim agency's political attitudes and behavior by putting justice at the center of this integrative framework.

This volume can also be situated within a different research program that puts Islamic justice at the center of scholarly inquiry. In this vein, a study by Dina Abdelkader[19] provides the first account of Muslim activism and Islamist mobilization through the lens of Islamic jurisprudence. In her *Social Justice in Islam*, Abdelkader shows that the goals of Islamic law (*maqāṣid al-sharīʻa*) may motivate contemporary Islamic activism.[20] Abdelkader's volume is an important contribution that links a native theory of social justice to contemporary social activism. She proposes that Islamic law principles can motivate Islamist activism in Muslim-majority societies to the extent that these principles and social activists' demands overlap in seeking public interest and social welfare implementation. Abdelkader, however, does not fully explore the reasons for Muslims' acceptance or rejection of democracy according to the native theory of justice she employs in her analysis. This book explores this missing link between various conceptions of justice as a religious value and Muslim political preferences. In addition, and differently from Abdelkader, the current volume moves beyond the effect of Islamic legal principles on Islamic activism and highlights the role of historical and intellectual foundations of Islamic justice values in Muslim politics. The analysis also employs a mixed-method approach and brings considerable evidence from public opinion surveys, archives of Islamist journals, and in-depth interviews to establish the linkages between Islamic justice values, on one hand, and Islamist ideology, political attitudes, and behavior, on the other.

Two historical treatments of social justice in the Muslim world are also worthy of mentioning within this second research program. In *A History of Social Justice and Political Power in the Middle East*, Linda Darling[21] explores the historical origins of the essential notion of *circle of justice*. Since the early ages, this concept was foundational to state legitimacy and efficient governance in the Middle East. The circle of justice refers to the interdependence of the rulers, military, and people in governance. Such interdependence leads to adequate public goods provision, egalitarian welfare policies, and continued security to bring about state legitimacy.[22] Darling argues that the circle of justice has been part of the statecraft since before the Islamic period and is a cultural element of governance in the Middle East. This idea undergirded the state legitimacy in the gunpowder empires, but it lost its prominence with the rise of the Western political and economic models. However, the main principles of the circle survived in the popular culture to resurface in contemporary mass movements (e.g., the Iranian Revolution, the Arab Spring).[23]

In another impressive volume, *Justice Interrupted: The Struggle for Constitutional Government in the Middle East*, Elizabeth Thompson[24] challenges the conventional view that Islam and liberal democracy are antithetical. She argues that the people of the Middle East have revolted since the 1850s in the name of justice and the rule of law, but the domestic autocrats and the foreign powers complicit in repressive regimes silenced these democratic demands. From the Urabi Revolt in Egypt (1879–1882) to the Arab Spring, democratic movements and popular struggles for justice have been the rule rather than the exception. For Thompson, the ideals of justice and demands for the rule of law have motivated the leftist and Islamist movements. Overall, Darling and Thompson recognize the importance of the notion of justice, whether it has been invoked for the legitimacy of a traditional monarchy, an authoritarian government, or a constitutional democracy. They trace the lineages of Islamic justice conception related to the state, democracy, and popular mobilization, an inquiry this volume also undertakes. However, unlike these two studies, *Islam, Justice, and Democracy* investigates the religious roots of justice values. It also explores how justice as a religious value manifests itself in contemporary political preferences. For a full account of the interplay of Islamic conceptions of justice and democracy, we need to understand how historical and intellectual conceptions of justice engender democratic (or authoritarian) attitudes or whether they motivate political acts conducive to democracy.[25]

What are the historical origins of Islamic conceptions of justice? Are these origins related to such notions as legitimacy and popular sovereignty? Can we trace pluralistic or authoritarian ideas in the Islamic conceptions of justice? Are social justice values such as charity conducive to support for a democratic government or benevolent dictatorship? This book aims to answer these and similar questions by using a mixed-methods design. This volume's method is rooted in ethnographic research spanning over several years of fieldwork in Turkey. Many of this volume's insights come from participant observation and in-depth interviews. The methodological tool kit also includes a content analysis of articles obtained from the archives of Islamist journals and quantitative analysis of survey data in the Arab and Muslim-majority countries. This mixed-methods approach provides rich data and robust empirical tests about individuals' attitudes and behavior. *Islam, Justice, and Democracy* is a social scientific investigation to uncover and explain the microfoundations of the association between justice and democracy in Islam.

Islam, Justice, and Democracy: The Argument

Justice is a broad concept with many dimensions, including but not limited to its political, social, legal, economic, commutative, and distributive facets. We can start to examine the connections between Islamic conceptions of justice and democracy by focusing our inquiry on some of these facets. This is not to claim that specific dimensions of justice are more crucial than others, but such simplification is necessary to better understand the association between conceptions of justice and political preferences.

Some justice dimensions may become more prevalent than others in shaping conceptions of justice over time and across different contexts.[26] For example, in the West, economic distribution has gained significance in the study of justice, presumably due to the Industrial Revolution's unique conditions.[27] By and large, two important traditions have influenced the intellectual debate about social justice in the West. First, religion (Christianity) played a vital role in reconciling social tensions that arose with industrialization and modernization. This development gave way to social democratic and religiously inspired egalitarian ideologies such as liberation theology.[28] Second, a liberal ideology played an instrumental role in reconciling free market and social justice outcomes in the twentieth century.[29]

In the Muslim world, justice discourses evolved along two discernible trajectories. The first trajectory is the political justice dimension. The origins of this trajectory go back to the conflicts during the beginning periods of Islamic history over the political leadership. The disagreement about who would be the leader of the Muslim community, after the death of its religious and political leader Muhammad, gave way to political strife in a community that had seen only peace and unity during the span of its short existence.[30] The political struggles over the succession problem eventually led to the first civil war (*fitna*)[31] and culminated in the sectarian division between Sunni and Shia. Sectarianism consolidated over time as the rift between these two sects widened in the doctrinal realm. However, justice and its political implications always remained salient matters in Muslim politics. As Majid Khadduri succinctly says, "At the outset the debate on justice began on the political level. In a community founded on religion, it was indeed in the nature of things that public concern should focus first on the question of legitimacy and the qualifications of the ruler whose primary task was to put God's Law and justice into practice."[32] This debate gradually spilled over into the theological and philosophical fields to inform intellectual discussions about thorny issues like free will, predetermination, justice, and the Islamic government.

Apart from this scholarly vibrancy, practical political issues related to justice and governance continued to inform the politics over centuries. Naturally, conceptions of political justice continued to evolve in response to the changing contexts and problems of different ages. For example, Shia political theory evolved along the lines of a belief that the community deprived Prophet Muhammad's son-in-law 'Ali of his right to lead the community, creating an injustice. The emphasis on the importance of political justice and a just ruler among the Shia is perhaps the result of this initial position.[33] In the medieval period, conceptions of political justice concerned the qualities of a just ruler among the Sunni thinkers. In the age of modernity, conceptions of political justice resurfaced in the ideologies of Islamist intellectuals and the protesters' chants in various mass movements. Manifestations of Islamic justice ideals can be traced to the constitutionalist uprisings of the early twentieth century and postcolonial independence movements,[34] the Islamist ideology and the discourse of religious activism, the Iranian Revolution,[35] and the demands of antiregime protesters as most notably observed in the Arab Spring.

The second trajectory, social justice, is rooted in Islam's emphasis on charity and helping the poor. Scripture and hadiths (words of the Prophet) are replete with passages about altruism and giving. The notion of *'iḥsān*,[36] translated as benevolence toward people or graciousness in individuals' dealings with others, is a central aspect of Islamic social justice.[37] Despite this emphasis, conceptions of social justice were not utilized as political tools until the weakening and fragmentation of the Islamic Empire in the thirteenth century. During the weakening period of the Islamic Empire and especially following the Mongol invasion, social justice emerged as a significant social problem.[38]

The political conditions of that time required a positive definition of justice that would ensure general welfare and the provision of public goods. Although political justice continued to receive scholarly attention in the works of ethics (*akhlaq*) and the political advice texts, most scholarly attention gravitated toward the notion of public interest (*maṣlaḥa*), especially among legal scholars. For example, Ibn Taymiyya laid out the foundation of a new political theory called *al-siyāsa al-shar'iyya*[39] that put the notion of

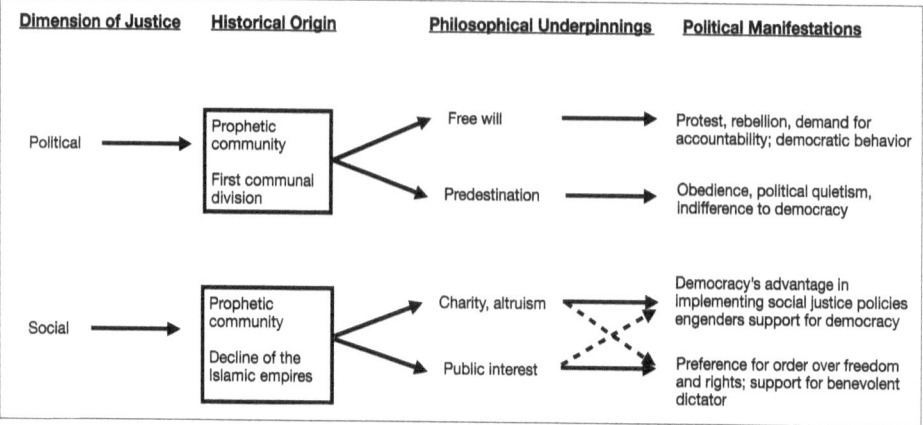

Figure 1.1 Trajectories of Islamic justice discourses and Muslim political preferences.

maṣlaḥa at the center of political thinking. The discourse of justice increasingly came to be defined by such norms as welfare, public goods provision, and security. Obedience to rulers was seen as an absolute necessity to ensure the implementation of these policies. In practice, the Islamic jurisprudential theory (uṣūl al-fiqh) came up with a theory of public interest, leading to what Abdou Filali-Ansary calls the "medieval compromise"[40] between the rulers and the scholars. In this arrangement, it was the duty of the scholars to keep the rulers in check. The balance tilted toward political authority and subjugated the religious authority to the rulers' will. Ahmet Kuru argues that this political formula and the end of scholars' independence from the ruling class due to a decline in trade are the leading causes of stagnation in Islamic societies.[41] Nonetheless, this model continued to inform political relations. Indeed, it conveniently served the rulers' interests, because of its capacity to create perceptions of legitimacy. The *siyāsa* model's legally bound and highly nuanced social justice paradigm played a significant role in these developments.

This study argues that the conceptions of political and social justice, as disclosed within the Muslim political experience, will inform contemporary political preferences, democratic or authoritarian, in two different ways. Figure 1.1 summarizes these different paths and their implications for political preferences.

The political justice trajectory originates from the early communal divisions over the question of choosing a leader. To reiterate, one outcome of this initial division is the development of sectarian differentiation between the Sunni and Shia groups. These political and sectarian divisions took on a life of their own over time. What started as a disagreement about politics spilled over into the areas of doctrine, culture, and lifestyle. The divergence within the Islamic political theory between the proponents of popular sovereignty/accountability axis and the proponents of obedience/social order axis follows the same division. The contrast between these two axes stands in sharp contrast to the idea of a unified political community, as seen during the Prophet's time.

One manifestation of this split emerged within theological debates between the proponents of free will and the proponents of predestination. The former implies that individuals have free will and they are responsible for correcting injustices and taking action against tyranny. This path is highly conducive to support for democracy and political accountability and leads to active engagement in political life. The latter advises obedience and quietism even under the political authority of an unjust ruler. Historically, proponents of free will and individual responsibility encouraged opposition and rebellion in the name of justice. The opposite camp's ideology has been conducive to unconditional obedience since they believed that God predetermines everything, including an unjust ruler's reign. This second path is likely to engender political apathy and indifference, if not opposition, toward democracy. This book demonstrates the evolution of these legacies by tracing their manifestations in contemporary Muslim politics.

The social justice trajectory also follows two different paths, but the transition from one path to another is possible, as shown with the dashed lines in Figure 1.1. All else being equal, a devout Muslim should hold economically egalitarian views due to the strong emphasis placed on altruism, benevolence, and charity in Islam. Pious Muslims should lean favorably toward democratic governance because democracy has an advantage in implementing egalitarian distributive policies.[42] This statement is also in line with Islam's doctrinal focus on benevolence. This path relies on the assumption that democracy has an advantage over other regime types, as the most compatible regime type with Islamic social justice.[43]

An alternative explanation may be in order given the historical evolution of conceptions of social justice, especially the increased emphasis on social order and public interest during the Islamic Empire's fragmentation in the thirteenth century. The need to institute social justice in a declining society gave way to a unique political coalition between religious scholars (ulema) and rulers to implement sharia as the quintessential governing formula. Ideally, this political arrangement necessitated constraining the rulers to ensure the implementation of justice. In practice, the rulers came to employ the ulema to create perceptions of legitimacy among their subjects.[44] Consequently, obedience to a benevolent but unjust ruler is legitimized as a necessary condition for ensuring social order and public interest. This second path implies support for nondemocratic forms of government.

The stylized distinction between two social justice paths is not as clearcut as the distinction in political justice paths because charity and benevolence may also underlie support for a benevolent dictator implementing egalitarian distribution within a supposedly Islamic political system. Meanwhile, public interest as the primary goal of sharia may engender support for democracy. This is because, in democracies, pious Muslims will find the necessary channels for contributing to society's general welfare, according to their religious beliefs, through deliberation and policy influence, which is not the case in nondemocratic regimes.[45]

Islamic law requires that certain religious norms constrain rulers. In settings where existing institutions give a ruler disproportionate power, such informal rules may be the only way for executive constraints. The process defined here is the norm of "institutional forbearance." Steven Levitsky and Daniel Ziblatt[46] define forbearance as "patient self-control; restraint and tolerance." Forbearance refers to the choice by those who hold power not to apply a legal prerogative. Sometimes, rulers may avoid a specific action they are entitled to because this would violate the spirit of the system or undermine it.[47] As Levitsky and Ziblatt argue,[48] forbearance norms have their roots in premodern government when the rulers had the divine right to rule. Even then, they would restrain themselves according to the accepted wisdom.

The notion of forbearance has direct relevance to the Islamic governance models. In the lack of institutions that could effectively constrain the ruler, religious norms may be the only path to forbearance. When followed by the rulers, these values could ensure general welfare. Specifically, Islamic justice requires that the ruler act wisely according to maṣlaḥa principle.[49] Any unjust act that violates citizens' rights or jeopardizes the welfare of society is against the spirit of religion. The classical Islamic state is a system of the past. However, its principles, especially those related to the general welfare provision based on forbearance norms are most similar to democracy. Devout Muslims' may not want to reinstitute the classical Islamic state, but they are likely to view democracy as a system that has the most significant potential to enact its normative outcomes. All else being equal, devout Muslims should prefer democracy over its alternatives because it constrains the executive either by formal institutions or by informal norms to protect the public interest and general welfare.

In conclusion, the historical lineages of political and social justice provide a foundation for understanding contemporary political preferences, especially those related to democracy. The analysis does not propose a causal relation linking historical patterns to contemporary political preferences. Nor does the theoretical framework maintain that the lineages of conceptions of justice shape current attitudes in an exclusive manner. A fuller explanation will clarify specific mechanisms that make democracy more (or less) preferable to its alternatives for pious individuals. The subsequent chapters elaborate on these mechanisms and present microlevel empirical evidence to explain Muslim support for democracy and authoritarianism.

Outline of the Book

This volume attempts to trace the lineages of political and social justice trajectories and their implications for Muslim support for democracy. It moves beyond the exclusively historical or empirical treatments of the subject to explain contemporary incarnations of justice orientations as they appear in Islamist ideology, mass protest movements, and public opinion. Chapter 2 surveys the scholarship on Islam and democracy to point to the lack of focus on "justice" as a crucial element of Islamic political theory. It first provides a review of the essentialist approach that is skeptical about the compatibility of Islam with democracy. The review shows that this skepticism is more nuanced than a simple rejection of Islamic faith's pluralistic origins. It then summarizes the counteressentialist scholarship that makes a case for the compatibility of Islam and democracy. This second line of research traces the roots of Islamic democracy in scriptural principles or in Islamic legal methodologies. This section demonstrates that the counteressentialist scholarship either neglects the role of justice as a constitutive principle of democratic thinking in the Muslim experience or it does not adequately examine the linkages between conceptions of justice and attitudes of Muslim agency. This chapter sets the stage for the subsequent analysis that explores the effect of justice values on attitudes.

Chapter 3 provides an overview of political and social justice trajectories to explain the connections between religious values and Muslim political attitudes. Starting from the first divisions in the early Muslim community and focusing on the paradigm shift from political to social justice during the decline of the Islamic Empire, it traces the development of justice discourses in political struggles and intellectual debates. This chapter does not claim to account for historical details of all important events in Islamic history but approaches the subject from a *longue durée* perspective[50] to provide a broad overview of the evolution of justice discourses. It focuses on the conceptual evolution of political and social justice rather than presenting a simple historical description of events. This chapter also discusses the linkages between historical trajectories of political and social justice and support for democracy and authoritarianism.

The remaining chapters examine the contemporary manifestations of political and social justice trajectories and their formative effects on Muslim political attitudes. These chapters bring evidence from the works of Islamist ideologues, archives of Islamist journals, the ideas of Islamist youth, widespread protests of the Arab Spring, and attitudes of ordinary men and women as reported in public opinion surveys. To that end, these chapters use a mixed-methods design, including such techniques as a close reading of primary texts, content analysis of Islamist journals, in-depth interviews, and statistical analysis of survey data.

Chapter 4 explores the Islamist justice theory in the works of 'Ali Shariati and Sayyid Qutb, arguably the two most influential Islamists of the modern era. For both scholars, the human agency plays a critical role in applying divine justice principles to the practical realm. Qutb believes that man can gain freedom of conscience through exclusive servitude to God and engagement in charitable acts. Shariati, on the other hand, focuses on man's capacity and free will, both of which can be realized by taking action against the polytheist world orders that have replaced the divine monotheist order. While Qutb is concerned about establishing a just order through inner purification and religious law, Shariati assigns this duty to the human agency engaged in continuous struggles against the oppressor. Man, for Shariati, can reach emancipation through the benevolent act. This chapter shows that building contemporary incarnations of Islamist justice is, in essence, a highly practical political project at the intersection of political and social justice. The main concern of Islamist justice theory is the emancipation of human agency through belief in an all-powerful single God and the establishment of a nonoppressive political order and harmonious society that can ensure social justice for all. Finally, Chapter 4 compares Qutb and Shariati's ideas to the views of Muhammad Baqir al-Sadr, Said Nursi, and Rāshid al-Ghannūshī. This chapter demonstrates that the lineages of Islamic conceptions of justice continue to inform the political philosophies of contemporary Islamists who appear to develop democratic utopias for an ideal Muslim society.

Chapter 5 uses a discourse analytic account of Islamist texts to demonstrate how social reformism and anti-imperialism emerge as the new manifestations of the classic debate between proponents of communal order and those who call for rebellion against an unjust ruler. It traces the lineages of the tension between social justice and political justice using the archives of the Turkish Islamist journals during the 1960–2010 period. This analysis provides the first systematic qualitative treatment of Islamist ideas about justice and democracy in the Turkish context. During the Cold War, Islamist writers presented a rudimentary treatment of justice conception to address the challenge of communist ideology. The primary focus of Turkish Islamists was public interest and social order at that time. Since 1980, Islamists have developed sophisticated theories to address the challenges stemming from the neoliberal economic system, globalization, and American hegemony. During this period, Islamists increasingly focused on ethics and politics, Islamic governance, and resistance to the new world order. The analysis in

Chapter 5 demonstrates that the early genealogies of justice discourses continue to shape Muslim political preferences.

Chapter 6 explores how pious individuals form cognitive pathways from a central value of Islam to inform their attitudes toward democracy and authoritarianism. It uses in-depth interviews conducted with the members of new Islamist movements in Turkey (2017–2019) to demonstrate how devout individuals problematize justice in forming their political preferences. As such, it presents a fine-grained empirical assessment of individual attitudes about justice and democracy and provides conceptual validation for the theory presented in this book. The interviews demonstrate no single uniform path linking religion to justice and justice to democratic orientations. While the quest for "justice" has been at the center of political debates concerning legitimacy, obedience, and rebellion against tyrants over many centuries, for contemporary Islamists, the mechanisms linking conceptions of justice to political attitudes and behavior, particularly those related to democracy, are ambiguous for the Islamist youth. The chapter argues that this should not come as a surprise to the extent that historical trajectories of Islamic justice discourses are characterized by dualities between free will and predestination, freedom and necessity of order, or rebellion against tyranny and obedience to a benevolent dictator. The analysis of Islamist outlooks implies that the legacy of complex historical trajectories concerning justice and democracy, although containing a gray zone, continue to inform Muslim political preferences. Finally, Chapter 6 highlights the main theoretical mechanisms underlying religion, attitudes, and support for democracy.

Chapter 7 explains the microfoundations of Muslim support for democracy. It proposes that distributive preferences and individualistic value orientations stemming from Islamic conceptions of justice mediate religion's effect on support for democracy. The statistical analysis of the extensive World Values Survey (WVS) conducted in two dozen Muslim-majority countries shows that religiosity increases distributive preferences. Meanwhile, pious individuals are less likely to hold self-direction values emphasizing individual autonomy but more likely to hold self-determination values cherishing individual resolve and control over life decisions. In turn, piety, egalitarian distributive preferences, and self-deterministic orientations increase support for democracy. Overall, the analysis demonstrates that legacies of political and social justice trajectories inform political attitudes directly or indirectly by mediating the effect of religiosity.

Chapter 8 focuses on protest behavior and examines the Arab Spring as an example of popular mobilization for political and social justice. It compares these protests to the constitutionalist movements of the nineteenth and twentieth centuries in the Middle East to demonstrate the continuities and ruptures in the discourse of these movements set one century apart. The chapter argues that the Arab Spring constituted a popular democratic movement demanding both social and political justice. The statistical analysis of the Arab Barometer data demonstrates that perceptions of political and social injustices played a large role in protest participation. Although religiosity's effect on protest participation is not consistent across statistical models, religion strengthens the association between indicators of political justice—including perceptions of corruption, access to state services, and political distrust—and the decision to protest.

Chapter 9, the conclusion, discusses the findings of this volume in the context of the vast scholarship on Islam and democracy. This chapter also discusses the policy implications of this volume for democratization in Muslim-majority societies. By putting justice at the center of democratic thinking in the Muslim world, the conclusion invites Islam and democracy scholars to reconsider Islam's potential for engendering democratic ideals and authoritarian preferences.

2

Islam and Democracy

A Never-Ending Debate

> All those who have been in the East, or in Africa, are struck by the way in which the mind of a true believer is fatally limited, by the species of iron circle that surrounds his head, rendering it absolutely closed to knowledge, incapable of either learning anything, or of being open to any new idea.
> —Ernest Renan, "Islamism and Science"

> Islam neither destroyed knowledge nor was it destroyed with knowledge.
> —Namik Kemal, "Renan Müdafaanamesi"

Democracy emerged as a by-product of complicated history in the West involving state formation, secularization, class struggle, and revolutions. It is associated with specific values and institutional structures such as freedom, accountability, popular sovereignty, elections, and representation. Democracy is a highly desired government type that "resonates in people's minds and springs from their lips as they struggle for freedom and a better way of life."[1] As Kenneth Amaeshi argues, although democracy is like value-free technology that can be implemented in non-Western countries, "to transfer it from one context to another, one needs to recognize the traditions and cultures of the place to which it is being transferred."[2] Common wisdom attaches the Western tradition and culture to democracy when exporting it to the Global South, usually neglecting the native culture, values, and practices. If democracy fails to take root or produces outcomes at odds with liberal democratic values in a particular setting, this failure is often blamed on cultural incompatibility.[3] In no other context was this outlook carried to its extremes more than in Muslim-majority societies where democracy is lacking.

Explaining the lack of democracy with cultural factors represents an ethnocentric worldview toward other religions (or civilizations) that views them from a lens similar to the *Orientalist* approach.[4] Western civilization, with its achievements—modernization, the scientific revolution, technological innovation, industrialization, political development—is taken as an ideal example to be emulated by the so-called "backward" civilizations. Since Islam is inherently incompatible with democracy, goes the argument, democracy can only succeed if Muslim-majority societies emulate the Western values. This perspective comes from the idea of "privilege of ignorance"[5] or the "problem of asymmetric ignorance."[6] That is, intellectuals in the periphery have to consider the Western history and traditions even when writing about their problems, but the Western scholars have the privilege of not reciprocating. Essentialist theorizing about the lack of democracy in Muslim-majority societies attaches Western values to democracy as prerequisites for its installment and does not consider the native traditions and culture, such as religious values or ethnic traditions.

The hegemony of liberal democratic discourse prevents us from seeing the other cultures' potential. We can indeed treat democracy as a neutral government type, but its legitimacy is contingent on its acceptability as a universal value.[7] Such acceptance in non-Western settings, in turn, can emanate from its justification through values that are most important to the members of these societies. Therefore, focusing on the approval of democracy by ordinary people will help us understand the normative/cultural foundations of support for democracy in the Muslim world.

This chapter presents the main contours of theoretical scholarship on Islam and democracy. To that end, it first provides a brief review of the origins and contemporary examples of essentialist theorizing on the subject that views Islam as hostile to democracy. Then, it discusses the counteressentialist theorizing and looks at the recent scholarship that sees a positive relationship between Islam and democratic ideals. The chapter concludes with a critical account of both approaches by emphasizing the role of Islamic values as cultural foundations of democracy.

Understanding the Essence of the Essentialist Theorizing

The origins of intellectual debate about Islam and democracy go back to the eighteenth century. According to the enlightenment philosophers, reason and science are the primary sources of authority and legitimacy. Reason and science give way to freedom, progress, democracy, and the separation of the state and church.[8] Positivist philosophers, similarly, attribute the progress of Western civilization to the advances in science. Comte argues that human societies will undergo social evolution stages, including the theological, metaphysical, and scientific phases.[9] During the scientific revolution stage, science replaces religious dogma, seen as the main impediment to progress. Only Western societies managed to reach the last stage of evolution in this scheme. Therefore, other societies should follow the example of Western societies and replace religious dogma with scientific ideas to achieve progress according to this approach. Comte's ideas greatly influenced scholars like Karl Marx, Max Weber, and Émile Durkheim. Although Islam was not the only target for the enlightenment and positivists, they viewed it as one of the primary impediments to economic development, scientific revolution, freedom, and tolerance in Islamic societies.

The enlightenment and positivist philosophies justified the subjugation and exploitation of colonies located within the territories ruled by classical Islamic empires. Thus, it is no coincidence that the nineteenth century witnessed the invention of a new science devoted to the study of Eastern societies, namely Orientalism.[10] For Orientalists, freedom, tolerance, and economic development are alien to Eastern and, especially, Islamic societies, because Islam, as monolithic and an all-encompassing religion, prevents its adherents from emulating the example of the West. In his famous treatise on Islam and science, French orientalist Ernest Renan refuted the religion and blamed it for the Islamic world's backwardness.[11] In response, two nineteenth-century modernists, Jamāl al-Dīn al-Afghānī and Namık Kemal, argued that Islam is open to progress and scientific revolution.[12]

That Islam is incompatible with economic development and democracy became a staple thesis in the Western academia. For example, Weber blamed Islam for the lack of economic development and freedom in Muslim-majority societies.[13] Following Weber's argument, contemporary scholars famously argued that Islamic faith principles are inimical to democratic ideals.[14] For example, Samuel Huntington contends that Islam is hostile to Western values such as rational thinking, freedom, and secularism.[15] According to Elie Kedourie:

> The notion of a state as a specific territorial entity which is endowed with sovereignty, the notion of popular sovereignty as the foundation of governmental legitimacy, the idea of representation, of elections, of popular suffrage, of political institutions being regulated by laws laid down by a parliamentary assembly, of these laws being guarded and upheld by an independent judiciary, the ideas of the secularity of the state, of society being composed of a multitude of self-activating, autonomous groups and associations—all these are profoundly alien to the Muslim political tradition.[16]

Ernest Gellner famously stated that "Islam is the blueprint of the society" and that its all-encompassing nature prevented the emergence of secularism and democratization in the Muslim world.[17] Similarly, Bernard Lewis states, "such central issues of Western political development as the conduct of elections and the definition and extension of the franchise therefore had no place in Islamic political evolution."[18] For these scholars, there is something inherent in Islam and Islamic culture, an essence, that makes it hostile to democracy. This incompatibility stems from the fact that (1) Islam is not conducive to the separation of religion and state, (2) it has a fixed set of rules that precludes popular sovereignty, (3) Islam provides a blueprint for the social and political life, and (4) in Islam, human-made legislation is not possible due to God's sovereignty. These factors leave little chance for establishing democracy in Muslim-majority societies.

Although Gellner, Lewis, and Kedourie contend that Islam is inherently hostile to democracy, a closer look reveals that these scholars do not merely use faith principles to substantiate their argument. Instead, they elaborate on the lack of social and political institutions that gave way to the rise of democracy in the West as the leading cause for the democracy gap in the Muslim world. These scholars employ a historical-deterministic approach for generalizing specific Islamic traditions or certain historical periods to all Muslim-majority societies over time, usually ignoring the vast diversity and temporal variation therein.

For example, inspired by Ibn Khaldun, Gellner uses a broad brush to confine a rich tradition and history to the duality of social structure.[19] Islamic society, Gellner states, "was divided into a 'high' form, the urban-based, strict, unitarian, nomocratic, puritan and scripturalist Islam of the scholars; and a 'lower' form, the cult of personality–addicted, ecstatic, ritualistic, questionably literate, unpuritanical and rustic Islam of the dervishes and the marabouts."[20] He argues that democracy cannot flourish in the Muslim world because the evolution and interaction of low and high Islam, as observed in the fourteenth century, created static political systems inhibiting democratization and secularization.[21] Gellner convincingly sets aside immeasurable changes and the vast diversity in Islamic societies, spread across the "Bosnia to Bengal complex."[22]

A similar reductionism takes place in the account of Kedourie, who argues that the first impact of European institutions on Middle Eastern governments came through enlightened absolutism rather than representative institutions lacking in the Muslim world.[23] Enlightened absolutism was similar to oriental despotism. Thus, it proved to be an efficient and attractive political model as the Middle Eastern states created modern military and bureaucratic institutions in the nineteenth and twentieth centuries.[24] In other words, the incompatibility between Islam and democracy is due to the unsuitability of Islamic traditional institutions and the impact of Western absolutist political ideas. Thus, the reductionism in Kedourie's account explains away complex social and political outcomes with accidental encounters by Western political institutions.

Lewis follows a similar line of reasoning, but he is subtler than Gellner and Kedourie. According to Lewis, for several reasons, autocratic rule (not despotism) has been the primary governance model for much of the Islamic political history.[25] For example, there was a distinction between revolutionary (Mecca) and quietist traditions (Medina) during Islam's beginning period. The former period represented an outlook of opposition, change, and rebellion against the status quo, whereas, during the latter period, political activities centered on lawmaking and establishing social order.[26] For Lewis, these two views prevailed throughout Islamic history, but the discourses of order took precedence over opposition's rebellious rhetoric due to the fear of fitna.[27] Although there were religious checks carried by the ulema, according to sharia, unconditional obedience to the ruler became the central political norm replacing the revolutionary spirit of the Meccan period. Furthermore, Lewis argues that modernization increased the prevalence of quietism by increasing the modern states' power while eroding the authority of religious checks on the rulers.[28]

Lewis also cites a lack of recognition of corporate bodies and accompanying legislation as one reason for the Muslim democracy gap.[29] Consequently, modern representative institutions did not emerge, and the state essentially turned into God's state ruled by divine law.[30] Other factors leading to democracy in the West were also not present in the Muslim world. For example, although private property was sanctified in Islam, its confiscation by the rulers was common practice. The merchant class was vibrant, but it never reached the power of the bourgeoisie in the West.[31] Religious scholars were economically independent because of familial ties to the merchant class, but this situation also disappeared by the eleventh century when ulema entered into an alliance with the rulers.[32]

By and large, then, for Lewis, the essence of the incompatibility thesis is not as much about doctrine as it is about institutions and their evolution in Islamic history. He does not entirely discard Islamic elements in the founding of democracy, leaving some room for the influence of traditional institutions and doctrinal principles.[33] For example, he notes the contractual nature of the ruler/ruled relation per the notion of *bay'a*. Lewis attributes a democratic quality to this notion by defining it as a "deal" rather than an "allegiance" or "homage."[34] Furthermore, he argues that the Islamic caliphate might be an autocracy, but since the law checks the ruler's power, it has never been despotic. More interestingly, Lewis argues that Islam's openness to diversity and emphasis on human dignity can provide the basis for democratic ideals.[35]

Overall, the analyses of Gellner, Kedourie, and Lewis are subtler than the presumption of Huntington, who links the principles of faith to a lack of democracy in the Muslim world. The former three scholars contend that while there might be potential for democratic ideals in Islam, the institutions that gave way to the rise of democracy in the West were lacking in the Muslim world. A combination of principles of faith, traditions, and accidental encounters with Western political models were the main reasons for the Muslim democracy gap. In response to this line of theorizing, some scholars argue that Islamic traditions, institutions, or values may inspire democratic ideals.[36] Usually, these scholars invoke principles of legal methodology such as *ijmā'* (consensus of scholars) and *ijtihād* (free reasoning, opinion) or scriptural principles like *shūrā* (consultation) to make a case for the Islamic origins of democratic ideas. The next section presents the main contours of this argument.

Counteressentialist Theories

Proponents of the counteressentialist approach (compatibility thesis) see no contradiction between Islam and democracy.[37] For example, they argue that Islamic legal methodology principles such as *ijmā'* and *ijtihād* or scriptural principles like shūrā can provide the basis for such ideas as popular sovereignty, elections, and legislative institutions. Next to the conceptions of legal methodology, the proponents of the compatibility thesis also frequently cite Islam's emphasis on values like justice and human dignity.[38] Rather than viewing the prevalence of religion in social life as an impediment to democratization, these scholars see a path to democracy through the reinterpretation or renegotiation of religious values.[39] To the extent that Islam determines religious outlooks, framing democracy as an Islamic model would increase its acceptability. A majority of people, however, viewed Western institutions with great suspicion. As Filali-Ansary insightfully says, "Muslim confrontations with European colonial powers in the nineteenth century gave birth to some great and lasting misunderstandings, as a result of which Muslims have rejected key aspects of modernity (secularization and, to some degree, democratization) as an alienation and a surrender of the historical self to the 'Other.'"[40]

Accordingly, it was necessary to convince a religious populace that democratic government was not in contradiction to the Islamic faith. In addition to overcoming the deep suspicion about Western institutions, building precise mechanisms that could convincingly link Islamic principles and values to democratic ideals proved to be challenging for the modernist Islamists. Examining the works of early modernists, some scholars conclude that concepts like tawhid (unity principle), khalifa, ijtihād, ijmā', and shūrā were instrumental in constituting the Islamic foundations of democracy.[41] Early Islamists responded to Western philosophies that viewed Islam as the leading cause of regression by demonstrating that Islam has significant potential to accommodate democratic institutions.[42] For example, Muhammad

Iqbal cites the principle of shūrā as the foundation of elected assemblies: "The transfer of the power of *ijtihād* from individual representatives of schools to a Muslim legislative assembly which, in view of the growth of opposing sects, is the only form *ijmāʿ* can take in modern times, will secure contributions to legal discussion from laymen who happen to possess a keen insight into affairs. In this way alone can we stir into activity the dormant spirit of life in our legal system."[43]

Simultaneously, the concepts utilized for justification of the Islamic democratic ideals may legitimize nondemocratic forms of government. For example, tawhid may inspire the notions of equality and dignity by creating a condition of exclusive servitude to God, but it could also be a source of nondemocratic government by prioritizing divine sovereignty over human-made legislation. Similarly, *ijmāʿ* could be seen as public opinion, but it may also justify a closed political system through authoritarian worldviews posed by religious scholars. Esposito and Voll refer to the challenges in specifying precise mechanisms explaining how these ideas could be foundational to democratic ideals. They highlight the need to develop a genuine Islamic theory of democracy based on ethics and moral values:

> Consultation, consensus, and ijtihād are crucial concepts for the articulation of Islamic democracy within the framework of the oneness of God and the representational obligations of human beings. These are terms whose meanings are contested and whose definitions shape Muslim perceptions of what represents legitimate and authentic democracy in an Islamic framework. However, despite the fact that within the Islamic world these terms are contested, they provide an effective foundation for understanding the relationship between Islam and democracy in the contemporary world.[44]

To address this issue, recent scholarship favoring the compatibility thesis develops precise mechanisms linking principles of faith to democratic ideals. This scholarship diverges from the approach focusing on principles of legal methodology by exploring the conditions that will make democracy acceptable to the pious Muslims. To that end, it has focused on the positive role religion can play in secularization and democratization by employing flexible interpretations of Islamic principles. The next section reviews this new genre of scholarship on Islam and democracy.

Authenticating Democracy within Islam

Democracy gains legitimacy when a majority of people view it as an acceptable form of government. This condition is especially significant for Muslim-majority societies where democracy is a rare commodity and suspicion about the democratic system abounds due to the perception that democracy and secularism are instruments of a Western imperialist project. For that reason, given Islam's primacy as a potent social force, any democratization attempt will have to acknowledge the importance of religious values in these societies.

Democracy is more than the sum of procedures or institutions. It provides a method for resolving differences over specific norms and values. As Philippe C. Schmitter and Terry Lynn Karl state, "Modern democracy, in other words, offers a variety of competitive processes and channels for the expression of interests and values—associational as well as partisan, functional as well as territorial, collective as well as individual. All are integral to its practice."[45] The peaceful resolution of contentious politics and the struggle between the poor masses and the wealthy elite are also essential prerequisites of democracy.[46] Insofar as actors and groups that hold different values and interests believe that democracy is the best option for resolving their differences, they will prefer it over other government systems.

Throughout Islamic history, significant contention has taken place about the role of religion in politics. A division between religious and political authorities started to materialize as early as the seventh century and consolidated during the reign of Abbasid caliph al-Ma'mūn in the early ninth century.[47] This separation was at odds with the communal governance model based on the unification of political and religious authority in Muhammad's person. In the medieval period, the separation of political and religious authorities resulted in a compromise between secular rulers and ulema. Consequently, rulers employed different political strategies, making it necessary for them to either obtain the blessing of religious authorities or subdue them to legitimize their rule. Religious authorities assigned a central role to Islamic law because they believed that law could provide the primary frame of social and political life and could be the only instrument for the livelihood of the ethically bound prophetic community model.[48]

On the other hand, in the nineteenth and twentieth centuries, state-religion relations came to be associated with secular policies and bottom-up social contention that at times gave way to democratic movements.[49] Despite this paradigmatic shift in social and political spheres, the theoretical debate on Islam and democracy continued to focus on the religion in politics. Consequently, making democracy acceptable to the Muslim public requires addressing the role religion will play in any political system. This is precisely the idea that motivated the recent scholarship of An-Náim, Hashemi, and El Fadl.[50]

Abdullahi Ahmed An-Náim[51] argues that a secular state guaranteeing the expressions of civic reason and allowing the religious people to contribute to policy making will bring about the acceptance of democracy among the pious Muslims. An-Náim's position rests on several assumptions. First, he believes that free choice should determine religious belief and adherence. Second, there is no room for the compulsory practice of religion by a state in Islam. Only a secular state can ensure religious freedom. Third, historically, religion and state were not as intertwined. There has been a great deal of struggle and altercation between political and religious authorities.[52] Furthermore, An-Náim argues that the modern state cannot accommodate the pluralistic and complex nature of sharia.[53]

Rather than seeking the theological roots of democracy, An-Náim proposes that a secular state that allows both the negotiation of sharia among different groups of Muslims and its reflection on public policy is the most important condition for democratic governance in Muslim-majority societies. Democracy is superior to the Islamic state as a governance model because it facilitates public deliberation, strengthens civic virtues, allows representation of Islamic policy positions, and engenders consensus among the Muslims, whether they are in the majority or the minority. For An-Náim, while the separation of state and religion (or religious law) is necessary, it is important *not* to separate religion from politics so that Muslims can accept democracy as a viable political system. Devout Muslims should be able to participate in politics and influence policy in democracies. This arrangement should take place even if Islamic law informs their policy positions.[54] In sum, An-Náim views the secular state as a precondition for the Muslim public's acceptance of democracy because devout Muslims will be treated impartially by a secular state and be able to influence policy making according to their religious values. Religious values and even the principles of sharia can affect policy outcomes through the participation of devout Muslims in a secular-democratic order. These conditions will make democracy acceptable to the pious Muslims.

Nader Hashemi[55] also points to the positive role religion can play in the democratization of Muslim-majority societies. Like An-Náim, he views secularism as a prerequisite for democracy and tries to address a significant puzzle. Democracy requires secularism, but the inspiration of the Muslim democrats is the Islamic theology. The outcome of this paradox is the incompatibility of Islam and democracy, a puzzle that Hashemi aims to resolve in his book *Islam, Secularism, and Liberal Democracy*.[56] Hashemi is critical of accounts that see religious ideas as antithetical to liberal democratic order. He invites scholars to rethink the relationship between religion and political development in the West. Religion, particularly reform movements, played an integral role in secularization and political development as the church came to accept legitimate political authority. The liberal democratic order had to deal with religious ideas before it had gained widespread acceptance. In societies where religion remains a potent force in social and political life, secular and political development has to pass "through the gates of religious politics."[57] As Hashemi neatly states:

> Both Christianity in the early modern period and Islam today had to grapple with the idea of the moral basis of legitimate political authority. More importantly, they had to do so in the context of rival notions of political legitimacy rooted in the Scripture. The emergence and social construction of an indigenous version of political secularism was an integral part of this development trajectory. Overcoming religious opposition to emerging liberal democratic ideas was also part of this long-term political process that scholarship on the development of liberal democracy has generally ignored.[58]

For Hashemi, just as secular and liberal democratic order emerged through renegotiation and transformation of religious ideas in the West, religion should have a role in Muslim democratization. As a prerequisite of liberal democracy, secularism lacks authentic roots in Muslim-majority societies. Since its top-down implementation has created hostile attitudes toward it,[59] Hashemi calls for an "indigenous theory of Islamic secularism" as a necessary step toward establishing democracy in the Muslim world.[60] Like An-Náim, for Hashemi, the emergence of secularism will require the input and participation of religiously inspired movements, especially the political Islamists that came to occupy an important place in the public space in the late twentieth century. Just as religion was at the center of the contentious politics for the religiously inspired movements in sixteenth-century Europe, Hashemi argues that participation by political Islamists of the contemporary times can play a significant role in the democratization of Muslim-majority societies. Hashemi states that Islamism "has been responsible for bringing new social groups into the political process, particularly from the previously marginalized sectors of society."[61]

An-Náim and Hashemi make a case for the constructive role of religion in the democratization of Muslim-majority societies. For An-Náim, a secular state is necessary for allowing the devout individuals to participate in policy making based on their religious preferences. Since this is possible in a secular-democratic system that protects religious freedom and allows rival groups' participation in policy making, democracy should be the most appealing form of government for devout individuals. For Hashemi, liberal democracy becomes an acceptable form of government to the extent that religious values inform secularism. Islamist activism plays a vital role in mobilizing religious masses and making Islam a constitutive element of secular liberal democracy. Both scholars focus on secularism as a prerequisite of a democratic system and highlight the instrumental role of religious values and religious identities for genuine acceptance of democracy by devout individuals. However, they do not comment on specific religious values that may inform the participation of religious actors. Such values are important because they emanate from religious norms that are likely to influence the attitudes and behavior of the devout. Khaled Abou El Fadl addresses this issue in his masterful essay on Islam and democracy by exploring the role of justice as a central concept that could provide the normative basis for acceptance of democracy by ordinary Muslims.

Justice as a Normative Principle of Democracy

According to El Fadl, the central paradox in Islam and democracy is the tension between procedures of democracy and theological sources of political norms.[62] The founding principles of democracy, including limited government, popular sovereignty, free elections, and representation, imply that people are the source of law. This understanding poses a challenge for Islamic political theory, according to which "God is the only sovereign and the ultimate source of legitimate law."[63] It is necessary, then, to reconcile the conceptions of people's and God's authority. To resolve this paradox, El Fadl acknowledges the dual conditions of the desirability of democratic institutions and the primacy of theological doctrine in Islam.

El Fadl starts to develop his theory by highlighting the importance of values in a democracy. Much of the theorizing on Islam and democracy focuses on specific institutions that facilitated democratization in the West. While procedures and institutions matter, "democracy and Islam are defined in the first instance by their moral values and attitudinal commitments of their adherents—not by the ways that those values and commitments have been applied."[64] Thus, it is imperative to explore the moral values that will show that Islam has practical possibilities for democracy.

According to El Fadl,[65] pursuing justice, the consultative method of governance leading to nonautocratic states, and mercy and compassion in social relations are essential values in Islam. Man is the vicegerent of God on earth, and this gives him the responsibility to pursue justice in this world. Given the primacy of justice as a social and political value, it is logical to expect that devout individuals will look into the practical possibilities of cherishing the pursuit of justice. As such, for devout Muslims, political systems that facilitate justice will be preferable relative to other systems.[66] For El Fadl, the greatest likelihood of implementing justice is found in democracy because democracy has moral and institutional standards that may facilitate this potential.[67] These standards include civil rights, religious freedom, the rule of law, and political accountability. While there is no guarantee for implementing justice in democratic systems, at a minimum, it provides an institutional basis for fulfilling the primary responsibility of man as vicegerent of God on earth; namely, the pursuance of justice as directed in many verses in the scripture.

Democratic policies are based on the principle of popular sovereignty, not God's sovereignty. If the latter ensures true justice, how can democracy and human-made legislation be the best option for implementing justice? El Fadl finds a solution to this paradox in the flexible sharia interpretation. For El Fadl, "when human beings search for ways to approximate God's beauty and justice, then, they do not deny God's sovereignty; they honor it."[68] If the state claims a monopoly on interpreting and implementing the divine law, excluding alternative interpretations, this condition will likely result in the justification of authoritarian government. This conclusion echoes An-Náim's theory citing the existence of a secular state that does not attempt to define or implement sharia as the prime requisite of democracy. Democracy with its representative and deliberative institutions will better facilitate the interpretation and implementation of sharia than a regime that claims to be the only authority implementing religious law.

After establishing the conditions that support his argument about the acceptability of democracy as the most preferred political system, El Fadl lays the foundation for his argument about justice being a constitutive principle of democracy. According to El Fadl, there is no clear guidance about the relation between the ruler and the ruled in Islam. The central paradigm is that the ruler implements the divine law and obtains the obedience of the ruled. There is supposedly an 'aqd (contract) between the ruler and the people, and, as a result, the people have the power. Within this framework, it is easy to justify the rule of law that ensures that specific regulations bind the government. The contractual nature of political authority and the rule of law are based on normative values inherent in sharia. As El Fadl states, the rule of law "might be interpreted as requiring the government to be bound by processes of making and interpreting laws, and even more important, as requiring that those processes themselves be bound by fundamental moral commitments—in particular to human dignity and freedom."[69] For El Fadl, putting restrictions on a ruler in consideration of public interest (al-maṣālih al-mursalah) or blocking the means to illegal actions demonstrates the primacy of Islamic values as guiding principles of procedures.[70] This reasoning is similar to engaging in forbearance according to informal norms.

The proponents of the compatibility thesis also refer to shūrā or consultation as a founding principle of democratic government in Islam. The Koran instructs the Prophet to consult with Muslims, and his life is replete with examples proving that he had frequently used consultation. Inspired by this principle, modernist scholars attempted to use the shūrā principle to justify representative democracy.[71] To that end, there were attempts to broaden the meaning of shūrā from consultation to wide-ranging discussions or deliberation by the public[72] or to the individual rights to form representative assemblies.[73] El Fadl accepts the significance of shūrā as a foundational principle of participatory democracy. Ultimately, however, it is the moral relevance of this principle that matters:

> so even if *shūrā* is transformed into an instrument of participatory representation, it must itself be limited by a scheme of private and individual rights that serve an overriding moral goal such as justice. In other words, shūrā must be valued not because of the results it produces but because it represents a moral value in itself. As a result, regardless of the value of specific dissenting views, dissent would be tolerated because doing so is seen as a basic part of the mandate of justice.[74]

Islamic justice has substantive implications for democratic procedures and norms. It is closely associated with the notion of "promoting good and forbidding the evil" (*al-amr bi-l-ma'rūf wa-n-nahy 'ani-l-munkar*), considered as an obligation to God and one another.[75] In addition, echoing Abdulaziz Sachedina's conclusion, El Fadl argues that the principles of justice and diversity lay the foundation for respect of differences and dissent.[76] This reasoning extends to the political realm by turning these two principles (justice and diversity) into the core values that democracy ought to protect.

In conclusion, El Fadl develops an Islamic theory of democracy by treating justice as the main principle of Islam. His theory relies on the importance of Islamic values in shaping society and politics. El Fadl's account of the human interpretation of God's law requires a paradigm shift that entails the primacy of justice as a determinant of law rather than the law determining justice.

Conclusion

Democracy emerged as a result of a complex social process in the West. It is also closely associated with liberal values. To explain the democracy gap in Muslim-majority societies, one stream of scholarship blames religion, culture, and values, invoking an incompatibility thesis due to a lack of liberal values or Western institutions that gave way to democracy in Europe.[77] In response, some scholars argued that Islam is compatible with the democratic ethos. Early Islamists responded to positivist and Orientalist views by arguing that democratic institutions were not alien to Islam. This line of reasoning used the shūrā principle and procedures of legal methodology to make a case for the Islamic roots of democracy.[78]

A new genre of scholarship focused on the positive role Islam can play in engendering democratic ideals. One of the proponents of this new approach is Nader Hashemi,[79] who proposes that Islam can play a positive role in justifying a secular order as a prerequisite of democracy through the contribution of Islamists. Similarly, An-Náim[80] argues that the most important condition for the acceptance of democracy by Muslims is a secular state. While Hashemi looks at the participation of Islamists as a condition for the acceptance of secularism and, consequently, democracy, for An-Náim, deliberative democracy, which can be possible under a secular state, would be the main route to engendering support for democracy in the Muslim world. The third group of scholars, including Tariq Ramadan,[81] Abdulaziz Sachedina,[82] and Abou Khaled El Fadl,[83] justify the religious origins of democracy through Islamic values such as mercy and justice. El Fadl's approach is especially noteworthy because he aims to develop the moral base of democracy from within the Islamic value system. This recent wave of scholarship on Islam and democracy contributed to our understanding of Islamic origins of democratic ideals. The scholars justifying democratic government by Islamic values are especially unapologetic in responding to essentialist scholars. They aim to authenticate democracy from within the Islamic paradigm.

Scholars can build on insights from this scholarship to advance our knowledge of Islam and democracy in two ways. First, principles of faith or religious traditions do not inform democracy in only one direction. Rather, religion and religious values have the "double-edged sword" quality that may engender democratic or authoritarian ideals. In other words, Islam can engender rival discourses of legitimacy. We need to unfold the mechanisms through which Islamic values can inspire both democratic and authoritarian ideas. Second, while it is important to elaborate on Islam's compatibility with democracy, we also need to understand the microfoundations of Muslims' support for democracy. While recent scholarship assigned a significant weight to the role of Muslim agency, generally, the focus has still been on "Islam and democracy" at the expense of paying attention to the issue of "Muslims and democracy." As a central value of Islam, if justice matters, how do individuals relate this notion to inform their views about democracy? What are the microlevel implications of Islam's ethical values for political preferences? How do individuals construct the meaning of religious values to form their opinion about different political systems? These questions, in essence, relate to the attitudes of Muslim agency.

This book explains how devout Muslims understand and interpret central religious values to form their attitudes. It puts justice at the center of its investigation into understanding the microlevel perceptions and behavior related to justice of devout Muslims and how these perceptions shape their acceptance or rejection of democracy. Its main contribution rests in its ambition to connect theoretical scholarship on Islam and democracy with the burgeoning empirical studies explaining Muslim political attitudes to understand the puzzle about Islam and democracy better.[84] Building on the research reviewed in this chapter, this book calls for a new approach that examines the role of values rather than principles of faith, legal methodology, or grand traditions for explaining democratic orientations. The analysis in the subsequent chapters builds on this approach to explain the synergies among conceptions of justice, Muslim agency, and support for democracy. The next chapter introduces the theoretical and conceptual foundations for this analysis by exploring historical trajectories of Islamic justice and the microlevel implications of conceptions of political and social justice.

3

Historical and Conceptual Foundations of Justice Discourses in Islam

> A Divine rule can be established only by a man, who, where justice and equity are required, neither feels deficient nor weak and who is not greedy and avaricious.
> —'Ali Ibn Abi Talib (Jafri, *Peak of Eloquence*)

The second Caliph 'Umar is best known for his iconic legacy as an ardent pursuer of justice. History books and folk culture are replete with stories that venerate his acts of justice. It is reported that in a letter sent to the governor of Basra, he said: "When people come to you for a hearing or when you gather a council, treat people equally. In this way, the weak will not despair of your justice. And the strong will not get the feeling that you may oppress others for your own gain."[1] In addition to pursuing political justice in his administration, he also set an example for future generations in economic justice through charitable acts and distributive policies. Being a just ruler in 'Umar's image has been an aspiration of many caliphs and sultans over the centuries. The *mazalim* courts, an administrative court designed for hearing ordinary people's grievances, were inspired by 'Umar's administrative style. It was not uncommon for the rulers to show acts of generosity or check on their subjects by joining the crowds in the marketplace or wandering around the streets at night while hiding their true identity, also a practice of 'Umar. Sultans aspired to be just rulers, impartial in their administration and caring for the welfare of their subjects following his example.

Political and religious authorities eventually separated in the Muslim world as the Islamic empires expanded. Religious values still mattered in politics to the extent that rulers used them to legitimize governance.[2] Justice principles exactly provided such validation. Inspired by the exemplary conduct and policies of 'Umar, scholars developed guidelines for the rulers to help them fulfill this ambition. These guidelines, known as goals of Islamic law, concerned the implementation of Islamic justice and included the protection of religion, life, mind, offspring, and property.[3] Implementation of these guidelines was vital for pursuing general welfare or public interest (maṣlaḥa).[4] In effect, a ruler abiding by these principles was demonstrating forbearance, a norm that provided an impression of political legitimacy.

Shahab Ahmed argues that the interplay of justice and provision of welfare was the essence of Muslim politics.[5] For example, Islamists of the modern era explicitly tied the notion of justice to the divine law and popular sovereignty. Two well-known intellectuals of the nineteenth century, al-Afghānī and Kemal, argued that despotism and foreign intervention—not Islam—were the main reasons behind injustices and that Western political institutions could be conducive to implementation of public interest in accordance with the Islamic law.[6] In the same vein, the democratic movements of the nineteenth and early twentieth centuries used the Islamic concepts to frame demands for accountable government and social justice.[7] Contemporary Islamists like Qutb, Mawdudi, and Shariati grounded their theories of political justice in religious doctrine.[8] Notably, the interplay of religious values and demands for justice was explicit in the chants of protesters during the Arab Spring. Protesters called for justice by voicing their concerns about corruption, economic decline, lack of economic opportunities, repression, and violation of human dignity. The language of these demands is, understandably, different from the jargon used by the group known as Kharijites protesting all parties during the first civil war in the seventh century. Similar differences will surface if one compares the chants of Arab Spring protesters demanding justice to the demands of the Ottoman constitutionalists who were mainly concerned with the state decline and constitutional government.

It is only natural that religiously inspired justice values and their relation to political reality would differ across contexts. However, despite differences in the language and style, we can observe certain continuities in the legacies of Islamic conceptions of justice throughout the centuries. These conceptions are significant markers of political legitimacy and pluralistic ideals in Muslim political experience. For example, the development of political and social justice trajectories was visible in competing conceptions of justice between the ethical and the realist views of politics[9] or this distinction resurfaced in the cleavage between traditional and modernist Islamists in the modern era.[10]

This chapter illustrates the evolution of "justice" as a normative principle in Islamic political theory. Throughout Islamic history, political struggles, social welfare, and unjust rule have been the fundamental problems of politics. These struggles triggered profound debates about the politics of justice, including state legitimacy, obedience to authorities, right/duty of rebellion against tyranny, and popular sovereignty. The subsequent analysis neither provides a detailed historical treatment of the subject nor attempts to present a literal analysis of justice as a scriptural concept.[11] It is rather selective in its scope. It aims to understand the development of conceptions of justice within the plurality of Muslim political experience. Since Muslim political experiences are not static,[12] the analysis explores historical ruptures and continuities. This approach helps depict the linkages between various conceptions of justice and contemporary political preferences of devout Muslims from past to present.

Conceptual Continuities and Variations of Islamic Conceptions of Justice

Research on religion and politics has widely explored religious identity, belief, and behavior to explain the interplay of faith and political attitudes.[13] This study adds to this research program by focusing on the relationship between religious values and political preferences. Religious values are likely to have substantial effects on individual attitudes and behavior.[14] Of Islamic values, justice is best situated to help scholars understand how religion shapes individuals' preferences, especially those concerning politics. This is because justice as a core value of Islam concerns prescriptions about the self, the community, and the government at the same time. It is no coincidence that the doctrinal principle of the oneness of God (tawhid), the discourse about the role of man as vicegerent within the cosmology of divine order, and the general theory of Islamic governance are all, in one way or another, connected to the concept of justice.[15]

Conceptions of political and social justice originate from the beginning of Islam, particularly the political struggles and debates about selecting a community leader as early as the seventh century. During the medieval period, social justice was defined in terms of security, order, and welfare of society.[16] As the first Islamic Empire expanded and various rulers started to create an independent body of legislation (qānūn) next to the vast religious rulings, justice came to be associated with the ruler's qualities and the compatibility between qānūn and sharia.[17] Much later, following the first Muslim encounters with a triumphant West, traditional Islamists began to associate justice with the renewal of religion (tajdīd). Modernists turned to Western ideas such as popular sovereignty and constitutional government to provide prescriptions for removing the injustices in their societies.[18] In these examples, we see the evolution of conceptions of justice in response to the changing social and political problems of the age.

We need to consider various interpretations of faith principles to explain the formative effect of values on pious Muslims' preferences. In this vein, studying the conceptual evolution of justice will help elucidate its implications for individual attitudes and behavior. Before providing the analysis of conceptual variations in justice trajectories, a quick note about its literal meaning will be helpful: the Arabic word for *justice* stems from the root *'adl*, which in its verb form means to straighten, depart from one path to the other, be equal, or balance.[19] Several other concepts are used in the Koran and hadiths to highlight the different aspects of justice. Some of these include *qisṭ* (installment, fair share), *mizan* (balance), *wasaṭ* (middle), and *istiqamā* (direction).[20] In Arabic, the opposite of *'adl* is *jawr*, literally oppression or tyranny. There is no lack of words for articulating the opposite of justice, including *ẓulm* (wrongdoing, tyranny), *ṭughyān* (extremity), and *inḥirāf* (deviation).[21] The word *'adl* is mentioned twenty-four times in twenty-two verses in the Koran.[22] Some of these verses refer to divine justice and others to just dealings in social life.

Building on this rich semantic field, scholars used different conceptions of justice to address the tension between the idealized interpretations of divine justice and its practical applications in human societies. A classic interpretation of Islam states that God is the ultimate sovereign, the legislator, the protector, and the sole provider. Since divine justice emanates from these principles, the faithful believe that God's justice is perfect. The challenge, however, arises when individuals try to implement the ideal justice in this world. The disparity between the idealized notions of sacred justice and the real-world conditions restricting its realization, here and now, forms the main background for the endless intellectual debates in Islamic political theory.[23] One needs to closely examine the special moments in the history of Islam, some of which could be viewed as critical junctures, to better grasp the political and social implications of this divergence.

The analysis proposes two such moments to explain the development of justice trajectories and their long-lasting influence on devout Muslims' attitudes. The first of these moments occurred in the seventh century when the first civil war broke out to create political divisions in the early Muslim community, eventually giving way to the sectarian separation into Sunni and Shia camps.[24] The second moment took place during the decline of the Abbasid rule and the Mongol invasion of the thirteenth century. The interaction of the scholarly and practical political fields at these critical moments resulted in two distinct justice trajectories, political justice and social justice. Various debates and struggles around these trajectories continued into the modern era, creating continuities and variations in the notion of justice and its strategic deployment by political actors. Through the analysis of such historical foundations of concepts, we can better understand Muslim political preferences.

Lineages of Political Justice

The political justice trajectory contains some essential issues, including political succession, qualities of rulers, and sources of legitimate authority. The intellectual debates dedicated to resolving these issues, especially the tension between the necessity of obedience and the duty of rebellion against an unjust ruler, undergirded the central tenets of the political justice trajectory. This debate's main parameters resurfaced in times of crisis (ruler succession, wars) with significant adjustments to the justice discourse.[25]

Of primary importance for understanding the connections between the trajectory of political justice and the preferences toward government is the prophetic community and the first civil war (A.D. 657). As stated above, the first civil war followed a disagreement about political succession upon the passing of Prophet Muhammad. The prophetic community was essentially a political organization, yet its members were bound by religious and moral principles. Patricia Crone describes this unique model with the metaphor of a caravan, where the whole community moves toward one direction (rightful path) under the guidance of the Prophet.[26] Upon Muhammad's death, umma's unity—inextricably linked to the Prophet's persona—came to an abrupt end. The debates about political authority and succession loomed large in a divided community, searching for new directions amid the unfolding turmoil. At this moment in history, conceptions of political justice informed much of the political theory, still in its infancy, that speculated on such issues as legitimacy, the duty of obedience, the right to rebellion, the selection of a just ruler, and benevolent absolutism.

The prophetic community as an example of social organization was elevated to a special status, an ideal vision, or the *golden age* to be followed by subsequent generations of believers.[27] In sharp contrast to this utopian vision, the reality brought about deep political divisions.[28] When 'Ali accepted arbitration in the first civil war to resolve the issue of political leadership against the claims of Mu'āwiya, a group known as Kharijite (or Khawarij, those who defected or left) took a unique position disagreeing with both parties. For Khawarij, arbitration meant the violation of the main principle of God's rule, namely, there is no sovereign other than God (*lā ḥukma ilā lillāh*). This group protested the arbitration method for the resolution of the leadership crisis. According to Khawarij, this method was illegitimate because sovereignty belongs to God, who is the sole authority for selecting the imam.[29]

This early schism's long-lasting legacy is the division between Shia and Sunni sects that initially concerned the political succession problem.[30] The

Shia believed that being a member of the Prophet's family is necessary for becoming the leader of the umma. They argued that the Prophet designated his son-in-law 'Ali to be his successor and passed him the vital knowledge for this task. Through blood ties to the Prophet and other qualifications, the rightly designated imam would be infallible and is the only one who could implement justice in this world. In contrast, the Sunni doctrine argues that choosing the imam is the responsibility of the whole community based on consensus.[31] The community's agreement on selecting the leader is the principal prerequisite for implementing justice because popular sovereignty is considered a foundation of just government.[32] The Kharijite position firmly adhered to this argument. They argued that since sovereignty belongs to God, its exercise cannot be a privilege of a few men. Since everyone is equal, all umma members should have a right to participate in a leader's selection. However, Khawarij went one step further by contending for the community's right to remove a corrupt and unjust imam. For them, God could not have willed such an injustice.

The debates on predetermination, free will, and justice resulted in various political approaches about selecting and deposing the imam (or sultan, caliph).[33] The Khawarij were the first to raise the question of *qadar* (power) as a quality that all believers possess, including the ruler. For them, it was critical to hold any individual responsible for the injustices that he may commit because man has to bear the consequences of his free will. In contrast, the *Jabrī* School supported the idea of predetermination, attributing all acts of creation, including both just and unjust acts, to God. This school of thought viewed the ideas of human choice and responsibility as irrelevant or nonissues.[34] The intellectual controversy about predetermination and free will has been the foundation of political divisions throughout Islamic history.[35]

This debate has significant implications for the notions of justice and political legitimacy. According to the *Qadarī* School, free will makes it incumbent on the ruler to act justly. For the ruled, it is their responsibility to elect a just imam and depose an unjust ruler. The Qadarī School took the implications of free will and human choice to its logical extremes to develop the conceptual foundations of popular sovereignty and political accountability. The proponents of the *Jabrī* School, in contrast, inferred legitimacy from the premise of predetermination insofar as the logical implication of their theory concerned the legitimacy of all acts of the ruler regardless of justice.[36]

The duality between Qadarī and Jabrī Schools was only the beginning of future incarnations of the dichotomies concerning free will and predetermination, reason and revelation, justice and oppression, and democracy and tyranny. These dualities were concentrated in creedal and philosophical spheres, leading to endless debates among kalam scholars, philosophers,

Sufis, and theologians.[37] However, such dualities are also clearly visible in the parallel universe of practical politics. As with theological positions, political behavior was also informed by conceptions of justice. Abdelwahab El-Affendi, who believes that a specific tension came to define Muslim politics from the very beginning, wrote an account of Muslim political history that succinctly captures these dichotomies.[38] For El-Affendi, the *ethicalists* held a puritanical worldview and called for the implementation of a social order reminiscent of the ideal prophetic community (i.e., Medina model), whereas the *realists*, championed by the Umayyad rulers, aimed to grab the political power at the expense of the ideal communal vision (i.e., Damascus model).[39] This cleavage consolidated at the height of the Umayyad Empire (A.D. 692–750). The growing size of non-Arab and non-Muslim populations in the first Islamic Empire brought about the questioning of the *jamā'a* model,[40] which stemmed from the notion of Arab tribal allegiances. Depicting this division as a schism between Marwani caliphs and the *piety-minded opposition*, Marshall Hodgson argues, "Gradually the ideal of benevolent absolutism attached itself to the caliph's court, confronting the ideal of Islamic egalitarianism in the opposition."[41] In effect, Hodgson's characterization of the political divisions in the Islamic Empire is no more than the projection of creedal duality between *Qadarī* and *Jabrī* positions into the realm of practical politics.

Representing the main opposition and building on the discourses of injustices committed against the family of the Prophet, the Shia groups were instrumental in developing political justice theory. However, the weight of various Sunni groups in this development should not be ignored. As the Umayyad Empire expanded and the Muslim rulers aimed to build social solidarity according to an Arab-dominated aristocratic order, and, hence, introducing hierarchies and inequalities, the new political reality was put under scrutiny by individuals who "envisaged a society which should embody justice on earth, led by the most pious among the Muslims."[42] Most notably seen within the Shia tradition, such piety-minded leaders bred the idea of rebellion against unjust rulers. They introduced a theology of legitimacy by linking political behavior to Islam's ethical values.[43] Consequently, the emerging justice principles of piety-minded opposition, next to egalitarian social commitments, included such values as human dignity, denunciation of corruption, and the necessity of rebellion against unjust rulers.

Piety-minded opposition, or ethicalists in El-Affendi's framework, can be viewed as one of the first religiously informed political groups striving to constrain the ruler in Islamic history. At times, this opposition led to rebellions against the oppressive rulers.[44] In other cases, pious leaders used their religious authority to constrain the oppressive and corrupt elite.[45] Therefore, this ethical dimension of political behavior somehow introduces a democratic quality into Muslim political discourse, constraining the executive for the sake of justice.[46] Simultaneously, an alternative vision restricted collective action against the ruler to encourage obedience for avoiding political chaos, regardless of injustices. Throughout the centuries, this tension, or duality to be more precise, inspired social revolutions and protests, on the one hand, and legitimization of authoritarian governance, on the other. The ideologies developed regarding the first schisms in Islam became potent ideals informing the notions of political justice, its application in practical politics, and political attitudes of the devout until today.

The historical origins of political justice trajectories have implications for Muslim political attitudes. For example, the dichotomies of justice versus tyranny or rebellion versus obedience have resurfaced in the modern age with references to religious values, but these concepts also utilized modern political language. Nineteenth-century Tobacco Protest and the subsequent constitutional revolutions in Iran combined the religious terminology of justice with the modern notions of popular sovereignty and constitutional government. One can trace the lineages of justice discourses in the language of popular resistance to domestic dictators or the fight against imperialism, as presented by 'Ali Shariati, one of the ideologues of the Iranian Revolution. It is possible to trace the reconstruction of legacies of justice discourses also in the ideologies of the 1960s Islamist movements in Turkey. These ideologies propagated political obedience for the sake of establishing public order (*kamu düzeni*). In the 1990s, the Turkish Islamists shifted their preferences toward an ideology of resistance, followed, after 2010, by another shift involving religious-nationalist justification of obedience to an authoritarian regime with Turkey's democratic backsliding under an Islamist party. The lineages of political justice constitute one side of the coin in the study of justice and democracy. On the flip side, the social justice trajectory completes the full picture.

Lineages of Social Justice

The social justice trajectory has primarily concerned welfare provision and security. As proposed by Khadduri[47] and Ahmed,[48] these policy issues, especially from the thirteenth century onward, preoccupied the intellectuals and religious scholars seeking to remedy the ills of a declining society. One implication of the Islamic social justice conception is the installation of a just ruler who could be a guarantor of order and prosperity. Given such historical origins, it can be argued that governance styles that consider human dignity and accountability and those that prevent arbitrary rule would be more appealing. Since general welfare and egalitarian policies are more likely to occur under democratic institutions, it is likely that Islamic social justice values would increase the appeal of democracy vis-à-vis an authoritarian regime among the devout Muslims. On the flip side, the same conception may lead to the justification of authoritarian rule. Economic justice and rulers' generosity in charity toward his subjects could be primary justifications for benevolent absolutism.

Historically, Islamic rulers tended to prioritize order and security as preconditions of welfare provision over freedom to gain legitimacy as benevolent but authoritarian rulers. This tendency has been and is still being used by authoritarian rulers in contemporary Muslim politics. Middle Eastern states, for example, deployed Bismarckian welfare policies in the 1960s and 1970s to aid authoritarian survival.[49] The rentier states frequently utilize distributive policies to quiet dissent.[50] Notably, the oil-rich monarchies have upped their game of welfare provision in the wake of the Arab Spring, including improvements to social security to buy citizen loyalty and quell the demands for democracy.[51] Religious justifications of these regimes are also not uncommon as exemplified by the Wahhabi scholars' support for the Saudi rulers or Sheikh Bin Bayyah's fatwas legitimizing the authoritarian policies of the United Arab Emirates.[52] By and large, then, examining the Islamic social justice trajectory may help us comprehend the extent of linkages between various social justice interpretations and political preferences tilted toward favorable views of democracy or authoritarianism.

The intellectual origins of Islamic social justice theory can be found in the medieval era corresponding to the period of political fragmentation of Islamic states starting in the tenth century. Khadduri explains these origins with two factors.[53] First, the central power of the Abbasid state was weakened with the emergence of smaller states that ruled stretches of the vast Islamic Empire. Second, the Mongol invasion and the destruction of Baghdad in A.D. 1258 had devastating effects on the well-being of Islamic society. These conditions necessitated a positive definition of justice that could ensure public order.

The practical origins of social justice, in contrast, can be traced back to the pre-Islamic notion of the circle of justice, an idea that created perceptions of political legitimacy in the Middle East for many centuries.[54] The circle of justice refers to the harmony among the sovereign, the army, the law, and the subjects in a just society. While all of the elements within the *circle* matter, the ruler's right to make the law and political accountability became especially important during the medieval Islamic period. The welfare provision according to Islamic law is particularly relevant to the idea of the circle. The ruler's law is conceived as the embodiment of the goals of divine law, which are the same as the maṣlaḥa itself, according to Abdelkader.[55] As Ahmed succinctly says, "The ruler's *siyasat* [politics], then, is precisely the making of laws in accordance with the general principles of shariat by observation and reason of what is necessary for the goal of human welfare in the context of the needs of the time and place."[56]

In general, politics revolved around the notions of security, order, and the provision of welfare services during the classical Islamic period.[57] Whenever deviations occurred, these acts were seen to be outside the realm of Islamic justice.[58] This synergy between Islamic law and just governance continued to be relevant when the economic and political decline in relation to the West became visible in the seventeenth century. For example, this condition gave way to intensified internal reform efforts in the Ottoman Empire. As early as 1631, the Ottoman statesman Koçi Bey prepared a report for Sultan Murad IV addressing corruption, nepotism, and domestic reform to rehabilitate the rotten state institutions.[59] This first report marked a series of reform efforts continuing with the nineteenth-century *Tanzimat*[60] and culminating into the first Ottoman constitutional government in 1876. These reforms highlighted the need for effective state institutions, eliminating corruption, and welfare provision to remove injustices. The primary legacies of the Islamic social justice trajectory were among the main reference points in these reform efforts.

Islamic conceptions of social justice also have their roots in scriptural emphasis on benevolence and charity. Just as in the political justice trajectory, the prophetic community serves as an ideal model to be emulated by the devout Muslims. Although such idealized versions of prophetic benevolence and charity or 'Umar's example have been important elements of social justice theory, the medieval paradigm of social justice was based on the notions of Islamic law and welfare provision. Notably, medieval scholar Ibn Taymiyya developed an elaborate social justice theory focusing on the provision of public goods, security, and distributive policies.[61]

The Islamic social justice paradigm was mainly a practical political project to be carried out by a just ruler holding particular virtues and who is bound with the principles of Islam. Social justice rested on three pillars. Legally, it relied on intellectual vibrancy in the area of law (sharia vs. *qānūn*).[62] Theoretically, it drew liberally from Islamic ethics and law to define the characteristics of the just ruler. Practically, this paradigm proposed a government model based on a division of labor and cooperation between the legal scholars (ulema) and rulers.[63] In practice, however, as Kuru argues, the last condition resulted in the encroachment of secular law into the religious law and the ulema's subordination to the sultans.[64]

The social justice paradigm does not solely rely on the work of legal scholars. Like the developmental trajectory of political justice, the social justice paradigm was also influenced by philosophers and scholars of ethics who focused on the virtues of rulers and social justice. Al-Farabi's masterpiece, *On the Perfect State*,[65] had been the definitive source for the scholars of ethics, including the highly influential work of Nasir-ud-Din Tusi, *Akhlāq-i Nāsirī*, the main text that inspired future generations of scholars of Muslim politics. For al-Farabi, a just ruler should have certain qualities, including wisdom, love, fairness, good memory, and physical health. The ruler's most important function is to uphold the law toward justice and happiness in his utopian *virtuous city*. One of the most important qualities of the just ruler is his knowledge of religious law and his ability to create and implement it for the public interest.[66]

Building on al-Farabi's ideas, a lively political advisory literature, *mirrors for princes*, became widespread to guide rulers in the virtues of ruling.[67] The essential wisdom of this literature concerns the application of religious law and the implementation of justice. In this approach, a ruler can govern effectively by providing security and public goods.[68] General welfare and happiness of the umma were seen as the most significant issues also according to scholars like Ibn Taymiyya and Ibn Khaldun. They correctly identified the instrumental value of law in solving the crisis of the Islamic world. Although Taymiyya was a jurist and Khaldun was a sociologist, both were concerned about social welfare.[69] They searched for religiously justified, positive rules to facilitate the implementation of social justice. According to the overarching goal of justice, rulers' engagement with the law seems to be the most significant element for these scholars. As Khadduri states in his account of Ibn Taymiyya:

> The unity of Religion and Law (state), which exists in principle, must be carried out in practice. Without the effective power (shawka) of the state, he [Ibn Taymiyya] held, religion and Law would be in danger. Conversely, without the constraints of the Law, the state (presided over by despotic rulers) degenerates into an unjust and tyrannical organization. Only in the pursuit of justice can the state be expected to fulfill the ends for which it was established. The justice that Ibn Taymiyya strove to achieve was obviously a new concept enshrined in the Siyāsa Shar'iyya which might be called social justice, as its aims were to serve the public interest.[70]

Although the proposed constraints on the ruler, whether through law or the activism of ulema, introduce a democratic quality into Ibn Taymiyya's model, this approach may also be conducive to the justification of authoritarian politics. Insofar as the ruler maintained the religion, prevented the vice, and provided public goods, it would not be appropriate to rebel against him even if he was unjust. In practice, Ibn Taymiyya's theory proposing to place constraints on the ruler by the power of law was not realistic. This theory relied on the norms of forbearance,[71] which were not always closely followed by the rulers who relied on the divine right discourse. It assumed that the rulers who claim to have a divine right to power would follow religious norms and not transgress or violate the religious norms of governance. In reality, as the secular rulers increasingly came to define religious law, ulema became the servants of the rulers.[72] Rather than checking the executive using religious authority, the ulema were at the mercy of the rulers. In fact, they had no choice but to assume the rulers would follow the norms of forbearance. This development undermined the democratic potential implied in this medieval model in the *longue durée*.[73]

The devastating effects of the Mongol invasion accelerated the implementation of this authoritarian model. The classical Islamic state was replaced by the absolutist state models that relied less on ethical concerns than on the discourses of order and security. The codification of religious law and experimentation with new constitutional orders in Iran and Turkey[74] deemed both the Taymiyyan model and absolutist incarnations of state obsolete. Encounters with the West and modernity gave way to new ideologies replacing this elitist classical model with a populist project in the hands of intellectuals, rulers, and Sufi orders,[75] a development leading to Islamism's appeal in the twentieth century.[76] Riding on the power of Western democratic ideals such as popular sovereignty and constitutional government, legacies of social justice resurfaced in the nineteenth and twentieth centuries in the demands for domestic reforms and calls to ending injustices. Despite widespread democratic movements, enlightened despotism using religious justifications and co-opting the religious scholars became the dominant model in many Muslim-majority societies.[77]

Justice Trajectories and Political Preferences

This chapter presented a stylistic description of political and social justice trajectories in Islam. The analysis relied on a selective reading of Islamic history to flesh out the main elements of justice theory related to Muslim political preferences. Critical historical moments during the early period of Islam formed the foundations of the political justice paradigm, primarily revolving around leader selection and qualities of the rulers. Informed by the philosophical arguments about predetermination and free will, political theory attempted to resolve issues like imamate, political obedience, executive constraints, and rebellion. Communal divisions and violence shaped the politics on the ground. Different intellectual traditions came up with explanations to make sense of the emerging divisions and violence within the Muslim community. The philosophical debates concerned man's role within a cosmological order. One camp proposed that man is free, whereas the other believed that everything is predetermined. In the long run, the first path of the political justice trajectory provided religious justifications for modern ideas such as popular sovereignty, executive accountability, and constitutional government. These justifications relied on the assumption that man is rational and free as a vicegerent of God. This assumption implies that man has the power and responsibility to correct injustices. This includes the right to elect a just ruler and the duty to depose an unjust one. Therefore, this first path of the political justice trajectory introduces a democratic quality into Islamic political theory.

In the modern era, Islamists built the intellectual foundations of Islamic democracy using the religious philosophies of rationality, freedom, and equality while also utilizing different conceptions of justice to make a case for democratic ideals in Islam.[78] Islamists were not merely reacting to the West's ascendance; they were also motivated to reverse the state's decline through deep reforms. Their main solutions were popular sovereignty and constitutional government because they believed these institutions were inherent to Islam and closely related to the conception of justice. For example, al-Afghānī believed that the grave injustices harming the public interest in the Muslim world were the result of despotism and foreign intervention.[79] He proposed that domestic reform and participation of people in public affairs through elected bodies could bring justice. Ottoman Islamists, al-Afghānī, and later his disciple Muhammad Abduh were trying to reconcile the popular demands of the democratic protests with Islamic principles.[80] Since the nineteenth century, the constitutionalist movements of the modern era and widespread mass protests were inspired by the conceptions of political justice like freedom, human dignity, and popular sovereignty. Some examples include the Urabi Revolt in Egypt, the constitutional revolutions in Iran and Turkey, anticolonial independence movements, and, most notably, the Arab Spring. Consequently, with its continuities and variations extending over centuries, the political justice trajectory has significant potential for engendering contemporary political preferences that could be conducive to democracy.

The political justice trajectory, however, is Janus-faced. It could be used to justify obedience and legitimize the authoritarian government. This statement follows the implications of predetermination perspective. Insofar as God predetermines every aspect of life, leaving little or no room for individual choice, whatever happens in the political sphere must be "just" by definition. Since God will not ever desire injustice, a ruler's reign, regardless of how he comes to and maintains power, reflects God's justice. By the same token, any act of the ruler is also just. Thus, obedience to the ruler is not only required but a duty upon the believers.

Consequently, individuals who hold religiously orthodox beliefs stemming from the predetermination doctrine will be indifferent toward any political system, democratic or authoritarian. This attitude is likely to swing toward proauthoritarian attitudes when a benevolent dictator provides order and security. Research shows that dictatorships that implement popular economic policies, mostly providing material benefits for citizens, survive longer.[81] The rentier states of the Gulf region combining Islamic values and oil monies are examples supporting this proposition. Research also shows that religious individuals with communitarian views prefer the authoritarian government to democracy due to social and political benefits they may obtain from the state-sanctioned religious participation of others.[82] Together, these research findings demonstrate that the implications of the political justice trajectory may lead to political indifference or support for the authoritarian government among the devout.

The roots of social justice ideals, on the other side, are related to Islam's emphasis on charity and benevolence. Rulers may utilize Islam's doctrinal focus on charity and benevolence to give distributive policies a sacred quality. Exaggerated acts of generosity by the authoritarian leaders or charitable acts of Islamist political actors in settings where electoral competition matters provide examples of utilitarian exploitation of Islam's emphasis on charity.[83]

During the medieval period, social justice was hardly concerned with developing a religious ideology to propagate distributive policy. At that time, the Islamic social justice paradigm concerned the general welfare of society.[84] The authorship and guardianship of religious law were the central problems of politics. One interpretation gave the upper hand to the religious scholars who created and guarded Islamic law. However, in reality, religious scholars were subservient to the secular authority and provided the religious justification for his supremacy. In both conditions, general welfare or public interest played a crucial role. Today, various Islamic states, including Iran and Saudi Arabia, are political arenas where the struggles over the nature and extent of the social justice policies concerning wealth distribution, social security, public goods provision, and Islam's role in these policies constitute the primary political issues.

The legacies of social justice may shape contemporary political preferences in two different ways. First, Islam's emphasis on charity and benevolence necessitates the implementation of religiously inspired welfare policies in Muslim-majority societies where devotion remains at significant levels. Since democratic institutions are more conducive to egalitarian policies to benefit the largest group of people relative to the authoritarian institutions,[85] it follows that the best path to society's general welfare is the implementation of policies upholding Islamic justice. As such, democracy should be more acceptable to the devout who cherish charity and benevolence ideals. This idea is compatible with Carles Boix's[86] and Daron Acemoglu and James A. Robinson's[87] theories, who argue that democracy is more acceptable to the poor, because egalitarian distribution is more likely to take root in democratic systems. This is because the leaders who impose a tax policy can be rewarded or punished in the polls based on the extent of distributive returns to the public.

Second, Islamic social justice discourses may also inform authoritarian preferences. In the medieval Islamic period, either religious scholars had the responsibility to ensure political accountability mechanisms or the abstract notion of the supremacy of religious law constituted the main constraints for the rulers' policy execution. This is what would be implied by the forbearance norm that is invoked in contemporary social science research as an important condition preventing the erosion of democracy.[88] However, during the medieval period, religious authority was transformed into a tool of authoritarian government insofar as it created an alliance between the religious scholars and the rulers where the latter commanded the former.[89] Thus, justification of authoritarian policies by religion resulted in a discourse of obedience to an unjust ruler in the name of order, security, and common good. This would imply a preference toward authoritarian rule insofar as the subject of obedience was a benevolent dictator who managed to ensure social order and provide an acceptable level of social welfare. Consequently, Islamic conceptions of social justice may generate support for authoritarian regimes.

Conclusion

What makes democracy more acceptable to ordinary Muslims is its potential to uphold human dignity and social order because democracy has a relative advantage in implementing political and social justice. At the same time, democracy allows Muslims to affect policy making through political participation according to their religious beliefs[90] or by hosting institutions conducive to the implementation of Islamic justice.[91] This argument relies on the assumption that democracies have an advantage, compared to autocracies, in participatory policy formulation compatible with Islamic religious values. It also assumes that, given the opportunity, pious Muslims should understand the comparative advantage of democracy in both political and economic justice fronts. Evidence suggests the feasibility of the first assumption. Many studies find that Muslim religiosity and values are not hostile to democracy.[92] We also know that Muslims living in the West prefer democracy and actively engage in democratic life.[93] The demands of the protesters in the Iranian Green movement or the Arab uprisings since 2010 are also suggestive that Muslims do prefer democracy for its potential in implementing economic and political justice.[94]

The subsequent chapters further develop these insights and provide empirical evidence to explain the associations between Islamic conceptions of justice and Muslim political preferences. To examine the continuities in justice trajectories, Chapter 4 traces the theories of political and social justice in the works of contemporary Islamists Sayyed Qutb and 'Ali Shariati.

This chapter demonstrates that the tensions inherent in the development of social and political justice trajectories such as free will versus predetermination and the duty of obedience versus the right to rebellion resurface in the contemporary manifestations of Muslim political outlooks. This book also brings significant empirical evidence to test several hypotheses about various conceptions of Islamic justice and Muslim political preferences. For example, in Chapter 5, the content analysis of the Islamist writings reveals a tension between discourses of order and discourses of freedom in Islamic political theory. Chapter 6 demonstrates that lineages of justice continue to shape Islamic worldviews among the Islamist youth. It provides evidence from in-depth interviews to show how Islamists continue to use some of the same arguments developed over centuries to inform their preferences about democracy and other regime types. Chapter 7 tests the individual-level implications of social and political justice trajectories related to support for democracy and authoritarianism using public opinion surveys conducted in the Muslim-majority societies. Finally, Chapter 8 examines the protests as a manifestation of the right to rebellion and a call for just government during the Arab Spring.

4

Islamist Justice Theory

> Oppression and tyranny are the worst companions for the hereafter.
>
> —'ALI IBN ABI TALIB (Jafri, *Peak of Eloquence*)

Islamic justice trajectories involve both social and political dimensions. Disagreement about leader selection in the early Muslim community resulted in deep intellectual and political divisions. Debates about political justice were at the center of these divisions. In the medieval period, the focus shifted toward social justice to deal with the declining social order. These political and social justice trajectories shaped political philosophies over centuries. Contemporary Islamists utilize the language of Islamic political and social justice,[1] but social justice has become especially significant in Islamist political strategy.[2]

This chapter explains the philosophical foundations of Islamist justice theory developed by Sayyid Qutb and 'Ali Shariati, mainly focusing on conceptions of social justice. Qutb and Shariati do not merely use static religious resources to develop a political philosophy of justice; instead, they define social justice as praxis.[3] Primarily inspired by Islam's cosmological framework, Qutb and Shariati argue that only a *free agency* defined as God's vicegerent can implement justice. Specifically, free human agency and the voluntary practice of benevolent/charitable acts are constitutive social justice principles. Qutb and Shariati revert to the spirit of the political justice proponents from the early period of Islam rather than using the conceptions of the medieval period to construct new social justice paradigms. However, the line between political justice and social justice is generally ambiguous in their writings.

Qutb and Shariati build their social justice theories as *metanarratives*[4] within the universal *truth-claim* of Islam. Both employ highly flexible interpretations of Islam to inform their conceptions of social justice instead of a scriptural literalist position. This approach helps them avoid utopian narratives that fail to address the practical social problems. In one broad stroke, they recast Islam as the sole panacea to modern social ills, and, with that, they hope to undermine the appeal of the Western ideologies. Their method, practice-oriented and flexible interpretation of religious principles, helps them legitimize Islamist social justice policy over the Western models (a.k.a. "Islam is the solution").

This chapter derives insights from Qutb and Shariati's political philosophy to explain the political attitudes and behavior of pious Muslims. The analysis deliberately focuses on "Muslims" rather than on "Islam" in studying conceptions of social and political justice. This approach is different from the Western-centric, Orientalist approaches. Orientalists study Islam using the concept of "religion" as defined in the Western intellectual sense. As Shahab Ahmed argues, the history of church-state relations in the West resulted in a compartmentalized social order where religion as a universal truth-claim involving "private religious norms" exists in separation from the "public political norms" such as the secular truth-claims like capitalism, liberal democracy, or communism.[5] However, there is no church in Islam. Hence, the institutionalization and compartmentalization of Islam as a *religion* will fail to understand Islam's diffuse and distributive nature, which Ahmed describes as a "way of life" (*din*) that require the continuous participation of human agency in both public and private spheres. As Ahmed succinctly states, "When we organize the world in terms of the sacred/religion vs. secular/nonreligion binary, this just does not help us in—indeed actively obstructs us from—recognizing and grasping central ways in which Muslims have conceptualized being Muslim."[6] The importance of this statement cannot be overstated, as it should guide us in avoiding the essentialist approaches regarding such questions as "Is Islam compatible with democracy?" or "Does Islam establish social justice with zakat?"

As discussed below, Qutb and Shariati take Islam as a way of life without using the sacred and secular binary to build their social justice theories. Liberal justice theories are strictly secular and imply a consensus about minimally acceptable rights and secular distribution.[7] In contrast, the Islamist conception avoids the religious/secular dichotomy, takes religion as a way of life, and, subsequently, uses divine principles to provide solutions to the worldly injustices through active engagement of free and conscientious individuals. Islamic democracy models follow similar reasoning.[8] Islamic justice theory stems from a cosmological worldview that views man as the vicegerent of God on earth. Within this cosmology, man's actions are part of and serve a balance between God and his creation. Political and social justice are manifestations of this balance.

The treatment of *Qutbian* and *Shariatian* texts in this chapter and the application of Islamist social justice theory to the analysis of Muslim political attitudes and behavior in other chapters of this volume also utilize a specific method in the study of the Muslim agency. This method is used by a prominent student of Islam, Abdullahi Ahmed An-Náim. In his seminal study dealing with global justice and human rights from an Islamic perspective, An-Náim states, "This emphasis on the agency of the human subject in determining what justice means for her, and striving for realizing her own conception, leads me to focus on Muslims as believers seeking justice, rather than speaking of Islam as a religion."[9] By promoting and applying this approach, this chapter shows that Islamist social justice is not merely a transcendental idea but rather a praxis carried by human agency's free will. This chapter argues that contemporary Islamists merge conceptions of social and political justice within a single model of justice. Furthermore, in that model, the Muslim agency plays a critical role. The analysis shows how the fundamental ideas related to justice trajectories are utilized in the modern age, not only by Qutb and Shariati but also by other prominent Islamists, including Mawdudi, Al-Ṣadr, Nursi, and al-Ghannūshī.

The chapter first discusses how Qutb and Shariati build their philosophy on the central tenet of Islamic faith, tawhid, or belief in God's unity. Second, it proposes that both intellectuals put particular emphasis on human agency. They are deeply concerned about free will and freedom of conscience as fundamental prerequisites of Islamic social justice. Third, this chapter demonstrates that Qutb and Shariati employ the golden age, the early prophetic community, as an ideal social justice model rather than reverting to the social justice paradigm in the classical Islamic state. The former embodies the praxis of social justice and the ideal Muslim agency, as seen in the persona of different historical figures. Finally, the analysis puts Qutb and Shariati's ideas in a comparative perspective by providing a short discussion about the justice theories of other Islamist scholars. Consequently, this chapter provides several insights about some contemporary issues in the Muslim experience, including the protest movements in the Arab world, the tactical use of "justice" as a dominant concept in the political party ideologies, and anti-imperialist attitudes in the Muslim periphery. The subsequent chapters provide empirical investigations of these insights in Muslim-majority societies.

Sayyid Qutb: Law and Social Justice

The Egyptian scholar Sayyid Qutb is known as the ideologue of the Egyptian Muslim Brothers and some violent transnational organizations. However, his ideas in *Social Justice in Islam*, *Milestones*, and his Koranic exegesis,

In the Shade of the Quran, have deeper philosophical connotations. His work is an example of a sophisticated religious philosophy that puts individual freedom and sharia at the center of a proposed harmonious society where economic and political justice prevail.[10] Another defining characteristic of his work is the criticism of Western societies, because, in his view, they neglect either the spiritual or the material side of humans.

Social Justice in Islam was published in 1949, in the aftermath of two devastating world wars and at the dawn of the Cold War. In response to the *capitalist* and *communist* systems as grand economic models, Qutb developed an Islamic theory, acknowledging man's spiritual and material needs. His social justice theory builds on divine principles (e.g., tawhid) to address man's spiritual side, but it also recognizes the material needs. As detailed below, the *Qutbian* social justice theory relies on the twin pillars of inner purification and the necessity of law. In an Islamic society, freedom of conscience, emancipation, and charitable acts play a central role in upholding these pillars.

Tawhid and Justice

The divine principle of tawhid plays a vital role in Qutb's social justice theory. Tawhid can be translated as oneness [of God], unity, that God is One (*al-'Aḥad*) and Single (*al-Wāḥid*), and it is patently the most important pillar of the Islamic faith. Qutb and Shariati employ this concept as a foundational principle of a harmonious society.[11] From the same principle, they also derive the elements of justice theory, namely, equality, freedom, and human dignity.[12]

In *Social Justice in Islam*, Sayyid Qutb explains social justice in a grand theory of Islam that deals with God, the universe, life, and humanity.[13] Qutb develops his theory in rather broad terms to encompass interactions among these elements. In this complex picture, tawhid (unity) connects everything, integrating diversity into a meaningful whole. As he states, "Because, then universe is a unity emanating from a single Will; because man is himself a part of the world, dependent upon and related to all the other parts; and because individuals are as atoms, dependent upon and related to all the other parts; and because they must have the same dependence upon, and relation to, one another."[14]

This theory has important implications if considered in conjunction with Qutb's analysis of Western civilization. He argues that a duality characterizes Christianity and modern Western civilization. Some manifestations of this binary framework include the distinction between the earth and heavens, religion and state, or the material and the spiritual. In contrast, tawhid makes Islam a unity and gives it an all-encompassing nature that combines the work and prayer or religion and state. It does not put the material at odds with the spiritual.[15]

Just as life, the universe and the world constitute a unity despite being composed of different things. Human personality is also a unity made of different desires (mud and spirit). In its servitude to God and through his prayers, humanity joins with God in unity. Qutb describes a harmony that does not favor the material over spiritual, society over the individual, or one generation over another. This harmony is related to a single goal, "namely, that the freedom of the individual and of society should be equally recognized without any mutual opposition and that the generations, one and all, should work together for the growth and progress of human life and for its orientation towards the Creator of life."[16]

For Qutb, social justice is not limited to material needs or economic distribution as in communism nor merely to spiritual needs as in Christianity. Life consists of not only material desires; in Islam, it also consists of "mercy, love, help, and a mutual responsibility.... There are, then, these two great facts. The absolute, just, and coherent unity of existence, and the general mutual responsibility of individuals and societies. On these two facts, Islam bases its realization of social justice, having regard for the basic elements of the nature of man, yet not unmindful of human abilities."[17]

In effect, Qutb refers to a kind of cosmic balance, a perfectly harmonious social order in which man is given no duty beyond his capacity. Neither the needs of man nor the welfare of society is neglected. In contrast to communism, Islamic justice does not require absolute economic equality because individuals differ in their material and spiritual endowments. However, Qutb acknowledges that desert (based on effort and hard work) and equality in opportunity are essential pillars of social justice.[18] Islam demands that every individual gain competence by freeing himself from the constraints of material needs. In Qutb's words, Islam "prescribes the claims of the poor upon the wealth of the rich, according to their needs, and according to the best interests of the society, so that social life may be balanced, just, and productive."[19] How can one establish this balance between individual and society? To answer this question, Qutb elaborates on social justice principles and assigns a central role to the human agency.

Human Agency and Social Justice

For Qutb, three principles form the foundation of social justice in Islam: absolute freedom of conscience, the complete equality of all men, the firm mutual responsibility in society (or *solidarity*).[20] All three require the active involvement of human agency. Social justice depends on the fulfillment of man's spiritual and material needs. There should be an inner conviction about the value of social justice (as in Christianity) on the spiritual side. On the material side, an individual should be willing to pay the cost and be ready to defend social justice (as in socialism).[21]

Inner conviction and desire for social justice will be possible to the extent that man obtains profound freedom of conscience, "by freeing the human conscience from servitude to anyone except Allah and from submission to any save Him."[22] Here, the idea of tawhid, the concept of *rizq* (provision), and the particular psychology at the intersection of these notions is significant. First, the unquestionable oneness of God, who holds a monopoly as the sole provider (*ar-Razzāq*), leads to a direct relationship between God and his servant. In Islam, the emphasis is on servitude to God and on banning any distractions that will lead to servitude to any other creature/notion. Second, the belief that provision is in God's monopoly results in a feeling of security that keeps man free of fear and anxiety. Since exclusive servitude will require the belief that any other creature is incapable of cutting or preventing any part of the provision, this makes individuals free from the anxiety of earning a livelihood. While this mechanism is not automatic and, according to Qutb, does not rule out causality or the role of material transactions, it nonetheless "strengthens the human heart and human conscience; it sets the poor man who is anxious over his livelihood on a level with a man who thinks that his provision is in his own hand, to be won with all his strength and resource."[23] He acknowledges that conscience is not immune to social forces because it may fall prey to the consequences of holding particular values like materialism. However, when Islam intervenes, it will reduce the effect of material values, put these values in the proper place, and equip man with dignity.[24]

The second foundational principle of social justice, equality, will be possible to the extent that man can obtain the freedom of conscience. When man frees himself from fear of livelihood and poverty and engages in exclusive servitude to God, he will gain his dignity and honor. This condition will lead to full equality between the poor and the wealthy.[25] As a foundational principle of justice, equality originates from the God-given nobility and the unity of humanity sharing one origin and similar experiences. Qutb cites a famous hadith of Prophet Muhammad: "All people are equal as the teeth of a comb."[26] To sum up, Qutb defines equality within the all-encompassing nature of Islam that deals with material and spiritual life. It is established with freedom of conscience from "all artificial values, from all outward appearances, from all material necessities."[27]

The third principle of the *Qutbian* justice system is the mutual responsibility, a principle that requires solidarity within the umma. While Islam helps an individual obtain freedom and equality in the perfect sense, it also places some restraints concerning mutual responsibility. As Qutb succinctly states, "Society has its interests, human nature has its claims, and a value also attaches to the lofty aims of religion. So, Islam sets the principle of individual responsibility over [against] that of individual freedom; and besides that it sets the principle of social responsibility, which makes demands alike on the individual and on society."[28]

The human agency plays a vital role in realizing this principle. Every individual has a duty toward social welfare and safety and for helping the poor and the orphans. Every individual also has the responsibility to prevent the vice because the whole community will be harmed if evil takes root. Society, in turn, has a responsibility to help its poor and destitute members. In effect, "the whole Islamic community is one body, and it feels all things in common; whatever happens to one of its members, the remainder of its members are also affected."[29]

Qutb's theory of social justice starts from the idea of tawhid and locates the human agency within a divinely inspired integrated order that combines the earth and the heavens, and the material and the spiritual. Man's relation to God, universe, world, society, and other individuals gains its meaning within a cosmological unity that integrates diversity in these different realms. Man, as the agent of social justice, emerges from this unity-oriented worldview. Freedom of conscience and absolute equality breeds the feeling of mutual responsibility and solidarity that makes social justice possible. However, Qutb is aware that social justice cannot always be possible even when man is free. Practical implementation of social justice is neither easy nor automatic. How can, then, an Islamic society establish social justice by free human agency situated within a "unity" worldview?

Social Justice as Praxis

Qutb is aware that human nature is selfish and inclined to the love of material wealth. However, establishing an Islamic just society will require a comprehensive justice model above and beyond material wealth distribution. At a minimum, legal measures are necessary for implementing social justice, but more important is the purification of the soul to overcome human ills like selfishness, greed, and the love of money.[30] Educating individuals in freedom of conscience helps them work toward the good of society and motivates voluntary behavior in protection of the law. This is unquestionably the critical first step in the implementation of Islamic social justice.

Qutb presents examples of zakat and charity to demonstrate how the praxis of social justice works in Islam. In Islamic law, distributing a fixed rate of wealth (zakat) is obligatory, and the state can enforce its collection. However, more important is the institution of charity imposed without a fixed rate. Engaging in charity is left to the discretion of believers. For Qutb, charitable act is the essential foundation of social justice policy. The charitable act matters a great deal because "it is the outward sign of charity and brotherly feeling, to both of which Islam attaches a supreme importance; it is an attempt to establish the mutual ties of mankind and social solidarity by means of an individual perception of what is necessary and a personal concept of charity."[31]

Charity is not only about helping the poor or distributing material wealth; for Qutb,[32] any act of kindness toward humanity, society, animals, or the environment is considered an act of charity. Human agency's engagement in this act is the foundation of the inner purification of conscience and the belief in solidarity. The psychological mechanism highlighted here stems from the notion of sacrifice. Since human nature is conducive to selfishness and love of money, the charitable act works its way toward purifying human conscience by helping the man give up what is dear to him and what has a powerful grip on him.

Reaching spiritual purification through charitable acts is a necessary but not sufficient condition for implementing social justice. The existing political and economic system should also be compatible with the ideals of Islamic social justice. For political governance, Qutb introduces his political theory of Islam involving three principles: "justice on the part of the rulers, obedience on the part of the ruled, and consultation between ruler and ruled."[33] Rulers should implement and maintain complete equality among citizens regardless of origin, race, and religion. In exchange, the ruled should be obedient to the ruler, but this is not unconditional. Obedience should not be about a ruler's privileges or his outstanding qualities. Rather, a ruler is obeyed only because he obeys God and follows Islamic law. Qutb argues that it is necessary to get rid of a ruler who abandons the law.[34] He believes that "no ruler may oppress the souls or the bodies of Muslims, nor dare he infringe upon their sanctities nor touch their wealth."[35] If this happens, this leader should be held accountable as he loses his qualification for being a leader. Finally, there should be consultation between the ruler and the ruled. While it is not clear what Qutb exactly has in mind as a political model, his ideas are reminiscent of those scholars' views who propose that Islam can play a positive role in the founding of the pluralistic institutions.[36]

In economic governance, Qutb invokes the well-known maxim of "there should be neither harming nor reciprocating harm (lā ḍarar wa lā ḍirār)."[37] Within this general maxim, both law and inner conviction are necessary for implementing social welfare. This general framework, however, does not ensure that distributive justice and charitable act will occur. Therefore, Qutb introduces additional principles that ensure the compatibility between an Islamic economic system and social justice. Islam accepts private ownership and wealth; however, this does not come with irresponsible economic freedom. There are certain restrictions on the disposal of wealth because "property belongs to society and is merely administered by an individual, so that if he leaves no issue, the property reverts to its original ownership by the community."[38] This is different from communism because Islam firmly established the property right. The property owner serves as the steward of property and is required to use it for the good of society after meeting his or her needs. This restriction is necessary because Islam forbids lavish spending and prohibits wastefulness, as seen in the capitalistic systems. Such lifestyles, according to Qutb, destroy society and create great injustices.[39]

Qutb believes that man is the vicegerent of God and needs to fulfill his spiritual and intellectual capacity to realize his God-given nobility. If man spends his whole life pursuing his basic material needs, he cannot fully realize this capacity. Through institutions like zakat and charity, a portion of wealth is given to the poor to remove the fear of provision and allow every individual to satisfy their spiritual needs and fulfill their intellectual capacities.[40] Only then will individual emancipation, human dignity, and ultimate justice be possible.

In conclusion, Qutb embeds his social justice theory within the divine principle of tawhid, builds it on freedom of conscience and equality, and maintains it through inner conviction and law. He presents a detailed account of political and economic governance and specific laws for sustaining the ideal just society in Islam. In this complex picture, social justice is not merely about economic redistribution but rather about human dignity, freedom, and Islamic law to protect these qualities. Law has a unique role in this system because obedience to the law does not restrict freedom. In contrast, it allows the individual to be free and governed because of the law's compatibility with human nature (*fiṭrā*).[41]

Is Qutbian social justice a utopia or a realistic praxis? To answer this question, we need to study the role of the prophetic community in Qutb's writings. Qutb anchors his theory in the praxis of social justice during the golden age. The political theory accompanying Islam's just order, according to Qutb, was in place even after the death of the Prophet during the reign of Abū Bakr, ʿUmar, and ʿAlī. However, due to ʿUthmān's weak rule and Umayyad family's lack of understanding of the Islamic spirit and their tendency toward greed and corruption, Islamic political theory was separated from the spirit of Islam. He mostly blames Muʿāwiya for corrupting Islam's true spirit and bringing a governance model not compatible with Islamic social justice. "The greatest crime of Muʿāwiya, therefore, was that he destroyed the spirit of Islam at the very beginning of his reign by a complete suppression of its moral elements."[42] This was the result of some unfortunate decisions of community leaders who failed to select ʿAlī as the caliph. These developments ended the social justice implementation that was so well established during the time of Prophet Muhammad.

However, this historical transformation does not point to an ever-deteriorating linear process. Qutb believes that Islam's spirit and the praxis of justice have always remained alive. He uses such examples as 'Ali against 'Uthmān and Mu'āwiya, rebellions against the Umayyads, and the later example of 'Umar ibn 'Abd al-'Azīz to show that ideal models of Islamic social justice continued to exist in different periods. The best embodiment of praxis of justice, in effect, appears to be the second caliph, 'Umar, who had the inner conviction and established the justice through charity and perfect implementation of sharia. Qutb provides many examples demonstrating how 'Umar had helped the poor, distributed all of his wealth in charity, put public interest above his personal gain, and always applied the law equally regardless of race, religion, or origin. A similar treatment can be traced for his account of Abū Bakr and 'Ali, but, in general, he cites many stories about 'Umar to demonstrate the perfect praxis of social justice.[43]

The golden age is not meant to serve as a distant ideal. Taking a revivalist position, Qutb aims to educate a vanguard generation that will practice social justice.[44] His emphasis on 'Umar is hardly a coincidence as it allows him to integrate inner conviction and the perfect application of sharia, according to the spirit of Islam. For Shariati, however, the law is an entity that should be viewed with suspicion as it sometimes serves the goals of despots. Henceforth, Shariati focuses on Islam's spirit and chooses to present the noble struggle of 'Ali, not 'Umar, as an example demonstrating the ultimate praxis of social justice.

'Ali Shariati: Rebellion and Social Justice

Marx, Fanon, and Shia scholars shaped 'Ali Shariati's interpretation of Islam and world history. Primarily inspired by Marx's historical materialism, Shariati provides a dialectical account of Islam, history, and class struggle. According to Ervand Abrahamian, Shariati rejects institutionalized Marxism of communist/socialist parties and accepts Marx as "predominantly a social scientist revealing how rulers exploited the ruled, how the laws of 'historical determinism'—not 'economic determinism'—functioned, and how the superstructure of any country, particularly its dominant ideology and political institutions, interacted with its socioeconomic infrastructure."[45] With this selective and critical reading of Marxism and Western philosophy, Shariati presents Islam as a revolutionary ideology, reminiscent of liberation theology. One can trace the resemblance of his thought system to that of Qutb, especially in the role of tawhid and human agency in social justice.

Tawhid and Justice

Tawhid plays a central role in Shariati's social justice theory. In a lecture titled *Worldview of Tawhid*,[46] Shariati puts the *tawhidi* worldview (monotheism) at odds with *shirk* worldview (polytheism) using a dialectical framework. For Shariati, tawhid directly relates to the social and political order and the historical struggles of the oppressed masses against tyranny (ẓulm). Shirk, on the other hand, is a worldview that involves a multiplicity of gods, which results in duality, or multiplicity, in the physical world. In contrast, in the tawhidi worldview, the physical and social world is perceived as unity or harmony. Just as tawhid does not accept duality between the body and spirit or contradiction between man and nature, tawhidi worldview does not accept class differences, divisions between the rulers and the oppressed, or racial and economic contradictions in the social realm:

> One further consequence of the worldview of tawhid is the negation of the dependence of man on any social force, and the linking of him, in exclusivity and in all his dimensions, to the consciousness and will that rule over being. Tawhid bestows upon men independence and dignity. Submission to Him alone—the supreme norm of all being impels man to revolt against all lying powers, all humiliating fetters of fear and greed.[47]

Shirk, however, justifies these contradictions. The difference between tawhid and shirk is reminiscent of the distinction between materialistic and religious visions, as seen in the *Qutbian* philosophy. In effect, Shariati argues that humanity has always been divided into two opposing poles. Throughout history, "the pole that represented corruption, crime, exploitation, ignorance, slavery, racism, imaginary virtues, and impediments to human progress, has always been at odds with justice, human consciousness, growth, and those who struggle to unite humanity."[48]

Shariati metaphorically uses the story of Cain and Abel to depict various manifestations of this duality. Abel, as a herdsman, represents a phase in human history during which livelihood depended on nature, hunting, and gathering. On the other hand, Cain was a farmer and represented a phase in which private property and monopoly became the economic norms. He argues, "All men are of 'Abelian' character because resources are equally at everyone's disposal. Individualism, individual ownership, monopoly, 'mine,' and 'yours' have not yet developed in man. On the other hand, Cain exemplifies an order in which a person fences a piece of land, tags his name to it and begins to exploit and enslave others."[49]

Shariati's reading of Abel and Cain's story has some very significant implications about Islamic conceptions of justice. With this polarity, social polytheism replaces the monotheistic world vision. Monotheism unites the material and spiritual in man and creates a harmonious order and a just society. In contrast, polytheism's divine order creates an inherent duality in man and leads to a hierarchical social system. This system creates the subjective polytheistic religion, disguised as true religion only to justify objective inequalities.[50] That is, "social objectivity creates religious subjectivity in order that the latter can manifest itself as the creator of the former."[51]

Human Agency and Justice

Human agency and freedom are crucial components of Shariati's justice theory. Rebellion against the oppressors to institute justice and equality becomes possible when man acts freely as the vicegerent of God.[52] God created man from mud and breathed his soul into him, making him two-dimensional.[53] Man swings between the lowliness of mud and lofty ideals emanating from the spirit of the Lord. Man is free to choose either pole, and hence becomes responsible. Shariati states, "Possession of will and freedom creates responsibility. And so, from the Islamic point of view, man is the only creature who is responsible not only for his own fate, but he also has a mission to fulfill the Divine Purpose in the world. Thus, he is a trustee in the universe."[54]

Man needs a religion that will protect him from one-dimensionality, either tilting toward the materialistic or the ascetic side. Only Islam is capable of providing two-dimensionality. Consequently, man can struggle to bring justice to the world because of having responsibility and freedom. Just as man is defined with freedom of conscience and only serves God in Qutb's theory, human beings are free to make conscientious choices as vicegerents of God, according to Shariati's view.[55]

However, man is confined to four prisons preventing him from realizing his potential: nature, history, society, and self. Modern men can realize this potential only if they can avoid these deterministic prisons. Through learning and science, man can get out of the first three; however, it is more difficult to get out of the prison of *self*. To support this argument, Shariati distinguishes *ensan* and *bashar*, two terms used to describe different qualities of human beings. Bashar is the biological creature; it is a "being," whereas ensan is "becoming," an extraordinary creature with unique properties and significant potential. In Shariati's words:

> *Ensan* has three characteristics: a) he is self-conscious, b) he can make choices; and, c) he can create. All of man's other characteristics derive their origin from these three. We are, therefore, *Ensan* relative to the degree of our consciousness and our creativities. Accordingly, when the characteristics of an ideal *Ensan* is clarified, we must try to identify the factors that hinder man in his becoming, and by removing them we can pursue our inherent and instinctive movement in the process of becoming an *Ensan*.[56]

Shariati argues that Western civilization can release man from his three prisons (nature, history, and society) by using scientific knowledge and providing material needs.[57] Saving man from the prison of self, however, is quite challenging. As human beings gain material comfort, they end up with futility and rebellion, which directs man to asceticism and subjectivity. Hence, ideologies like existentialism or hippie movements had significant appeal in the West. The question is, then, how can man, as a free and responsible agent, make a difference? For Shariati, this is possible only with a lofty goal that can help man negate his self. Like Qutb, Shariati believes that *ithar* (benevolence, selflessness, altruism) can help bashar transform into becoming ensan. With love and benevolence, argues Shariati, man can become the agent of change, a responsible individual struggling for equality and justice:

> Thus, every man can free himself from the last prison—which is frightening and contains invisible walls—through the power of *ithar*. It is a love which, beyond rationality and logic, invites us to negate and rebel against ourselves in order to work towards a goal or for the sake of others. It is in this stage that a free man is born, and this is the most exalting level of becoming an *Ensan*.... We humans have been invited to this nature with a duty and a responsibility to devise a plot. What plot? A scheme in which man, God, and love are involved to initiate a new creation and a new *Ensan*. This is what I mean by human responsibility.[58]

Social Justice as Praxis

The tawhidi worldview corresponds to a just society free from transgression and oppression. In this society, prosperity comes from spiritual values, not materialistic values. Shariati aims to rejuvenate the role of religion in instituting justice in this society: "If religion does not work before death, it certainly will not work after it."[59] Instead of prescribing a utopian order, Shariati proposes a model—directly inspired by divine principles—with full equality and freedom.[60] Freedom is foundational to justice and it becomes possible as individuals obtain basic material needs. If an individual has to struggle for these needs, he cannot engage in intellectual activities and emancipate to complete his transformation from bashar to ensan.[61]

Shariati demonstrates the importance of praxis in social justice by bringing examples from the early period of Islam. Just as Qutb, and many modernists, he invokes the golden age and looks for an actual example of social justice as a replicable model. In his account, particular figures are ideal embodiments of ensan striving to establish an Islamic just order. Figures like Muhammad, 'Umar, and Abu-Dhar al-Ghifārīy engage in the historical dialectic of tawhid and always oppose social polytheism, oppression, and inequalities.[62]

The most apparent manifestation of this opposition is in the struggle of tawhid against shirk, 'Ali against Mu'āwiya, red Shiism (the religion of martyrdom) against black Shiism (the religion of mourning), working class against the capitalists, and the oppressed against the despots as exemplified in the struggle of Abu-Dhar, a close companion of Muhammad known for his egalitarian views. This duality puts one's preference for piety, ethics, equality, and justice against corruption, tyranny, exploitation, and aristocracy.[63]

In *The Reflections of a Concerned Muslim on the Plight of Oppressed People*, Shariati describes Prophet Muhammad as this simple person who is one of the poor and weak, someone who rebels against the aristocrats and struggles to empower the slaves, the poor, and the ordinary masses.[64] This shepherd (Muhammad), argues Shariati, established a just and equitable society ruled by one of the weak and poor; however, oppressive rulers eventually destroyed it.[65] This process started with the denial of 'Ali's right to be the successor of the Prophet. Meccan aristocrats, especially the Umayyad family, transformed this prophetic society and replaced its just order with inequalities and a simple pious life with luxurious lifestyles. The isolation of 'Ali, "the embodiment of spirit of this Revolution," after the death of the Prophet, according to Shariati, is a sign that "justice is separated from religion."[66] Shariati describes this stage as an "inclination of Islam to the right," where the masses leave the scene to the aristocrats and clergymen.[67] 'Ali emerges as the ultimate leader that is capable of reinstituting the just system of the Prophet. He represents the agent fighting for the weak against the tyrants to restore the order of tawhid:

> He ['Ali] did not draw his sword to defend himself, his family, his race, nor to defend big powers. It was done to rescue us at all stages. . . . He is a leader of the working class and those who suffer. He is the expressing power who struggles for the well-being of the community. Sincerity, loyalty, patience, steadfastness, and the concepts of revolution and justice were the main features of his daily messages to the masses.[68]

In *And Once Again Abu-Dhar*, Shariati presents the story of Abu-Dhar to demonstrate how ordinary people can struggle against injustices. Above all, Abu-Dhar desired to return to the piety of the Prophet's age, and, to that end, he engaged in a one-person rebellion against the Umayyad aristocracy. His struggle was to oppose class discrimination and fight the *kinz* (accumulation of wealth) to establish justice. Abu-Dhar always reminds his followers of the Prophet's simplistic, egalitarian, ethical, and pious life.

To sum up, Shariati favors a system conforming to the principles of the tawhidi worldview. The empowered and emancipated man transformed from bashar to ensan is at the center of this just social order. With absolute freedom, ensan struggles to establish equality, a just social order where class differences are minimal and luxurious lifestyles or aristocratic rules do not distort the unity of society. Neither economic greed nor tyranny prevails in this society. It is the active human agency that builds this system through a struggle shaped by divine instructions, free will, and benevolence.

The Foundations of Justice Theory in Islamist Ideology

Any theory of Islamic social justice should acknowledge a critical division that emerged in Islam's early period. This cleavage results from a conflict between those holding a pious worldview and those who desire power. The former favored a puritanical approach cherishing the ideal prophetic community and its just order. The latter inclined toward the grab of political power, class differences, and status quo.[69] This duality first emerged in the debate concerning 'Ali's right to the caliphate, and it crystallized during the reign of 'Uthman and Mu'āwiya. Further incarnations of this duality were seen at the height of the Umayyad rule (692–750) and in the reign of later Islamic empires. Shariati and Qutb use the prophetic community as an actual representation of their social justice model, yet they differ in interpreting this early schism.

For Qutb, the prophetic model and spirit of Islam was in place until the reign of 'Uthmān and came to an end due to some random events preventing 'Ali from assuming the caliphate. Abū Bakr, 'Umar, and 'Ali are the ideal embodiments of Muslim agency implementing social justice according to Islam's true spirit. Mu'āwiya was responsible for replacing the egalitarian order with a social order involving economic inequalities and political hierarchy. Within this historical account, Qutb especially praises 'Umar for several reasons. First, 'Umar sees wealth as the property of the umma and does not use it for personal gain or to reward his supporters. Instead, economic distribution during his reign is just, egalitarian, and helps social welfare. Furthermore, 'Umar is a leader who follows sharia. He is a leader who has inner conviction, responsibility, and respect for the law because of fear of God and charitable acts.[70]

For Shariati, the same schism emerged much earlier when 'Ali was denied his right to be the caliph. While the prophetic community in its ideal form continued under the reign of Abū Bakr and 'Umar, the first seeds of corruption transforming tawhid-oriented society into a social polyarchy were also sown at that time and culminated during the reign of 'Uthmān. In this picture, 'Ali emerges as the perfect embodiment of man (that is, ensan), tending toward humanity's spiritual side, an active fighter in the name of justice and a leader in the struggle of the oppressed masses against social inequalities. Unlike Qutb, Shariati is highly suspicious of law and sees it as an instrument legitimizing the class differences and tyranny. Therefore, the essential first cleavage marks the struggle of the oppressed masses against the despots. It also reflects the eternal struggle between the tawhidi worldview and shirk and the egalitarian just society versus social inequalities. Another important figure in Shariati's vision is Abu-Dhar, who carries a heroic one-man struggle to protect the prophetic egalitarian society against the Umayyad rule. Just like 'Ali, he is an agent participating in the eternal struggle between tawhid and shirk, who also continually engages in benevolent acts to free himself from the prison of self.[71]

One significant difference between the Western liberal and the Islamist theories of justice is the premise about the ownership and the disposal of private property. The Islamist view diverges radically from the former in that all wealth and resources belong to God, and the benefits should apply to all humanity. This difference has important implications for economic distribution. First, while Qutb believes that the right to private property is legitimate in Islam, the disposal of property is constrained by "responsibility toward society." An individual is not free to waste his wealth with a luxurious lifestyle because all wealth (*mulk*) belongs to God, and it should be used for the welfare of humanity. According to Qutb, the use of public treasure (*Bayt al-Māl*) for social welfare during the prophetic age stands in sharp contrast to the corruption and exploitation of these public funds toward personal and political gains under the rule of 'Uthmān and Mu'āwiya.

Shariati presents a slightly different argument than Qutb. For him, class differences and inequalities result from *kinz* and they are the foundation of a polytheist worldview. Abel represents an economic order where resources and wealth belong to everyone. Cain represents a system involving the practice of kinz, exploitation, and inequalities. Shariati depicts the prophetic community as *Abelian*, wherein public treasure belongs to the umma and is used for the common good. Public treasure should not be used for personal gain, as seen during the reign of 'Uthmān and Mu'āwiya. 'Ali and Abu-Dhar, in this account, are role models who struggle to establish the prophetic practices in economic justice.

Overall, the Islamist justice theory of both Qutb and Shariati is informed by the events during the beginning period of Islam and the first political divisions over the succession question. The struggle between historical figures longing for social justice and those who prefer a hierarchical political order and social inequalities is at the heart of the social justice theory. Both intellectuals also develop a philosophical account of social justice by justifying freedom of conscience and free will as scriptural principles that lay at the foundation of a just society.

Two conditions give way to a just, harmonious society: the tawhid principle and charity or benevolence (*'iḥsān*). Since Shariati and Qutb view Islam as a way of life and do not separate religion from worldly affairs, it is only natural to expect a foundational role for divine instructions in their social justice theory. For Qutb, tawhid leads to freedom of conscience through servitude to the one and only God. According to this belief, God is the sole provider (*ar-Razzāq*), and man does not have to be a servant of others. Consequently, according to Islam, an individual living his life will be free from the fear of livelihood, strengthen his heart and soul, and earn his dignity. This process also requires that society be governed according to the political and economic theory of Islam. This is necessary because only implementing sharia can ensure the distribution of public wealth toward establishing an egalitarian, just order where human emancipation can occur.

For Shariati, tawhid represents the unity worldview, justice, and equality, whereas shirk represents class differences and inequalities in the social realm. Within this dialectic of tawhid, free will is the most important quality that will establish unity for Islam's two-dimensional man. In the social polytheist order, man faces a constant struggle and sway between its mud-nature and spiritual side. In Islam, man can end this struggle and form his internal unity as vicegerent of God because he has free will and can resist the tyranny. Just as Qutb, Shariati believes that man can gain freedom when he meets his basic needs and makes a comfortable living.

While the tawhid principle provides a scriptural framework for explaining man's desire for freedom, equality, and justice, it is not sufficient to create a *self* that is the agent of justice in daily life. Voluntary acts are necessary, too. To address this issue, Qutb and Shariati use the scriptural instruction about charity and benevolence. In Qutb's theory, sharia is not sufficient for the implementation of social justice. Social justice also requires an inner conviction so that individuals choose to follow the law voluntarily. The best method for overcoming selfish human nature's limitations and creating selflessness (an indication of inner conviction) is the charitable act. Charity is not only about helping the poor or needy; it is an act that involves kindness and good deeds for humanity, nature, or society. Thus, charitable behavior engenders purification of the soul, strengthens inner conviction, and induces a feeling of responsibility and solidarity.

On the other hand, in Shariati's theory, the continuous struggle for justice is necessary but not sufficient to bring about the free will in man. To free man from the prison of *self*, Shariati argues that man needs religion and love. A passion for good actions and caring for others can be achieved only through the negation of the self. Only with *ithar* (benevolence, selflessness, altruism) can man negate himself and work toward lofty goals.

Consequently, the Qutbian and Shariatian Islamist justice theory depends on three pillars. First, individuals should have a strong belief in tawhid with all of its implications for the unity of the individual and society (or classless society for Shariati). Second, they should engage in the praxis of Islamic social justice, that is, the practice of benevolence and charity toward humanity, nature, and the universe. And third, individuals should gain freedom of conscience and realize their free will through conviction in tawhid and engagement in the praxis of justice. While the first pillar informs justice theory generally, the second pillar shapes social justice and the third has implications for the political justice paradigm.

Qutb and Shariati developed sophisticated political philosophies that directly address social and political justice as constitutive elements of Islamic society. They have had a significant influence since the 1970s on Islamist intellectuals and movements across Muslim-majority societies. While other Islamist scholars also assign a central role to justice, they do not put justice at the center of their inquiry or develop a complete theory of justice like Qutb and Shariati. For example, Mawdudi had drastically shaped Qutb's ideas about tawhid and the blueprint of Islamic society. He introduced the concept of theodemocracy to offer a native governance model based on sharia and popular sovereignty.[72] While justice and benevolence are central values in Mawdudi's thought, he is far from being a revolutionary, unlike Shariati.[73] Although he emphasized justice as a central virtue of Islamic society, he did not present a complete theory of justice like Qutb.

Another scholar who deserves mentioning is Muhammad Bāqir al-Ṣadr, who criticized capitalism and socialism and developed a novel Islamic economic theory. Al-Ṣadr views justice as an essential Islamic principle like tawhid and usually defines it as economic justice. His account of economic justice is embedded within the broader conception of justice that is integral to Islamic society. The most notable contribution of al-Ṣadr to justice theory is his strong advocacy for democracy. Like other scholars, he bases this support on the Islamic foundation of popular sovereignty stemming from man's vicegerent status. He believes that man's vicegerent status gives all members of umma the power and the right to govern their political affairs within a democratic system.[74] This is similar to the idea of a free individual proposed by Qutb and Shariati.

Two other scholars who left significant marks in the Islamist landscape, Rāshid al-Ghannūshī and Said Nursi, are worth mentioning. The Tunisian intellectual and party leader al-Ghannūshī views justice as the end goal of an Islamic political system. Like Qutb and Shariati, man's vicegerent status is the starting point for al-Ghannūshī, who derives principles of dignity, agency, and responsibility from this position to develop an Islamic democracy model compatible with the notion of Islamic justice.[75] This model relies on the active participation of Muslims through *bay'a* and active engagement in interpreting and making Islamic law. Al-Ghannūshī's most significant contribution is his political theology of popular sovereignty that suggests umma's participation in the political process and interpretation of sharia.[76] The end goal of his sophisticated theory is the creation of a virtuous and just society.[77]

Said Nursi of Turkey (1876–1960), a prominent scholar and activist with a lasting legacy on the Turkish Islamist landscape, is best known for his spiritual guidance for the *Nurcu* groups, especially the Gülen Community.[78] During the early years of his life, which he dubs as the period of "Old Said," he participated in the democratic struggle against the Ottoman sultan Abdulhamid II, by joining the Committee on Union and Progress, the main opposition group.[79] This was part of his quest for democracy and justice against the declining Ottoman state and the Western incursion.

After the Turkish Republic was founded, he took a different approach and started to write commentaries of the Koran to preserve Islam. His main goals were to counter the positivist and antireligious ideology of the Western-minded, secular elite by training individuals in "faith," which he viewed as the quintessential factor for protecting religion in the modern age. Although Nursi does not offer a complete Islamic justice theory, his writings and actions reflect the weight Nursi assigned to this concept.[80] Nursi's theory of justice relies on the idea of interrelationships among God, cosmos, and man. It is different from Qutb and Shariati's political philosophies in its political implications and lack of concrete prescriptions for an Islamic political system. He argues that a Muslim can obtain conscience only by conceiving the purpose of faith and God's creation. Only through understanding the true faith can individuals create a virtuous and just community. His main contention is to empower the faithful through strengthening the faith that will help emancipate the individual to fight positivism and the bureaucratic structures (i.e., the secular Western Turkish state). Like Shariati and Qutb, Nursi's justice theory is grounded in the emancipation and empowerment of the self by strengthening faith through the reinterpretation of the scripture and religion. He is mainly concerned with establishing a just society via this individualistic path of self-direction and emancipation.[81] At the same time, his actual praxis exemplifies a life fought for faith and democracy.

Overall, this review of Islamist justice theories demonstrates significant similarities among the philosophies of various scholars. In general, Islamist political philosophy grounds the justice theory within a cosmological worldview related to the principle of tawhid and the purpose of man's creation. The totality of existence connects man to nature, the universe, and the creator within a balanced order. Conceptions of justice stem from, or mirror, this cosmic balance. Islamist scholars believe that individuals have free will and choice and that, as God's vicegerents, they can be emancipated within this cosmology. This individualistic foundation is one legacy of the political justice trajectory that is compatible with democratic ideals.

On the flip side, Islamist justice theories differ in their scope and focus. For example, al-Ṣadr is mainly concerned with economic justice, though he endorses the struggle for democratic institutions. Nursi's main goal is to initiate a bottom-up process to empower the individual through faith for creating a just society. Mawdudi aims to develop a blueprint for an Islamic social and political system that is not exactly compatible with liberal democratic norms. While each of these scholars puts a premium on the notion of justice, unlike Qutb and Shariati, none of them provides a complete theory of justice connecting the cosmological, individual, and systemic aspects of justice.

Conclusion and Implications

The discussion of Qutb and Shariati's political philosophies, along with the ideas of other Islamist scholars, reveals that Islamist justice theory is markedly different from the Western theories of justice. In Western justice theories, the unequivocal principle is property rights and freedom to dispose of this property. The main puzzle is about finding an agreeable formula concerning the distribution of wealth. The answers to the puzzle range from utilitarian worldviews to communitarian solutions or to finding a procedural consensus that is acceptable to all individuals regardless of their real-life conditions.[82] According to Islamist social justice theories, property belongs to God, who has given this property to all humanity. The puzzle in Islamist thought concerns how to establish a just order according to God's will. Since Islam, as a way of life, does not separate religion and the worldly affairs, or the spiritual and the material, the starting point for Islamist justice theory is the criticism of the materialistic worldview. While distributive justice is an important end goal, the main problematic in Islamist justice theory is to establish a just society through voluntary behavior. This does not necessarily require a utopian vision but necessitates a constant struggle against oppression through freedom, for Shariati, and inner purification of the soul accompanied by the flawless implementation of Islamic law, according to Qutb.

Since all property ultimately belongs to God, man is not free to use it for his own selfish needs. Its disposal should help social welfare and public interest, which requires voluntary and selfless action, according to sharia. Shariati is highly skeptical of religious law and believes it serves the interests of the oppressors, whereas, for Qutb, the law can free man and bring justice, but its implementation requires inner conviction. It is imperative to free man from his shackles, help him obtain his conscience, and act with free will to voluntarily engage in selfless behavior that benefits society or humanity.

Benevolence is the key in Islamist justice theory. However, neither Qutb nor Shariati propose that belief in tawhid is sufficient to create benevolent acts. The strong and wealthy can escape from selfish behavior by engaging in a variety of beautiful acts, such as charity, protecting animal rights, keeping the environment clean, helping the immigrants, or raising responsible children. Benevolence allows the rich and powerful to escape the prison of *self* and creates motivation toward solidarity in society. On the flip side, it will help the needy meet their basic needs and avoid the fear of livelihood. Only then, Qutb's free conscience and Shariati's free will should become a reality and result in the praxis of social justice.

Islamist justice theory provides insights for understanding several pressing issues that have been the subject of many inquiries among the scholars of Muslim politics. For example, the extraordinary uprisings in the Arab region are best remembered for the chant "bread, freedom, and human dignity," representing the calls for social and political justice. Islamic social justice principles might have played a vital role in motivating these protesters. A more interesting example is Turkey's Gezi Park protests in 2013. A broad coalition of civil movements, student organizations, and labor unions organized these protests, but the Islamist groups were also active in these demonstrations. They provided a religious justification for the protests representing the Islamist opposition against an arguably Islamist government. As I demonstrate in Chapter 6, the ideologies of these groups include the central tenets of the Islamist social justice theory, especially of Shariati's ideas. Furthermore, some elements of the Islamist social justice theory are evident in the party programs and policies of Islamist parties. It is hardly coincidental that many Islamist parties use the word *justice* in their names or emphasize this concept in their party programs. This preference represents their mobilization strategy of prioritizing economic and political justice.

5

Between Order and Freedom

Islamism and Justice Discourses

> Law that cites justice is the pillar of the heaven; if the law goes corrupt, heavens crumble; principality can survive with law; law is like water; tyranny destroys everything like fire. You streamed pure water and put out the fire. (Author's translation.)
> —KUTATGU BILIG (as cited in Arat, *Yusuf Has Hacip*)

"To put everything in its proper place" is the most common definition of *justice* that a reader would encounter in the pages of Turkish Islamist journals since the 1960s. As simple as this definition is, a closer analysis of Islamist journals' archives reveals highly complex and multifaceted conceptualizations of this notion. For Turkish Islamists, justice refers to many things at once, including but not limited to fairness, charity, rights, rebellion against an oppressor, anti-imperialism, social order, retribution, equality, and the rule of law. This chapter attempts to place order onto this complex semantic field. The analysis of Islamist writings in Turkey provides significant insights into Turkish Islamism, conceptions of justice, and political preferences.

Justice discourses have been instrumental in political struggles throughout Islamic history as far back as the prophetic community, the medieval period, and, more prominently, during the colonial and independence periods of the nineteenth and twentieth centuries. This chapter builds on the theoretical framework proposed in previous chapters for examining the evolution of justice discourses among the Turkish Islamists since the 1960s. Through close readings of 396 articles published in forty-three Islamist journals, it examines the meaning and political instrumentation of Islamic conceptions of justice against the background of significant sociopolitical developments in Turkey. The discourse analysis of Turkish Islamist texts corroborates the implications of the explanatory framework developed in this book. As has been the norm throughout different historical episodes and contexts, the debates about justice took place in very dynamic discursive fields within the Turkish context. These discursive fields are powerfully shaped by Turkish Islamism's reference frames and the significant sociopolitical events unfolding in the Turkish society in the Cold War and the neoliberal age. Two critical themes that shaped Islamist justice discourses are social order (*nizam*, or *kamu düzeni*) in the 1960–1980 period and resistance against economic globalization and American hegemony in the post-1980 period. While both of these themes are closely related to the lineages of social and political justice trajectories, their contemporary incarnations in the Turkish Islamist writings take entirely unexpected turns.

This chapter presents a brief description of the discourse analytic method and the suitability of Turkey as a case for the analysis of justice discourses. It then provides a general overview of Turkish Islamism, especially highlighting competing visions informed by the native and external Islamist ideologies. The chapter continues with discourse analysis of the texts published in the Islamist journals during the 1960–1980 and 1980–2010 periods. The conclusion discusses the implications of the analysis for understanding Islamic conceptions of justice and political preferences.

Explaining Islamic Conceptions of Justice through Discourse Analysis

This chapter uses discourse analysis to examine the development of the Islamic conception of justice in Turkey. The discourse analytic method is chosen over content analysis because it is more suitable for examining the Islamist texts within the social and political context. Discourse analysis does not treat the *text* as an objective body of information subject to quantification. Instead, it makes possible the social scientific analysis of meaning by using a systematic approach and considering the interaction of the *text* and social reality.[1] As such, discourse analysis focuses on the interaction between the text and the context and, subsequently, provides the necessary tools for observing the change in the discourse.[2]

The concept of discourse is used in the Foucauldian sense to signify the primary tool for creating knowledge and frames of action within the discursive fields. As stated by Weedon,[3] discourse refers to the "ways of constituting knowledge, together with the social practices, forms of subjectivity, and power relations which inhere in such knowledges and relations between them." Discourses help us trace the "genealogy" or "archaeology" of knowledge production.[4] As places of meaning-construction operating within the power structures and generating power itself, discourse can attach itself to knowledge production that can create domination or resistance strategies.[5]

As discussed in the previous chapters, justice discourses provided the main cognitive frames in the intraelite struggles and the political interactions between the rulers and the masses throughout Islamic history. The analysis up to this point has shown how justice discourses shaped the meaning systems and constructed *alternative truth claims* among the opposition groups during different episodes of Islamic history. Some examples include the first civil war during the early period of Islam, struggles between the ethically minded pious leaders and the Umayyad rulers,[6] the opposition of ulema to the sultans in the name of protecting the welfare of the masses in the age of the decline of the Islamic Empire and the Mongol invasion,[7] the constitutional rebellions of the late nineteenth and early twentieth centuries against domestic and colonial injustices,[8] and contemporary Islamism presenting Islam as the third way against capitalism and socialism.[9] This chapter adds to this book's central theme by tracing the evolution of justice discourses in Turkish Islamism.

From a discourse analytic perspective, the evolution of Turkish Islamism is replete with multiple variations in the interaction of texts and social reality. Since *justice* is one of the central concepts of Islamic political thought, it allows for studying the different moments of the construction of Islamist ideology under changing sociopolitical conditions. Turkish Islamism's origins go back to the nineteenth-century Ottoman intellectual tradition, the main goal of which was to save the state from collapsing.[10] However, during the republic period (1923–1930), the secular-authoritarian regime's restrictive religious policies severed Turkish Islamists' ties to their origins and the global Islamist movements. In effect, one can argue that Turkish Islamism entered a dormant period, until the 1950s, to awaken in the multiparty democracy era, post-1950. Various Islamist movements and organizations flourished in a context characterized by the activism and militancy of youth groups in the 1970s and 1980s. During the 1980–2010 period, among other sociopolitical developments, the alliance between the devout bourgeoisie and the Islamist/conservative political parties[11] resulted in the taming and incorporation of Turkish Islamism's political wing into the neoliberal economic order.[12]

In contrast to our knowledge about the sociopolitical context of the Turkish political Islamism, we know very little about how Turkish Islamists constructed ideology in their texts. The bulk of scholarly attention has focused on institutions and strategic behaviors of Islamist actors while paying little attention to knowledge production dynamics. For example, Turkish Islamist parties use justice or a related concept like welfare or prosperity in their names and make ample references to the notion of justice in their manifestos.[13] However, research has not looked into what Islamists mean by "justice" when they say "justice." The discourse analysis conducted in this chapter aims to address this shortcoming. It looks into how Islamist actors use the concept of justice in their texts to present Islam as a solution for all problems in Turkey and the world.[14]

Finally, discourse analysis of Islamist writings has the added advantage of compensating for the lack of historical survey data that could have given us a glimpse of public opinion about Islam, justice, and democracy in the past. Islamist journals have functioned like schools through which less sophisticated readers were educated about Islamist ideology since the nineteenth century. The articles in Islamist journals are mostly written with a nonacademic language to appeal to the common readers to increase membership. It can be reasonably assumed that the content of these texts provides a reliable proxy for gauging public opinion about such issues as justice and democracy compared to the scholarly works of prominent Islamist intellectuals.

The Sociopolitical Context

In contrast to the relatively vibrant Islamist intellectual field in the Middle East and South Asia in the first half of the twentieth century, Turkish Islamism had entered a dormant period until the Cold War era. Such inertia is a result of the Kemalist project's secular authoritarian policies, aiming to create a Western-style nation at the expense of eliminating all manifestations of religion from the public sphere.[15] These policies resulted in the abolishment of the caliphate and establishment of the Directorate of Religious Affairs (Diyanet), the closure of religious schools, the formation of a secular educational system, the banning of the Sufi orders, the prohibition of traditional attire, the adoption of a Western civil code, and the replacement of the Arabic alphabet with the Latin alphabet. In 1928, the constitution of the young Turkish Republic was amended to remove the phrases about state religion and, in 1937, to make *laïcité* a constitutional principle. In this context, some of the most prominent Islamists, including Mehmed Akif, Elmalılı Hamdi, and Said Nursi, were exiled (or went into self-exile) or prosecuted. İsmail Kara defines this period as the most challenging years of the Islamist movement in Turkey to the extent that "the publications of [Islamists] are shut down, they were barred from publishing books . . . their professions were discredited, their ideas were banned, religious education was minimized at every stage, the [government's] attempts to intervene and deform the religious sphere had increased, and the [Islamist] cadre was dispersed, disappeared, or went into hiding."[16]

While religious opposition primarily used grassroots activism focusing on educational activities, Islamists started to maintain a low profile and retreated to the intellectual field to preserve Islamic identity by infusing it into the nationalist ideology as an alternative to the Kemalist secular nationalism. Islamism was one of the three ideologies that fueled the intellectual energy toward the salvation of the Ottoman state in the nineteenth and twentieth centuries, with the other two being Ottomanism and Turkism.[17] While Islamists like Mehmed Akif first promoted a pan-Islamist ideology based on a rational, modern interpretation of Islam, this ideology was compatible with Turkish nationalism, primarily infusing an Islamic element into the Turkish national identity.[18] After 1913 and during the early republic period, Islamists like Mehmed Akif openly advocated the Turkish-Islamic synthesis. Although a secular nationalist identity came to dominate the political scene during the early years of the republic, Yavuz argues that this represents an exception in the history of Turkish identity rather than a norm.[19] In a way, Turkish Islamism remained dormant during the 1923–1950 period to only resurface as an element of religious-nationalist identity after the 1960s.

A similar retreat was also visible in the public presence of Islam. There were attempts to reinvigorate religion in the civil sphere and bring back the Islamist publishing tradition during the transition to democracy (1945–1950) and the multiparty era (1950–1960). The Democratic Party came to power in 1950 and appealed to the traditional religious groups, most prominently to various *Nakshibendi/Nurcu* groups who found ample opportunities to expand their educational, religious, and charity activities.[20] Islamism, however, came to prominence only in the 1960s. The primary stimulus behind this "reemergence" is the democratic effect of the 1961 constitution that had increased civil and political liberties. One result of this liberal constitution, the civil and militant activism of the 1960s and 1970s, eventually led the Turkish society into conditions approaching total social anarchy. Youth militancy and urban violence pitting the nationalist and leftist groups against each other are the defining characteristics of this period.

Against this background, Islamist movements resurfaced through the activism of publishing houses and civil organizations representing a "third way" against the nationalist and leftist ideologies. Islamist groups did not participate in the youth militancy and urban violence until the late 1970s. They focused their intellectual energy mostly on the development of Islamist ideology, separated from its roots for so long, and remained isolated from the influence of global Islamism during the dormant period. After the translation of Sayyid Qutb's works to Turkish, some intellectuals rejected his ideas in favor of native ideologies that fused Islam and nationalism. The most prominent figures of this era are Necip Fazıl Kısakürek, Nurettin Topçu, and Sezai Karakoç. All three aimed to develop nativist ideologies infusing Islam with the Turkish national identity.[21] These intellectuals had further developed the foundations of nationalist-religious (*milliyetçi-mukaddesatçı*) identity, providing the intellectual background for various nationalist and Islamist political parties.

Among these pioneers, Kısakürek held strong anticommunist views, which became prevalent among most Turkish Islamist groups.[22] This position resulted in the co-optation of certain Islamist and nationalist groups as regime elements to counter the challenge of communist ideologies, as seen in Egypt and Indonesia. Some organizations that opted out or unique figures who remained independent from the state are exceptions to such co-optation. Nurettin Topçu, who promoted native Islamic socialism and youth activism (*hareket felsefesi*) as a solution to underdevelopment in Turkey, and Sezai Karakoç, whose Islamist view involved a grand civilizational argument, are notable examples of such independence.

Developing native ideologies (*yerli ve milli*) fusing Islam and Turkish nationalism or utilizing civilizational discourses were not the only preoccupation of Islamists in the 1960s. More significant for the Islamists was the so-called "degeneration" of the youth falling under the spell of Western ideologies and culture. Islamists blamed the Republican policies for moral decay and strongly criticized the imposition of Western culture onto society. To counter this challenge, Islamists tirelessly worked on refining the nativist ideologies visiting the pre–republic era and reconstructing the images of the Seljuk and Ottoman Empires.[23]

Turkish Islamism's search for identity resulted from the crisis of Turkish modernization, visibly observed in urban sites. As mass migration to urban centers in the 1960s brought about a tension between traditional and modern forms of cultural belonging, religious ideologies were employed to facilitate the integration of the rural masses into modern urban lifestyles.[24] Rapid rural migration and urbanization remained at the top of the policy agenda from the 1970s to the 1980s. Militant organizations found fertile ground for recruiting in the mushrooming shantytowns (*gecekondu mahalleleri*). However, religious inhabitants of these towns turned to traditional and modern Islamist groups searching for a new identity that included both nationalist and religious elements.[25] The view that the state is an instrument for protecting religion and establishing order (*kanun ve düzen*) and Islamic national identity were central elements of the Islamist outlook that resonated among the devout urbanites.

Toward the end of the 1970s, Turkish Islamism started to change course through new translations and interpretations of the major works by the scholars of Middle East and South Asia such as Mawdudi, Qutb, and Shariati. The Iranian Revolution has also significantly contributed to the new direction of Turkish Islamism that increasingly expanded its sphere of influence in the 1980s and 1990s. As Turkish Islamists started to demarcate the boundaries of the Islamist ideology from the outlooks of traditional Sufi groups and religious-nationalist tradition, the social anarchy conditions resulted in the military coup of 1980. Like many groups, the newly budding Islamist actors, but not necessarily all Islamic groups, had also taken their share of repression and prosecution. Equipped with the intellectual ammunition obtained from Ottoman Islamism, global Islamist ideologies, and the foundations built in the 1960s, Turkish Islamists' separation from the traditional Sufi orders and conservative-nationalist groups gained pace in the 1980s. Turkey's transition to the free market system and its integration into the neoliberal economic order were additional parameters of this new sociopolitical reality.

Next to the reinvigoration of Islamist movements in the intellectual field in the post-1980 period, the most apparent manifestation of Islamic revival was the rise of Islamist political parties. Islamist Welfare Party won the plurality of the parliamentary seats to become the principal partner of a coalition government with the True Path Party in 1996. This outcome is partly the result of Prime Minister Turgut Özal's reforms in the 1980s, allowing the Islamist actors to expand their civil, economic, and political activities. Throughout the 1980s and 1990s, Islamists also established newspapers, journals, and TV stations to appeal to a broader social base. The financial support for this awakening was provided by the owners of small and midsize enterprises, the so-called "devout bourgeoisie" or "Anatolian tigers," who also had strong ties to various Sufi orders, Islamist movements, and conservative political parties.[26]

The rise of Islamism in civil society and the political arena was perceived as a severe challenge to the establishment elites' secular ideology. In the 1990s, the publishing houses served as the focal points of Islamist activism. Seeing a threat in this vibrant intellectual and civic activism, the military, in cooperation with other political and bureaucratic elites, intervened in democratic processes to reverse the rising tide of Islamism. Under the tutelage of generals, the establishment elite started to repress Islam's public manifestations (e.g., headscarf ban). The 1997 military intervention (the February 28 intervention) targeted Islamist civil society by banning Islamist organizations and political parties and closing down the publishing houses.[27] Some observers of Turkish politics view the February 28 intervention as the most significant moment of contemporary Turkish politics vis-à-vis the Islamist movements.[28]

One can reasonably argue that the February 28 intervention has shattered the vibrant Islamist intellectual and civic field. Most Islamist journals and religious organizations were perceived as a threat and shut down by the secularist establishment elite. The intellectual vigor and civic activism of Islamist actors in the 1990s remain unmatched in the recent history of Turkish Islamism. From İsmet Özel to Ercümend Özkan, Ali Bulaç to İhsan Eliaçık, contemporary representatives of Turkish Islamism vigorously developed the discourses of new Islamist ideology. This effort helped demarcate the intellectual and social boundaries of Islamism from Islamist credentials of political parties and traditional Sufi orders that have constituted the "religion side" of the state-religion complex in modern Turkey. Just like the

Islamists of the 1960–1980 period, members of this most recent wave have established numerous publishing houses and used Islamist journals to disseminate their ideas. At the same time, this period is considered the era of reinvention, moderation, and the Islamist movement's co-optation by the AKP (Justice and Development Party) government.[29]

During the post-1980 period, the rise of the Welfare Party and later the AKP is also viewed as a development integrating the religious bourgeoisie into the neoliberal economic order.[30] Not all Islamists integrated or were content with these developments. Those who survived the repression and prosecution of the February 28 intervention continued to criticize the moderate Islamism (political Islam) and its capitalist tendencies, mostly manifested in the changing lifestyles of the devout individuals.[31] Some Turkish Islamists also became fierce critics of the economic globalization and American hegemony. These tendencies have become salient, especially during the ethnic war in former Yugoslavia and international interventions in Iraq and in the new millennium after the AKP won the election to rule the country single-handedly.

Understanding the evolution of the Islamist justice discourses in response to this complex sociopolitical reality is important. This inquiry is likely to provide insights about conceptions of political and social justice, political preferences, and Islamist ideology addressing the contextual factors. The next section discusses the competing visions of Islamism to explain how different views within this ideology inform political and social justice discourses in the Turkish context. Then, the content analysis of the articles in Islamist journals since the 1960s is presented. The analysis elaborates on the synergies among contemporary manifestations of justice discourses, Islamist ideology, and regime preferences.

Competing Visions of Islamism and Justice Discourses

To recap, following a retreat and a dormant period between 1924 and 1960, Turkish Islamism entered a reconstruction period starting in the 1960s, within a political setting of increased freedoms and rights.[32] In this context, Islamist groups constituted a dynamic segment of the Turkish intellectual field. Turkish Islamist groups continued to flourish after the 1980 coup and in the new millennium despite periodic repressive policies undermining their activities.

Unlike the cases where a single group (Muslim Brothers in Egypt or Ennahda in Tunisia) is dominant, the Turkish Islamist landscape is a crowded field, including political parties, professional associations, literary movements, Sufi orders, and religious communities of many shades. This feature of Turkish Islamism allows researchers to carry the discourse analysis of Islamic justice beyond the empty rhetoric of party slogans into the substantive content of Islamist texts produced by various Islamist groups. The lack of scholarly interest in broader Turkish Islamism by scholars of comparative and Middle Eastern politics, save the vast literature about Turkish Islamist parties, comes as a sizable surprise given this movement's rich intellectual tradition and vibrant organizational capacities. Perhaps one reason for the lack of studies is the narrow focus of existing studies on political Islam or militant organizations.[33] Before we can discuss the evolution of justice discourses in the Islamist publications in Turkey, we need to define Islamism beyond this narrow focus. İsmail Kara,[34] the renowned expert on Islamism in the Turkish language scholarship, provides a broad definition of Islamism:

> Islamism is a thought and a movement of the 19th and 20th century, which is the total sum of the political, intellectual and scholarly studies/quests that are highly activist and eclectic and aim to re-establish the dominance of Islam in society as a whole (belief, worship, ethics, philosophy, law, education) to save the Muslim world from the Western exploitation, oppressive and tyrannical rulers, imitation [of the West] and the superstitions in order to civilize, unite, and help develop it [the Muslim world].[35]

Kara provides a broad definition avoiding the pitfalls of the scholarship in the West that usually confines Islamism to either political Islam or violence. He situates Islamism in its historical context by linking the current movements to their anti-imperialist origins of the nineteenth century. Furthermore, the main goal of Islamism is seen not only as a struggle with colonialism but also as establishing the dominance of Islam in society. This definition does not exclude political party activism for the sake of Islam. However, it expands the scope of Islamism beyond the political sphere. Prominent Turkish Islamist Ali Bulaç employs a slightly different approach:

> Islamism is an intellectual, ethical, social, economic, political, and international movement rooted in the primary sources of Islam aiming to establish a new model of human[ity], society, politics/state, and the world, and subsequently a social order and universal union of Islam. In other words, Islamism is to bring back Islam's livelihood, to implement its principles, and it is an ideal and struggle to rebuild the world for every historical and social condition.[36]

Bulaç's definition is as broad and ambitious from the perspective of a practitioner as it can be. He does not link Islamism to its apologetic and defensive origins but defines it as a movement with universal ideals that will solve humanity's problems (a.k.a. Islam is the solution). Bulaç is not alone in not invoking the anticolonial threads of Islamism. Turkish political scientist Mümtazer Türköne argues that Turkish Islamism differs from similar movements in other parts of the Muslim world due to differences in their motivations.[37] Islamism in non-Ottoman (non-Turkish) societies emerged as a resistance movement against foreign invasion and colonialism. Accordingly, these movements are generally associated with anti-imperialist ideology and a jihadi outlook. There was no direct foreign invasion in the Ottoman Empire, but a state in decline needed saving. Turkish Islamists' main concern, thus, was to protect and strengthen the state. At the onset, Turkish Islamism came to life as a modernization project that also promoted constitutional government according to the Islamic principles.

Several Islamists' works can be cited to support the above proposition. Nineteenth-century Ottoman poet, writer, and bureaucrat Namık Kemal argued that a new reinterpretation of religious sources according to a rational and modern outlook could bring Islam's original vision to life. Consequently, he believed that Islam could be a source of progress and constitutional government.[38] Mehmed Akif, another leading figure of Islamism, believed that Islam could inspire scientific progress and democracy if its real message is brought to life. He propounded a selective adaptation of Western science and argued that Islam is already compatible with science and progress in his poems and writings in Islamist journals (*Sırat-ı Müstakim* and *Sebîlürreşâd*). He viewed Islamic identity as a solution to the reversal of the state's decline and took an anti-imperialist position during the Turkish independence war.[39]

By and large, global Islamism encompasses two broad views. On the one hand, there is a view that takes an anti-imperialist reaction as an inherent characteristic of Islamism. According to the second view, Islamism is not a reaction, but, rather, it is a genuine ideology. It relies on the motto that "Islam is the solution," and it can solve the crises of humanity, the nation, and the world. This view also attributes a prescriptive quality to Islam, viewed as a panacea to social ills or a blueprint for constructing an ideal order. In this vein, Türköne argues that Turkish Islamism has not emerged as a reaction to colonial domination, but it is about saving or strengthening the state.[40]

These two views have divergent implications for justice discourses. The first view will take Islamism to a position of "resistance" or "rebellion" against oppressors. Such acts could be directed against foreign invasion, colonialism, economic exploitation by the global economic powers, or domestic tyrants. In this scenario, Islamism becomes an ideology of justice against all injustices and oppression. As Kara succinctly states, "We must not forget that almost all of the Islamist movements have continued to be, at the same time, movements fighting injustice as well as movements of solidarity with and protection for the oppressed."[41] By this account, Islamism is an ideology that fights for the rights of victims who are being exploited by colonial rulers or contemporary beneficiaries of the global economic order. The cause of injustices is usually perceived to be external to Islam. The culprits are the forces of modernity or the Western hegemonic powers, in most cases. Subsequently, devout Muslims are seen as agents, and they should rise and fight with imperialist powers and challenge all the inequalities and oppression created by these same powers.

This first view has been the predominant approach among the Islamist intellectuals and social scientists in the non-Turkish context. For example, Mohammed Ayoob[42] and Immanuel Wallerstein[43] view Islamism in these terms. For Wallerstein, Islamist groups are among the antisystem elements, but they will eventually be incorporated into the world system.[44] By invoking rebellion against a hegemon in the name of the oppressed masses, this view implicitly attributes a democratic quality of the revolutionary brand to Islamism. Finally, in this vein, Ali Shariati defines the world system as a constant struggle between the forces of the Islamic worldview and the polytheist worldview or the oppressed and the oppressor. In his account, the imperialist and capitalistic orders represent the oppressor, and the people are the oppressed who should fight against them.[45]

The second approach attributes a prescriptive quality to Islamism. In this view, Islam turns to a magic wand that could save the individual, society, and humanity. It can solve social problems, end the chaos, establish morality, and institute a just political system. In effect, the most important goal of early Ottoman Islamists was to save the order and prevent the state from collapsing.[46] Islamists like Mehmed Akif aided the founding of Turkish-Islamic synthesis as the primary identity to accompany this goal. Turkish Islamists have followed these pioneers' footsteps to focus on social order, national identity, and building a new civilization in the republic era. This view is especially visible in the writings of prominent Turkish poet Necip Fazıl Kısakürek in the 1960s.[47]

This second view does not preclude resistance against the corrupt systems, but its implications may also lead to political quietism to prevent fitna. Thus, one can argue that the Islamist ideology may inadvertently engender pro–status quo attitudes (and behaviors) even when the nondemocratic or illegitimate government is in place. This approach is akin to the doctrine of Sunni political quietism best expressed by the fourteenth-century Islamic scholar Ibn Taymiyya: "Sixty years with a tyrannical imam are better than one night without an imam."[48] As demonstrated below, political quietism and obedience have been the dominant attitudes among many Islamist groups in Turkey.

Given the complex sociopolitical reality and two visions of Islamism in the Turkish context, carrying the discourse analysis of articles published in Islamist journals will provide an excellent opportunity for moving beyond the analysis of political and violent Islamism. It is likely to helps us understand better the construction of discursive fields related to the concept of justice as the society and politics evolve. The analysis is likely to provide insights about the role of competing visions of Islamism in the construction of Islamic conceptions of justice. Finally, by analyzing the Islamist journal archives, scholars can shift their scholarly attention from the intricacies of party politics and electoral strategies toward understanding how Islamist movements reconstruct discourses of Islamic justice to create meaning that either triggers critical attitudes or encourages obedience within the existing power relations.

Understanding the Justice Discourses in Islamist Journals

Journal publishing has always been an essential tool for Islamist movements. Turkish Islamists have utilized journals to convey their ideas and educate their followers since the second constitutional revolution of 1908. Some students of Islamism perceive journal publishing to be so significant that they study Turkish Islamism by examining the historical trajectories of journals.[49] As discussed above, Turkish Islamist journals entered a lively phase of activity in the 1960s, a trend that continued after 1980. A close reading of the articles in these journals provides a window into the mindset of diverse Islamist groups operating within a dynamic sociopolitical reality. The analysis presented in this section is not limited to Islamist political groups. It also sheds light on the ideology of intellectual communities, literary movements, and antisystem groups. The analysis separates the post-1960 era into two periods, 1960–1980 and 1980–2010, following the scholarly convention about the evolution of Islamism.[50]

The discourse analysis utilizes the digitized archives of Islamist journals stored in the servers of İLEM library (*İlmi Etüdler Derneği*) in Istanbul.[51] The articles were selected in three stages according to a rigorous method. In the first stage, the main keyword, *adalet* (justice), was used to filter a large number of articles. In the second stage, a joint keyword search was conducted for additional filtering of the articles to capture the most relevant writings. Many articles were eliminated because they omit the keyword adalet or other keywords capturing different dimensions of justice, including *zulüm* (oppression), *hak* (right, desert), *zalim* (oppressor), and *adil* (just). In the third stage, the filtered articles were subjected to close reading to separate the articles that directly discuss the Islamic justice conception from those that simply use justice in passing and do not provide any substantive discussion of this notion.[52]

Table 5.1 shows the distribution of the articles by Islamist journals based on the availability in the İLEM archives. The table reports the publication

TABLE 5.1 PREVALENCE OF ISLAMIC JUSTICE DISCOURSES IN TURKISH ISLAMIST JOURNALS (1960-2010)

Journal	Publication Dates	# of Issues	# of Articles Referencing Justice	# of Articles about Islamic Justice
1960-1980 Period				
Yeniden Milli Mücadele	1970-1980	528	8	6
Büyük Doğu	1943-1978	512	11	8
Diriliş	1960-1992	396	2	1
Hilal	1958-1993	367	4	4
Sebil	1976-1992	269	13	8
İslamın İlk Emri Oku	1961-1979	209	9	7
Hareket	1939-1982	187	6	3
Edebiyat	1969-1984	157	2	0
İlahi Işık	1966-1973	135	9	9
İslam	1956-1976	108	5	2
Sönmez	1964-1972	77	5	4
Fedai	1963-1979	64	2	2
Kriter	1976-1984	48	2	1
İslam Medeniyeti	1967-1982	44	6	6
Sancak	1967-1968	10	3	2
Other	1960-1980	Variable	38	38
1980-2010 Period				
Kudüs	2003-2005	7	1	1
Bilgi ve Hikmet	1993-1995	12	1	1
Bilgi ve Düşünce	2002-2003	14	6	2
Yeni Zemin	1993-1994	18	5	2
Yeni Yeryüzü	1993-1995	20	3	2
İnsan	1985-2000	33	1	0
Bilge Adamlar/Adamlar	2002-present	44	18	2
Vahdet	1996-2000	48	11	3
Değişim	1993-1999	61	21	9
Anlayış	2003-2010	84	15	9
Özgün İrade	2004-present	152	87	12
Umran	1991-present	280	21	4
Haksöz	1991-present	320	15	5
İktibas	1981-present	464	66	17

The count of articles reflects the results according to the author's three-step method filtering a large number of articles. *Source:* İLEM archives.

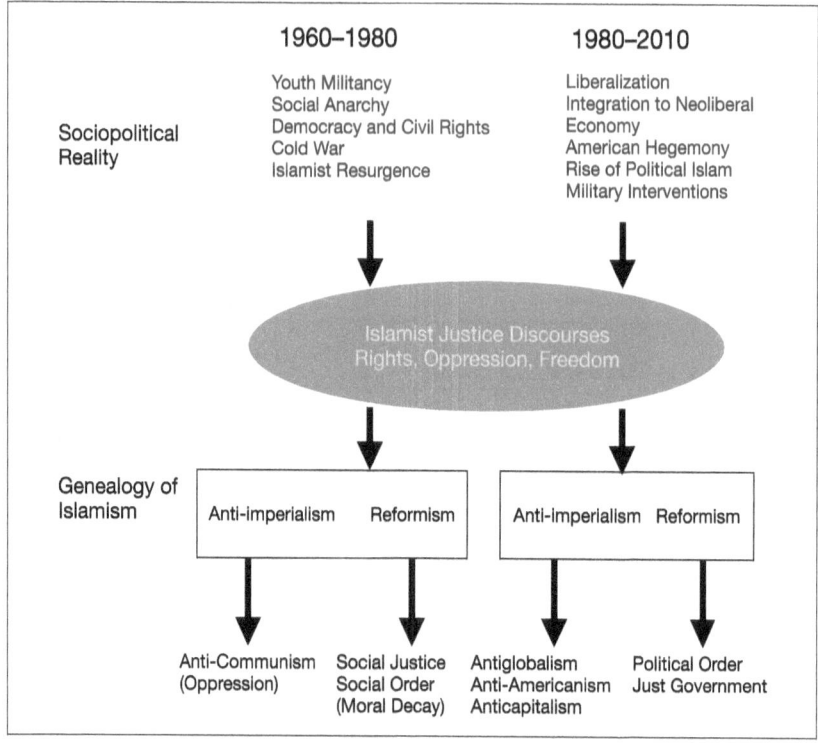

Figure 5.1 Evolution of justice discourses in Islamist journals (1960–2010).

dates, the number of issues published, and a count of articles referencing justice. This general count is also inclusive of the articles that specifically discuss Islamic justice. It should be noted that the numbers presented in Table 5.1 do not necessarily reflect the full coverage of Islamic justice conception in Islamist journals. Instead, due to the filtering method described above, the counts in Table 5.1 show the most relevant articles to be used in the discourse analysis.[53]

The analysis of Islamist articles published during the 1960–1980 and 1980–2010 periods takes place in three steps. The first step presents the semantics of the Islamic justice conception by providing examples from various definitions related to this notion's historical evolution. The second step involves an examination of how the meaning of justice is constructed by the Turkish Islamists against a dynamic sociopolitical background. Finally, the analysis traces the similarities and differences between Islamist conceptions of justice and discourses of political and social justice in the Turkish Islamist writings. Figure 5.1 shows a schematic representation of discourse analysis and the remainder of this chapter elaborates on the mechanisms depicted in this figure.

The Semantic Field of Islamist Conceptions of Justice

In thousands of pages of Islamist journals, the concept of justice takes center stage in a crowded semantic field of related terms like freedom, equality, right (*hak*), oppression (zulüm), merit, deserve, and moderation. References to justice usually involve these other related terms, whose semantic weight changes as the focus and prevalence of justice discourses evolve from 1960 to 2010 in the Islamist writings. As the sociopolitical reality changes, so do the meanings attributed to justice in these Islamist writings.

Zulüm or zulm is the most frequently used term in discussions of justice. Although this concept has a more significant role in Shia political thought,[54] it emerges as one of the principal justice notions in the Islamist writings of Sunni groups in Turkey. Zulüm originates from Arabic and is translated as oppression, tyranny, or wrongdoing. It appears as the quintessential opposite of Islamic justice in most articles analyzed here.[55] For example, one article states, "Justice is the opposite of zulüm. Zulüm means to violate rights, to harm, to break hearts. In contrast, justice means to give everyone their rights, to place everything in its proper place according to reason, logic, and wisdom."[56] Another article describes a just ruler by the quality of fighting with injustices and zulüm:

> Every ruler, every servant view [establishing] the justice and goodness in society as his first duty. He takes other rulers' palaces, splendor, and domination to be the indicators of zulüm. He believes that building palaces by exploiting others' rights or dominating citizens to that end constitutes zulüm. He knows that justice is the foundation of government, and zulüm is the greatest of all sins.[57]

A similar semantic construction is also visible in the post-1980 Islamist journals. For example, an article discussing the workers' rights states, "Justice is the government's foundation. Wherever justice lacks, there is zulüm. Wherever there is zulüm, there is no prosperity."[58] One notable difference between the two periods is the use of zulüm in conjunction with references to social problems in the 1960–1980 period and international politics in the post-1980 period. In this vein, many articles provide strong criticisms of foreign intervention in Chechnya, Afghanistan, Bosnia, and Iraq during the second period: "If the feelings of justice were remembered when the world was experiencing these events [wars], then these atrocities would not have occurred. The world still is indifferent to zulüm in Chechnya."[59]

Some writers use the notions of justice to denote distributive justice, rights, freedom, morality, equality, and mercy. A strong emphasis is placed on the notions of equality and rights in the 1960s. The Islamists aimed to counter the appeal of social justice ideals defended by the leftist groups with this strategy. For example, one writer states that justice means "to give everyone their material and spiritual rights. The just person ensures the provision of rights to the self and all individuals in society."[60] A similar definition takes place in another article published in 1979. "[Justice is] to give everyone their rights, to treat everyone equally in their rights, and make everyone equal in law."[61]

In the post-1980 period, the Islamist writers' substantive focus shifted from rights and equality to freedom and the main pillars of Islam, such as the unity of God, though zulüm continued to be a central concept. In an article about Prophet Muhammad, the author describes Islamic justice as one of the main pillars of Islamic civilization, along with freedom and rights. "However, Ibrahim's real tradition is tawhid. This tradition serves the creation of a civilization founded on rights, justice, and freedom."[62]

The transformation of the semantic field of justice is best explained by the interaction of Islamist ideology and the changing sociopolitical reality. First, the analysis of Islamist texts reveals that Turkish Islamists have intellectually increased in sophistication over time. In addition to the translation of major works about Islamism and the Western scholarship on the subject, new studies of Ottoman Islamists and classical Islamic texts have contributed to this sophistication. Turkish Islamists came to define justice in light of the Islamic unity principle of tawhid.[63]

Second, changes in the social and political context brought about differences in Islamist justice discourse in 1970s. The struggles between the left and the right and daily clashes among the youth organizations resulted in an anticommunist stand among the Islamists. In this context, justice was defined in relation to rights and distributive justice to counter the communist ideology's egalitarian rhetoric. In contrast, during the post-1980 period, the Islamist reaction to the neoliberal economic order, foreign intervention, and wars in various parts of the Muslim world and domestic repression of the Islamist groups in the 1990s brought about a new type of justice discourse emphasizing freedom and anticapitalist preferences.

The discourse analysis of Islamist journals demonstrates a considerable change in the Islamist conceptions of justice since the 1960s. These discourses evolved from the dislike of communism into nuanced criticisms of global capitalism. In the 1960s, Islamic justice was defined in relation to social equality, rights, and economic distribution to counter the appeal of the leftist ideology. In the post-1980 period, conceptions of justice concerned freedom, global injustices, and Islamic governance against the negative consequences of globalization.

Justice as Social Order and Political Reform

Just as Sayyid Qutb believed in an Islamic solution to end the corrupt systems, Turkish Islamists also aspired to bring order to a society they perceived as corrupt. The Islamists' writings of the 1960–1980 period emphasize social order and social morality. For an Islamist writer in the 1960s, justice brings about a harmonious social order (*nizam*), whereas injustice represents a catastrophic condition for society. One article states, "As far as justice, morality, virtue, and goodness prevail, whether it is aware of it or not, society will realize the best of reforms. The extent of the civility and vigor in this society can be best perceived relative to backward societies that perish within injustices."[64]

In the 1960–1980 period, a significant area of contention concerned delineating the conceptions of communist and Islamist social justice. It is not the social justice and equality promoted by the communists, according to the Islamists, that will bring about just order. For Islamists, the best social order is possible only in an Islamic society. The relationship between social justice and harmonious society is best seen in the Prophet's life and his companions' stories. Many articles refer to 'Umar's benevolence and justice to describe the ideal social order during the golden age. Some articles present the Ottoman political system as the perfect embodiment of just government.[65] These examples were instrumental for demonstrating that communist conceptions of social justice and equality will destroy morality, whereas Islamic social justice could provide true equality, prosperity, and happiness. Some articles particularly emphasize the ideal-typical "just ruler" (*adil lider*) as the most significant prerequisite for establishing justice, morality, and social order. This perspective encourages obedience to the ruler in order to achieve public interest. The focus on social and political order is reminiscent of the principle that requires political quietism in exchange for the public interest in the Islamic social justice trajectory. This principle was especially important during the medieval period, and it was formulated in the works of Ibn Taymiyya.[66]

Since 1980, the Islamists have turned their attention from the social order to political reform and just governance. While some articles focused on social justice and order in this later period, others focused on just government, political strategies, and an Islamic theory of just government. İhsan Eliaçık appears to be the dominant intellectual figure in debates about

Islamic justice with his sophisticated theory of "justice state" in this period. Eliaçık believes that just as divine justice is one and brings balance to the universe, a political system based on justice can bring unity and prosperity to the world. This theory's underlying logic is hardly novel as inferring justice discourses from the tawhid principle has been quite common among Islamists. Some examples include Sayyid Qutb, 'Ali Shariati, and Said Nursi. The novelty of Eliaçık's ideas concerns his attempt to make justice the foundation of the modern state. He states, "It should be evident that the unity of existence leads to right and justice (*hak ve adalet*). Just as cosmic justice creates a unity of existence, can there be any method other than political and social justice to unite humanity? . . . What else can be the state's *raison d'etre* other than justice?"[67]

Eliaçık develops his theory of "justice state" as an alternative to the theocratic and secular state models. His model is based on the togetherness of the state and religion according to a novel secular arrangement. In Eliaçık's words, "In the Turkish case, state-religion relations can be formed in the following way: 1. The state would have no power and responsibility in religious creed and religious duties, 2. The state can be responsible for the moral aspects of the religion, 3. The state would sometimes be responsible according to some aspects of religious law."[68]

The third condition is significant, especially given the close relationship between moral values and law in Islam. Here, Eliaçık comes closer to El Fadl[69] and An-Náim[70] by emphasizing the central role of moral values in Islamic political systems. Finally, Eliaçık views the justice state as the best means for restoring Islam's primacy in modern society within the state-religion relations he proposes. Other writers also discuss various aspects of politics as they relate to the notion of Islamic justice. One article looks at the importance of Islamic moral values in creating a legitimate political authority and cites justice, consultation (*şura*), and allegiance (*beyat*) as the main principles of Islamic political authority.[71]

Islamist authors also frequently mention the necessity of political reform and the protection of freedom and rights in the post-1980 period. They argue that Islamic justice protects freedom, human rights, and civil liberties. Sometimes, the justice principle serves as the basis of political opposition strategies against the domestic government, Western powers, or even Islamist organizations. Some Islamists, including Eliaçık, do not see this opposition emerging from traditional religious organizations or the Islamist political parties. Instead, Islamists are encouraged to focus on learning about the essential faith principles, such as unity of God, justice, and freedom, to form the necessary foundations for creating an Islamic government.

What explains this shift in the Islamist outlook? In the 1960s and 1970s, the main occupation of Islamists was the role of Islam in building a social order to confront the communist challenge. Islam was seen as a solution to society's perceived ills, including moral decay, and revolutionary ideologies were seen as incompatible with an Islamic social model. Therefore, a social order based on Islamic national identity and the twin pillars of justice—rights and equality—took center stage in the Islamist justice discourses. After the 1980s, the main preoccupation was with the politics and Islamic political reform due to increased political activism and Turkey's integration into the neoliberal global order. Liberalization policies of the 1980s, Islamist parties' first experience in government in the 1990s, repression of Islamist groups by the secular elite/military establishment in the late 1990s, and the rule of an Islamist party (AKP) unavoidably shifted the center of gravity in Islamist ideology from social order to politics and reform. The Islamic justice conception, now attached to the notion of freedom, was once again the principal semantic tool for constructing Islamist political ideology.

The Manifestations of an Anti-Imperialist Position in Islamist Journals

The second dimension of Islamism is the anti-imperialist position resulting from the colonial origins of Islamist movements.[72] As discussed above, some scholars argue that Turkish Islamism differs from its counterparts because it is not a reactionary movement against colonial incursion.[73] However, the analysis of the Islamist journals reveals that anti-imperialist ideology is a prominent dimension of Turkish Islamism, albeit in highly nuanced ways. During the 1960–1980 period, anti-imperialist ideology primarily took an anticommunist form. After the 1980s, Islamists diversified to present anticapitalist, anti-American, and antiglobalization discourses to express their discontent with the international system.

Anticommunist views frequently appeared in the pages of Islamist journals before the 1980s. Islamists criticized the communist and socialist systems for leading to a corrupt social order, injustices, and lack of morality. They presented these systems as ideological tools of the Soviet Republic, aiming to subdue and exploit the Muslim-majority countries. Some articles have a strong negative tone, also targeting capitalism and Western civilization. Nevertheless, communism is the principal target of Islamist writers for being a government type creating zulüm. Most of the criticism lacks a strong philosophical foundation and uses slogans. For example, one article states, "In Islam, there is divine justice, not social justice. . . . Every Muslim individual knows that almsgiving (*zakat*) is processed based on the property. Islam is like the sun; you cannot cover it. Muslimness means divine morality, whereas communism is about social immorality."[74] Another article provides specific references to the Cold War powers by stating, "While millions of people are suffering under *zulüm* in the Kremlin regime claiming to implement true equality, in the so-called civilized America the segregation becomes terrifying; however, both talk about social justice and democracy. Democracy in Red Russia or capitalist America, I do not think so."[75]

By and large, anti-imperialist discourse during the 1960–1980 period is constructed in the dichotomy of justice and oppression, where Islam represents true justice and Western ideologies represent the oppression. Of these Western ideologies, communism is particularly dangerous in view of some Turkish Islamists insofar as it threatens the social order, destroys morality, and prepares the ground for Turkey's colonization. In this period, most articles used slogans and stereotypes to describe the leftist ideologies.

In the post-1980 period, anti-imperialist discourse is not merely a critique directed at a single ideology or economic system; rather, the close reading of articles reveals a dynamic discursive construction involving anticapitalism, anti-Americanism, and strong criticism of international institutions and Western culture. Justice, once again, surfaces as the central concept in the construction of these positions. For example, one writer talks about injustices and the new world order:

> In effect, everything started with demands for "justice and freedom," but millions of individuals' calls for justice went unheard. Those who control and manipulate the world system and global capital have transformed the world into a war zone to silence the four-fifth of the global population. Although this war continues in Islamic geography, its primary goal is to force the silent majority into slavery.[76]

Islamist writers also frame anti-imperialist ideology as attacks targeting Islamic civilization. One article states, "Today, there is an attempt to modify Islam to ease the control of global power; they want to eliminate the noble Islamic bloc, seen as an eternal danger by M. Thatcher and S. P. Huntington."[77] On other occasions, Islamist writers discuss injustices taking place in other countries and blame the corrupt new world order for these outcomes. "There is no difference whatsoever between the hegemonic greed that oppresses (*zulmetmek*) the people with black skin and that of 'new world order' which is forced upon people like a straitjacket."[78]

The criticism of the new world order and neoliberal economic order involves criticism of international capitalism and its domestic supporters in the post-1980 period. Islamist writers argue that transnational corporations (i.e., global capitalism), and their domestic accomplices, try to confine religion to traditional interpretations and promote the notion of "moderate Islam" to exploit the Muslims. According to one article, since capitalism is built on the exploitation of people and charging interest, the Muslim businessman cannot avoid the vices of this system.[79] Global capitalist activities and the participation of the so-called devout bourgeoisie in this system are depicted as exploitation and injustice in the Islamist journals.

Conclusion

The archives of Turkish Islamist journals provide an excellent opportunity for examining contemporary manifestations of Islamist political and social justice discourses. Islamist journals function like schools where ideology is communicated to people using a simple language. Given the lack of historical elite and mass surveys for the period under investigation, the articles published in Islamist journals are the best proxy for exploring the Muslim attitudes about justice and political preferences.

The analysis conducted in this chapter reveals that justice is a crucial concept of Islamist ideology in Turkey. Its use as a central concept is anything but static as justice discourses evolve in response to changing sociopolitical reality. The articles published in the Islamist journals since 1960 reveal the central role of justice. During the 1960s and 1970s, Islamist justice is viewed as the most important condition for establishing social order. Islamists' primary preoccupation concerned communism as they tirelessly criticized this system for promoting false social justice and equality and for undermining social morality. For Islamists, Islam is the opposite of communism and is the only system that can bring order, implement morality, and establish social justice. The pages of Islamist journals in the 1960s included numerous references to the issues of rights, social justice, and equality, denying their central role in leftist ideologies and reconstructing these notions according to an Islamic framework. At the same time, references to communist conspiracy repeatedly appeared in multiple journals. Despite the high volume of attention concentrating on these issues, the treatment of justice as a central Islamic term is rudimentary and reduced to slogans at best before 1980.

After 1980, justice discourses became highly sophisticated within the Islamist worldview. Islamist writers described justice with such terms as freedom, human rights, and political liberties. The language of justice included references to politics and Islamic governance more than social order. Meanwhile, Islamists employed a cosmological outlook to construct justice discourses using the doctrine of tawhid. Rather than relying on common examples from the prophetic community or the religious slogans, Islamists developed sophisticated philosophies of just government to present a new image for Islam as the categorical opposite of the capitalist system, the new world order, and economic globalization. Turkish Islamists shifted their attention from the social order to the critique of capitalist ethics, American hegemony, and injustices seen in the major wars in the post–Cold War era. They presented Islam as the solution against oppression, exploitation, and injustices stemming from the ills of global capitalism and American hegemony.

The changing sociopolitical reality partly explains the differences in Islamist justice discourses between the two periods. In the 1960s, mass migration to urban centers, social problems associated with rapid modernization, and violence among the leftists and nationalist youth groups explain why Islamists focused on implementing an Islamic social order. They viewed the communist system as the categorical opposite of Islam. A crude image of leftist ideologies helped build a rudimentary justice discourse about the vices of the leftist ideologies and virtues of Islam.

After the 1980s, two developments might have triggered the new conceptions of justice among Islamists. First, international events, including the spread of neoliberal policies, economic globalization, and U.S. hegemony, had resonated deeply among Turkish Islamists. In responding to this new reality, Islamist intellectuals frequently referenced to various traumas—stemming from the various post–Cold War conflicts involving Muslim minorities and countries around the world—in developing new conceptions of justice. Second, domestically, Islamists gained influence in Turkish politics with the rise of Islamist parties and increasing the policy influence of religious actors. Faced with a highly complex social and political matrix, Turkish Islamists started to develop sophisticated accounts of the new global order and the rising prospects of Islamist parties. Subsequently, justice discourses concentrated on freedom, human rights, Islamic governance, anticapitalism, and anti-Americanism.

The analysis of Islamist journal articles also provides several insights about the synergies concerning the interplay of Islam, justice, and democracy. Democracy does not come up as a significant issue in the journals' pages, especially in the 1960–1980 period. In other words, the relationship between democracy and conceptions of justice is a nonsignificant issue in Islamist journals during this earlier period. Usually, democracy is mentioned in passing with no clear indication of what the authors mean when using it. Most accounts of democracy are not necessarily well informed. Those articles making references to democracy usually depict it as an instrument of Western imperialism. Neither do Islamist writers believe that democratic systems can establish justice or prevent zulüm. What matters is justice, not the type of political system in the Islamist outlook in these journals.

In the 1960–1980 period, Turkish Islamists seem to more clearly utilize the lineages of social and political justice trajectories in their writings, namely, freedom and order. Furthermore, these same lineages have been instrumentally used by the Islamist political parties as they made their way into government. Old and new incarnations of Islamist political parties, including National Order Party, Welfare Party, and AKP, have justified their policies either in the name of social order for a just, prosperous society or for the sake of fighting with injustices. This should not come as a surprise as the Islamists of the new millennium were members of various Islamist groups or students of prominent Islamist intellectuals during the 1960–1980 period.[80]

Ironically, however, the instrumentation of anti-imperialist discourse in foreign policy, a more visible discourse in the post-1980 period, helped the AKP leaders justify the domestic injustices with the pretext of the "social order," the dominant discourse of the 1960–1980 period. For example, AKP leaders have taken a very vocal stance and exploited the public's sensitivities about such issues as Palestinian independence, anti-immigrant policies in the West, or the Rohingya refugees in Myanmar. Foreign policy rhetoric employed the language of the Islamist anti-imperialism outlook and involved references to justice and oppression (*adalet ve zulüm*). In contrast, on the domestic scene, repression of the Kurdish minorities, the crackdown against the civil protesters, or violations of the rule of law were justified in the name of social order (*nizam*, or *kamu düzeni*). This dual strategy, while contradictory, contributed to the demise of Turkish democracy.

Despite the lack of interest in democracy in Islamist journals and the potential of the instrumentation of justice discourses to serve the authoritarian policies in a nascent democracy, the articles, especially those published during the 1980–2010 period, consistently used the jargon of democracy. More specifically, it is hard to find unequivocal references directly made to democracy in these journals. However, one can find ample use of notions that are, in fact, the building blocks of democratic institutions. For example, Islamist intellectuals made frequent references to the notions of equality, the rule of law, consultation, freedom, constraining the ruler, and civil rights in the pages of Islamist journals in the post-1980 period. However, they utilized these terms as part of Islamic justice, not as essential jargon of Western liberal democracy. This approach echoes the writings of the nineteenth century Islamists in the Ottoman Empire.[81]

This approach is symptomatic of a significant dilemma for the proponents of democratization in the Muslim world. It implies that Islamists believe that Islamic justice is compatible with democratic values, but they also view liberal democracy as a foreign system that is not suitable for Muslim-majority societies. From a policy perspective, these findings imply that top-down approaches to democratization that promote democracy by external actors or through the use of Western political culture may not resonate well in Muslim-majority countries, even in settings with a considerable democratization experience, such as Turkey. Democracy may be an acceptable form of government only when it is coated with Islamic notions such as justice (*'adalā*), consultation (*shūrā*), and freedom (*ḥurriyā*). On the flip side, the disapproval of Western democratic language may serve well to the authoritarian politicians' ambitions who conveniently hide behind the Islamist pretext of anti-imperialism and social order to undermine democracy.

The analysis in this chapter merely scratched the surface of rich variations in the Turkish Islamist landscape since the 1960s. The Turkish Islamist landscape includes a variety of movements that may not fit in this chapter's analytical framework. For example, some Islamists started to distance from the ruling AKP and its policies after 2011. The groups inspired by Eliaçık and the grassroots organizations like *Emek ve Adalet* took ideologically egalitarian and democratic positions against the AKP government.[82] These groups openly criticized AKP leadership and their policies and advocated for civil rights, labor rights, and egalitarian distribution. They also participated in the 2013 Gezi protests. Yenigun explains this schism among the Islamists as the new manifestation of the historical divergence between ethicalists and realists.[83] He points to the Akif Emre's[84] distinction between *Islamists* cherishing justice, democracy, and rights and *Muslimists* sacrificing justice principles for the sake of obtaining power. This new cleavage within Turkish Islamism started to materialize after 2011, a period that is not included in the analysis of Islamist journals in this chapter. The next chapter explores the association between justice discourses and democracy from the perspective of those who could be described as *Islamists* in the post-2011 Turkey. It presents the outlooks of justice-oriented new Islamist groups and their views about democracy using ethnographic research and in-depth interviews.

6

New Islamist Movements, Justice, and Democracy

> It is said that Allah allows the just state to remain even if it is led by unbelievers, but Allah will not allow the oppressive state to remain even if it is led by Muslims. And it is said that the world will endure with justice and unbelief, but it will not endure with oppression and Islam.
>
> —Ibn Taymiyya (Daily Hadith Online)

As the sun was setting, several people rushed to lay down the newspapers and plastic covers on the street. Others were carrying the meals, plates, plastic cups, and utensils and stacking them next to the beverages on the sidewalk. The crowd included university students, volunteers, observers, residents, and refugees from Syria and Africa gathered in this narrow street of Istanbul's poverty-stricken Tarlabaşı neighborhood[1] to break their fast (*iftar*) during Ramadan. "We have been organizing these meals for several years now. It is our way of helping the poor, the immigrants, and anyone in need. Ramadan is about blessing, humility, and human dignity, not about wasteful meals and vanity," said one of the organizers. He talked about what came to be known as *earth meals* (*yeryüzü sofraları*) organized by the new Islamist movements such as the Labor and Justice Platform and Anticapitalist Muslims since 2011 to protest the lavish lifestyle, corruption, and neoliberal policies of the ruling AKP in Turkey.

This iftar gathering in Tarlabaşı was an impressive scene of solidarity and benevolence. Its setting was a narrow and impoverished street next to Taksim, one of the most affluent areas and the center of Istanbul. The contrast between the communitarian and egalitarian spirit of this gathering was in stark contrast to another Ramadan dinner, the mayor's iftar at the center of the Taksim Square, only a couple blocks away from the first scene in Tarlabaşı. The Taksim Square dinner was sponsored by prominent businessmen, presumably devout and close to AKP circles. The guests were separated from other people in the square who were waiting in line to receive a free boxed dinner. The latter group was not invited to the tables, nor were they engaging in conversations with the guests. A new generation of Islamist social activists representing an egalitarian religious outlook organized the Ramadan dinner in Tarlabaşı. The other gathering, the Taksim dinner, reflected the changing political Islamist vision that has increasingly become elitist and hierarchical and has dominated the Turkish social and political scene in the new millennium under the AKP rule. The contrast in these iftar gatherings represents two competing outlooks, both rooted in the same religion and prioritizing justice as Islam's core value. The outlook associated with the Tarlabaşı gathering is representative of a new brand of Islamism, significantly different than the Islamism associated with the AKP.

The disillusionment of some Islamists with AKP's policies after its rise to power in 2002 was perhaps one of the main catalysts for the social justice–oriented civic activism of the new genre of Islamic groups.[2] Inspired by both leftist and Islamist ideologies, these groups represent a new brand of Islamic identity emphasizing egalitarian, pluralist, and social justice oriented views.[3] They resemble the horizontally organized new social movements that form counterhegemonic discourses in the public sphere,[4] especially using their Islamic identity.[5] One common element uniting these new groups is their quest for justice and the resulting social activism to help the most disadvantaged groups. From homeless adults to children living in the streets, the immigrants to the unemployed, the new Islamic social activism was an everyday protest movement empowering those confined to marginal urban spaces and left out of the "hegemonic charity structures."[6] The glue that held these groups and their socially conscious small charity activities together was their profound belief in Islamic justice. Specifically, they used justice as a discourse and engaged in social justice activism in accordance with their alternative Islamic political vision.

What do social activists mean when they say justice? Does one's conception of justice influence her political attitudes? Do perceptions of justice, for instance, shape one's attitudes toward democracy? At first sight, the answers to these questions might seem too evident, especially given the central role of justice in Islam's ethicopolitical system. However, a closer look reveals that the picture is much more complicated than it initially appears. There is no uniform path in the Islamist mindset leading from religion to justice and from justice to democratic orientations. While the quest for justice has been at the center of political debates concerning legitimacy, obedience, and rebellion against tyrants over many centuries, the mechanisms linking conceptions of justice to political attitudes and behaviors, particularly those related to democracy, are not always clear.

Previous chapters examined the historical and ideological underpinnings of Islamic conceptions of justice and their relation to political preferences. They examined the mechanisms linking Islamic conceptions of justice to perceptions of legitimacy, political obedience, and social welfare. This chapter builds on this analysis to explain the cognitive pathways linking perceptions of justice to support for democracy and authoritarianism. It aims to explore how religious individuals problematize justice to inform their political preferences. The analysis provides a fine-grained assessment of attitudes about justice and democracy using two dozen in-depth interviews conducted with the members of new Islamist movements in Turkey in 2017 and 2019. The subsequent chapters further explore the insights from this analysis by conducting statistical tests of public opinion surveys.

New Islamist Movements in Turkey

Turkey's new Islamist movements, ironically, teamed up with the opposition groups in the Gezi protests against a political party with Islamist credentials. Against the realist pursuit of power by the ruling Islamists at the expense of ethical principles, "seeking justice" has been the central notion motivating these movements before and after these protests.[7] These protests were the most significant demonstrations against the AKP government unfolding in a small park in Taksim Square in 2013. The demonstrators were from different civil organizations and they represented a broad ideological spectrum. Protesters came together to oppose an urban development plan involving one of the few parks in central Istanbul.

The Islamist Labor and Justice Platform was one of the first groups to come forward by signing a declaration supporting these protests. In this declaration, the group frequently referenced Islamic justice as a panacea against the unjust and corrupt government.[8] Arguably, this oppositional stance is the new incarnation of the everlasting cleavage in Islamic history[9] between ethically minded pious individuals and those who seek power at the expense of religious principles. The group's manifesto and the Gezi declaration highlight justice, morality, and human dignity, making them the centerpiece of their criticism of the AKP government. Islamist writers raised a similar criticism about the consequences of neoliberal economic policies in the post-2000 period, as discussed before.

The Labor and Justice Platform was not the only group to come forward during the protests. The Anticapitalist Muslims movement (Antikapitalist Müslümanlar) was another religious group participating in demonstrations. Inspired by the writings of influential Islamist intellectual İhsan Eliaçık, who has written extensively about social justice and the political role of justice in an Islamic government,[10] the members of the Anticapitalist Muslims strongly opposed the AKP government. Gezi provided an opportunity for the group members to voice their concerns about such issues as justice, oppression, and workers' rights. The group's ideology is reminiscent of a leftist critique of the AKP government, viewed as corrupt and authoritarian. Just like the Labor and Justice Platform, Anticapitalist Muslims strongly emphasized justice as a core value of Islam and viewed its implementation as a panacea against the "unjust rule" of the "conservative Islamists." The doyen of the group, Eliaçık stated that the protesters' real fight is for social justice and that "the young people who were with us on the square were rebelling against authoritarianism, totalitarianism and the patriarchy."[11]

These new Islamist movements represent one side of a split between Islamism and Muslimism, as defined by prominent Islamist intellectual Akif Emre.[12] According to Emre, Islamism is a movement, an ideology claiming to provide new solutions and projects, whereas Muslimism is a pragmatist political view. Muslimists aim to win power and use religion as an element of political strategy. Islamists, on the other hand, focus on apolitical vision grounded in Islamic ethics. Yenigun finds a family resemblance between Emre's classification and the historical cleavage between ethicalists (i.e., Islamists) seeking justice and realists (Muslimists) striving to maintain political power.[13] This cleavage is a contemporary manifestation of rival ideologies of legitimacy going back to the distinction between the piety-minded opposition and proponents of benevolent absolutism in early Islamic empires, as described by Hodgson.[14] One can argue that AKP's renunciation of Islamism to consolidate its power and the party's turn to the so-called conservative democracy as a model are the most visible manifestations of this cleavage. Yenigun succinctly summarizes this trend by arguing that "a new generation of Islamist youth, who was already disgruntled over the victims of the AKP's neoliberal development model as well as rampant corruption and nepotism within its ranks, had emerged. Banding together under new youth organizations with a particular focus on social justice issues, they began speaking up against the AKP."[15]

As discussed above, these groups included the Labor and Justice Platform, the Anticapitalist Muslims, some branches of the Islamist human rights organization such as the Association for Human Rights and Solidarity for the Oppressed (Mazlumder), Islamic feminist group "Muslims' Initiative against the Violence toward Women," and some other smaller groups. Gezi protests served as a catalyst that increased the activities and awareness of these groups. They reached out to secular, liberal, and leftist groups to convey their support for the protests. Labor and Justice Platform's declaration proved to be highly controversial from the perspective of the AKP leaders and traditional religious elites. Groups like "Muslims' Initiative against the Violence toward Women" resolutely challenged AKP's attempts to label Gezi as an anti-Islamic protest.[16]

Some of these groups were active long before Gezi. Social justice has been the main motto of these groups who criticized the developmental model of AKP for creating new inequalities and exploiting the working class. For example, Mazlumder organized an activity in Istanbul's Fatih Mosque to demand justice for Uludere victims.[17] The Labor and Justice Platform organized Ramadan dinners in front of five-star hotels to protest the lavish lifestyle among the AKP rank-and-file members since 2002.[18] Later, Anticapitalist Muslims organized street iftars calling for social justice policies. They criticized the ruling party's corrupt policies and exploitation of Islam. Another group, an intellectual brand of the new Islamist youth, gathered around the Istanbul Think House (İstanbul Düşünce Evi-İDE) voicing similar ideas. Members of these groups were interconnected. They engaged in social justice activism by helping homeless children, women, the poor, and immigrants.

Overall, the new Islamist movements opposed the religious conservative AKP government. They are critical of AKP policies, which they view as unjust, corrupt, and authoritarian. They have a socially conscious agenda resulting in charity activities geared toward bringing justice to the most marginalized segments of Turkish society. Members of these groups actively engage in labor unions, workers' mobilization campaigns, and anticapitalism protests. Given their social justice focus, how do members of these groups view democracy? This chapter provides an analysis of in-depth interviews conducted with the members of these groups to answer this question.

The Interviews

In-depth interviews with the members of new Islamist groups and other religious youth were conducted in Istanbul during the summers of 2017 and 2019.[19] I made the initial contacts before my travel and looked for opportunities for additional interviews during my stay. The interviews were semistructured and lasted between thirty-five minutes and one hour. I recorded the conversations when permitted to by participants and also took notes during the interviews.[20] These interviews provide a unique opportunity for understanding the cognitive mechanisms linking justice to support for democracy among the devout individuals. Most interviewees were members of new Islamist movements, including Labor and Justice Platform, Anticapitalist Muslims, and Islamic feminist groups. Other interviewees (students, part-time workers, professionals) were highly devout, but they were not affiliated with any of these groups. I also participated in several street iftars in Tarlabaşı and closely observed the interactions at these events.

A preliminary look at these interviews reveals that members of these groups define justice in broader terms and link these conceptions to their political preferences. The interviews also show that religion plays a significant role in the development of different conceptions of justice. Most interviews point to a healthy dose of skepticism about the existing political system. The chapter continues by presenting the deeper insights from these interviews in two sections. First, the analysis discusses interviewees' perceptions and interpretations of Islamic justice conception. Second, the discussion elaborates on attitudes to explain the synergies between justice values and support for different regime types (e.g., Islamic state, Muslim democracy, and authoritarian systems). This analysis helps us understand specific cognitive mechanisms linking justice orientations to support for democracy. The next two chapters build on these insights to conduct statistical tests of this relationship using the survey data collected in the Muslim world.

Conceptions of Justice

The interviews demonstrate that the Islamist youth define justice with a broad set of concepts, including equality, rights, entitlement, economic distribution, and oppression.[21] Conceptions of justice are at the center of a crowded semantic field among the religious youth, as has been the case in the writings of Islamist intellectuals as demonstrated in Chapter 5. Of these concepts, equality appears to be an essential dimension of conceptions of justice. However, this egalitarian outlook is rarely related to economic distribution or financial aspects of social justice as in the Western tradition.[22] For example, Cüneyt, a twenty-five-year-old doctor, defines justice as "equality in opportunity and equality in legal matters," whereas Türkan, a thirty-four-year-old female dorm manager, states that justice is "equality in having the right to live, or in equal distribution. It is everyone's right to use the opportunities, regardless of their race, ethnic origin, or religion."

Those affiliated with the new Islamist movements also recognize equality as a central element of justice, but they define it using such notions as deserved reward or punishment (desert), right, entitlement, and conscience. The interviewees from the Islamist groups also explicitly relates justice to political reality and power relations. One interviewee's response succinctly captures this perspective: "Justice (*adalet*) shares the same root with the word equivalent (*muadil*). It means equivalent and maybe even equality. We separate equality and justice, but in fact, these are not different from each other. Justice is about the perception that all human beings are equal and at the same level without one trying to establish authority or sovereignty over the others by despotic means" (Kemal). Similarly, Murat (graduate student) also invokes power relations: "It is easy to be just or care about equality when one is powerless. What is important is one's behavior toward the weak once they obtain power." Most interviewees eschew defining justice in terms of absolute equality. One of the former members of the Anticapitalist Muslims movement was highly critical of this attitude and presented an alternative view:

> We grew up among the Islamists in Turkey. We were told that equality is a problem for the leftists, and justice is a concern for the Islamists. The main focus of Islamists has been on justice at the expense of treating equality with a left-phobic (*solfobik*) mindset. In his book El-Mufredat, Râgıb el-İsfahânî argues that justice can be maintained only when equality is present. El-İsfahânî is a highly respected source among Islamists, so how come they say "justice matters, but equality does not." I do not understand (Ferdi).

While few interviewees define justice in egalitarian terms, most of them refer to such terms as "deserving," "to have the right to something," or "entitlement." In this sense, justice is similar to desert. Some interviewees define justice as "to treat the others as they deserve it" (Ayşen), "to provide the rights to someone as s/he is entitled to" (Ferit), or "to take the rightful entitlements" (Şener).

For some interviewees, to talk and care about justice is a means of criticizing the existing power relations and status quo. For example, when asked about the opposite of justice, many choose the Koranic term *zulüm*. Among its other meanings, this Arabic word also means to displace or not put something in its right place. Zulüm is also interchangeably used with such political terms as oppression and tyranny. Kadir defines zulüm as "to prevent someone from getting what s/he is entitled to or to violate a person's rights." Murat states that "*zulüm* is directly linked to power. It is about having the mindset of 'I have power, so I can do anything,'" a statement echoing other interviewees' mindset:

> Zulüm can be about taking a kid's candy by force or the state oppression against its citizens. In essence, it is the tyranny of power (Şener).
>
> The opposite of justice is wrongfulness. Maybe repression or being repressed, imposition, or tyranny [zulüm] (Talat).

As these excerpts from the interviews reveal, the Koranic term zulüm plays a vital role in Islamist youths' narratives as they form their attitudes about justice and power relations. The cleavage between ethical and realist outlooks seems to resurface in contemporary Islamists' worldviews. As stated earlier, the lineage of this cleavage goes back to the first political divisions in the early Muslim community and in the medieval compromise of the classical Islamic state.[23] According to this cleavage, justice and tyranny represent polar ends. Since there will be oppression and tyranny in the lack of justice, one can legitimize rebellion against the unjust ruler or justify the executive constraint (classical Islamic state) to prevent zulüm. This position is evident in a long line of intellectual tradition, including Khawarij, Qadarites, Mu'tazila, constitutionalists of the nineteenth and twentieth centuries, and contemporary Islamists. Although traditional ulema had also occasionally opposed tyranny,[24] political authorities eventually co-opted them to serve the state.[25] Based on this background, two questions require further investigation to understand the perceptions of the religious youth. First, are these perceptions formed according to the Islamic conceptions of justice? Second, do Islamic conceptions of justice shape political preferences?

Most interviewees cite justice as a universal value, but they also give the lion's share to Islamic tradition as the primary determinant of conceptions of justice. They bring evidence from the Koran, the Prophet's life, and the rightly guided caliphs when asked about justice in Islam. For example, Türkan states, "All religions have something to say about justice. You do not have to belong to a specific religion to carry a feeling of justice. . . . Islam, however, preaches justice for all regardless of religion, language, or race." Tarık is more specific about the significance of justice in Islam: "According to my definition of an Islamic order, justice will inevitably be served, I will call Islam, justice. There is a saying which states, 'state's religion is justice.' I feel very close to this position." The Islamist position that equates Islam with justice emerges very prominently among the interviewees. Similar to the Islamists of the twentieth century,[26] the new Islamist youth continues to use "justice" as a catchall phrase and a panacea for all social and political problems:

> In Islam, justice refers to an individual's conscience about knowing her limits and obeying the just. It is about avoidance from engaging in tyranny. Justice is criticism toward tyranny, as seen in the Koranic argument against the religious leaders who play God's role. I prefer to think about justice in terms of servitude to God (*kulluk*). . . . I believe Islam can establish justice in this sense. . . . At least this notion of servitude will remove the tyranny. I am mainly interested in the social implications of this notion. I am trying to look from a general perspective. We can establish justice only with Islam (*Şener*).

The notion of servitude (*kulluk*) comes up in almost all interviews. The participants view servitude to God as an essential principle within Islam's cosmological hierarchy that creates absolute equality among God's servants (*kul*). This approach is reminiscent of Qutb and Shariati's conceptions of justice.[27] In the above quote, Şener also refers to conscience as an important precondition for justice. As discussed in the previous chapters, one legacy of the political justice trajectory concerns free will, individual autonomy, and human dignity as conditions resulting from man's vicegerent status. While not explicitly referring to the historical events that brought about this legacy, many interviewees invoke individual conscience and freedom from servitude to others as significant requisites of Islamic justice in their responses.

The interviews also reveal that the Islamist youth use novel concepts to define justice. In addition to the role of man within a divine hierarchy, conscience, and equality, "being a just witness" or the "just testimony" (*adil şahitlik*)[28] are also frequently cited as elements of Islamic justice by the interviewees:

> When I think about justice in Islam, I remember the verse about "just testimony." I remember the verse warning about the "hatred of other nations" and the recommendation about "treating the other as your own." There is also the equality aspect. I am thinking about the verse about devotion (*takva*). This one establishes equality among human beings in their relation to God, but equality is not always possible among human beings [in other aspects]. (Talat).

The interviewees mention equality among human beings as a universal value when describing justice as "just testimony." They also believe that just testimony or just witness principle implies pluralist outlooks and tolerance. This principle also motivates political action, as some respondents stated that they would engage in various civil and political acts to counter an unjust ruler because they want to be just witnesses. Thus, in addition to informing attitudes about political preferences, a unique manifestation of the Islamic justice conception may bring about increased civic engagement among the Islamic youth who care about justice as a core ethical value of their religion. Chapter 8 tests this relationship and finds statistical evidence confirming the relationship between perceptions of justice and protest behavior using survey data collected during the Arab Spring.

Justice and Political Attitudes

Although most interviewees inform their value orientations using Islamic justice principles, these orientations do not necessarily engender support for democracy or Islamic governance. Most interviewees demonstrate a healthy dose of skepticism about different governance formulas, whether an Islamic state or a Muslim democracy. However, the in-depth interviews and my ethnographic observation reveal that they prefer secular democracy as the most viable political path for social justice implementation. In contrast, they view the authoritarian system as un-Islamic and unjust.

Interviewees were highly critical of political systems presented as Islamic states. Respondents brought up Saudi Arabia and Iran as cases of authoritarian government. The repressive policies of these states were a common point of criticism across different conversations. Opinions ranged from total rejection of Islamic statehood to conditional acceptance of this model with significant skepticism. The respondents frequently emphasize the need for alternative applications. For example, Talat, a nineteen-year-old college student, expresses his distaste of the "state" as a political institution and questions the notion of Islamic government:

> I reject this notion of the state according to Islamic principles. In the expression "lā 'ilāha 'illā -llāh," the "ilāha" [gods] also refer to the "state.". . . We need to reject this notion of state. I mean, a categorical rejection. For example, we need to do so when we are supporting the oppressed [mazlum]. If the state is in an equation, we need to approach the state from minus one and directly oppose it. Those states that describe themselves as "Islamic" are simply executing things per the definition of the state; they are directly, and by definition, producing zulüm. I reject the state according to the just testimony principle [adil şahitlik].

Others voice skepticism about using Islam as an adjective for describing the state (Ferdi), refer to the utopian nature of the prophetic society (Hale), or mention the difficulty of implementing such a political model in modern societies (Filiz). Kadir succinctly summarizes this last point: "When we talk about an Islamic state, we are referring to the modern state, a highly complex structure, a powerful mechanism that is likely to use force against its citizens. Religion cannot be more than a tool that legitimizes this kind of policy." Under such skepticism, the interviewees disassociate the implementation of justice from the Islamic state as its provider.

The respondents also hold a great deal of cynicism about the possibility of implementing justice policies in political systems using religious justifications for legitimacy. Kadir makes this position very clear when he says, "The provision of justice is not about state policies. This superstition about the state is one of the most common mistakes of Muslims. Unless the society becomes just, it is impossible to provide justice, especially with a state that uses a religious label." Filiz expresses a similar opinion from a different perspective: "The provision of justice entirely depends on the person who executes policies; it depends on the perspective. It does not matter what the label of the state is or whether Muslims hold political power. If justice is not implemented in society, it does not matter how you label the state."

By and large, members of new Islamist movements oppose "Islamic state" models due to their potential to inhibit just governance and facilitate oppressive policies. This finding echoes the scholarship that makes a case against the Islamic government, Islamist political models, and state control of religion.[29] In addition, putting the goal of justice above Islamic state models, as many interviewees do, is reminiscent of critical medieval ulema's political preferences, particularly of Ibn Taymiyya, who view justice as the most important principle and essence of politics.

The conversations with the Islamist youth reveal an interesting divergence between the opinions of interviewees who are active in civil platforms and other interviewees who are highly devout but are not active in Islamist organizations. The latter group believes that justice can be established in a regime ruled according to the principles of Islam or a model depicted as Islamic state. For example, when asked about whether justice can be achieved in a government ruled by Islamic principles, Türkan expresses a strong opinion: "Absolutely, justice can be established in this system. During the prophet's time and the reign of the rightly-guided caliphs, an Islamic state was in place. Ömer is best known for his just policies." However, this acceptance is conditional on the existence of a "true Islamic state that is not repressive but a state that maintains universal values" (Ayşen).

In contrast, Islamist youth active in civil platforms voice substantial doubts about establishing justice even in a government abiding by Islamic principles. These doubts arise from the disagreement about Islamic principles, the lack of trust toward the rulers, or the practical impossibility of justice maintenance. Ferit believes that "Islamic principle means it will be a state governed according to the stereotypes of the *sunni* tradition, and hence establishing justice will be very difficult. They will use şura (blah blah) to do things clandestinely." Ediz argues that it will be easier to quiet the opposition in this kind of political system. Hale presents a sophisticated argument about the sustainability of justice even in the existence of an Islamic government:

> These kinds of societies can emerge only when decisions are made according to a social contract, when consultative mechanisms allow participation of all, or when there are leaders who are there to serve and who can take criticism [that] are in control rather than the leaders who only care about staying in power. Whenever this society prefers growth and development over justice, then it cannot establish justice.[30] We can establish justice for a moment, but this can change ten years later. This is like Moses leaving for Mount Sinai and coming back to a corrupt society.

While the interviewees apply their sophisticated accounts of religion, politics, and justice to inform their perceptions of democracy, this is not a linear process. Some skepticism emerges about Islamic democracy or Muslim democracy as governance models suitable for justice implementation. Many respondents view democracy as a Western project and voice their reservations about implementing democracy in Turkish society. Based on their perceptions of the ruling AKP's use and abuse of majoritarian institutions, some respondents condemn the majoritarian interpretation of democracy.

The interviews also include references to contemporary Islamists such as Rāshid al-Ghannūshī, Yūsuf al-Qaraḍāwī, and Mawdudi. However, rather than unquestionably accepting the theoretical models presented by these thinkers, the interviewees ask many questions about the utility of "democracy" or its "Islamic" character. For example, Ediz says, "I do not think there is anything that Islam can add to democracy." Kemal states, "democracy emerged due to certain contextual factors. Therefore, it can be problematic to assign a universal character [Islam] to democracy." Notwithstanding these critical stances, most interviewees think that Islam and democracy are compatible. For example, Ferdi argues that "if democracy is truly implemented and if all human beings and their property are protected, Islam and democracy can coexist in this system. I do not think these concepts are separate. I believe the principles of these concepts are the same."

Does the Islamist conception of justice inform preferences about democratic, Islamic, and authoritarian governance? To answer this question, the interviewees were presented with four regime types and were asked to choose one according to their Islamic conception of justice:

- Secular democratic
- Secular authoritarian
- Democratic regime with Islamic principles and a religious ruler
- Autocratic regime with Islamic principles and a religious ruler

Most interviewees preferred a secular democratic regime because they believe that this regime is most conducive to implementing Islamic justice. They also believe that this outcome will be contingent on several factors, including the interpretation of Islamic values, societal actors, and political realities. For example, Şener argues, "There will be many factors here. You can establish justice also in other regimes. However, justice is more likely to emerge due to political struggles among different groups in a secular democratic regime." This point echoes An-Náim's argument stating that democracy can be acceptable to religious Muslims in secular systems where Muslims freely deliberate on and contribute to the policy according to their religious values.[31] However, some others make a strong statement against the possibility of establishing justice in a democratic system:

> Some people argue that democracy is polytheism (*şirk*). Recently, I have suspicions about democracy as an ideal regime. Let us talk about an example. Let us assume that the society [majority] came to an unjust decision. What can you do against this in a democracy? ... Let us say Islamist democrats are in power. For example, let us assume that our current president [Recep Tayyip Erdoğan] is a democrat, he is a Muslim, and he did everything according to the election results. However, this does not make me feel that the society I live in is just (Hale).

Despite visible skepticism, democracy appears to be the most preferred regime type among the respondents for several reasons. First, it is seen as "the lesser of two evils." Second, interviewees view it as a better alternative for establishing justice. Third, they believe that its working principles are more compatible with Islamic conceptions of justice. For example, Filiz states, "I believe that democracy can be more comprehensive about these concepts (about social justice in the whole society) than monarchy. It will be easier to establish justice in a democracy." Murat most succinctly expresses this position:

> I believe democracy will be more just than other systems. Various religions will have different notions of justice. A secular democracy will also differ in its justice conception. If we consider justice in a secular democracy, this may be viewed as injustice relative to the perception of justice in a given religion. Regardless, I still believe that establishing justice will be more likely in a secular democracy. And this will be compatible with Islam.

Kemal voices a more reserved opinion and believes that justice will be realized if democracy is defined as "government by people." Meanwhile, Kadir believes that while authoritarian regimes may also implement justice, it will be easier to achieve this goal in democracies. Nevertheless, like many of his peers, he appears to be very concerned about a religious leader's possibility of exploiting democracy and causing injustice:

> You can implement justice in authoritarian systems, too. For example, there could be a just king who uses his authority in a very just way. He can build a just system encompassing the poorest and the most disadvantaged people. In a democratic system, a religious or secular person can establish justice. I have one reservation about the

possibility of exploitation of religion. A religious person can be just today, but tomorrow, he may justify injustice and oppression with religion. Therefore, I believe justice can be best served in a secular democratic system (Kadir).

Conclusion

The analysis in this chapter shows that, rather than formalistic approval of a regime type, the Islamist youth are mainly concerned with the realities of the political world and substantive outcomes of different regimes. The Islamic conception of justice emerges as the dominant discourse in shaping their political attitudes. In effect, justice almost serves as a yardstick for evaluating the desirability of a regime. Based on Turkey's existing political reality, the interviewees demonstrate their cynicism about democracy, even if the ruler is a devout person. The Islamist youth take an ethical position prioritizing such notions as desert, equality in servitude, and opposition to tyranny. This position stands in sharp contrast to the pure power-seeking agenda and corrupt practices of rulers who use Islam as a political instrument of power games. In the interviews, not a single respondent agreed to support a religious but unjust ruler. All of them find protest acceptable against an unjust ruler regardless of his religious devotion or the ruler's use of Islamic discourse. At the same time, they criticize democracy with a healthy dose of skepticism akin to "critical citizens"[32] of advanced democracies.

The in-depth interviews revealed that Islamist youth define justice as a general principle and explicitly link it to the resistance against oppression. Most of the time, the concept of justice is juxtaposed with Islam and used as a term that encompasses freedom, social harmony, human dignity, and equality in servitude to God. The terms zulüm and individual responsibility expressed in terms of being a just witness are especially prominent in Islamist discourses of justice. The analysis of the interviews, thus, lends support to the theoretical proposition about the lasting influence of different lineages of Islamic justice.

The interviews also shed some light on the puzzle of Islam and support for democracy by depicting specific cognitive mechanisms. The essentialist argument theorizes an inherent incompatibility between Muslim culture and democracy and, hence, implies that the religious will be less supportive of democracy.[33] The interviews with the Islamist youth reveal that essentialists and their critics may be oversimplifying the problem at hand. Rather than asking whether Muslim culture or being religious affects their support for democracy, we need to understand the different ideological positions that generate a reservoir of attitudes that may be in favor of or against democratic (or autocratic) government.

7

Distributive Preferences, Individualism, and Support for Democracy

> Indeed, Allah will not change the condition of a people until they change what is in themselves.
> —The Koran (13:11).

> Take, [O, Muhammad], from their wealth a charity by which you purify them and cause them increase, and invoke [Allah's blessings] upon them.
> —The Koran (9:103)

The global rise of the antiausterity movement since the 2008 Great Recession marked the beginning of a new global protest era. From the squares of the Middle East to Wall Street and from the slums of Brazil to the skyscrapers of Hong Kong, people took to the streets in unprecedented numbers within the past decade. According to a recent study,[1] global protests increased by a rate of 11.5 percent annually between 2009 and 2019, making this period one of the most remarkable eras of mass mobilization. Echoing the wishes of the protesters in the Arab Spring, demonstrators across the globe have demanded justice in their chants for freedom, political accountability, and public services. For example, during the remarkable mass demonstrations against the government before the 2014 Soccer World Cup in Brazil, a protester dressed in a Batman costume told the reporters that "he dresses as Batman because the character is a symbol of the struggle against oppression . . . in [my] opinion Brazil is a dictatorship posing as a democracy, and I will continue to appear at protests as the Caped Crusader until people get the housing, education, and health they need."[2] Similarly, referencing the antigovernment Gezi protests in Turkey in 2013, İhsan Eliaçık stated that their real fight is for social justice and people in these protests were chanting against authoritarianism.[3] In short, the language of global protests involved calls for freedom, democratic government, and, importantly, social justice.

Given the strong desire for democracy in the language of these global protests, it is crucial to understand the underlying attitudes, which, presumably led the people to take the streets. This chapter examines support for democracy as a significant precondition for civic participation in the Muslim world. The analysis builds on two assumptions. First, religion is a significant factor shaping attitudes toward democracy in Muslim-majority societies. Second, Islamic faith informs value orientations, especially those concerning social and political justice among the devout. The main proposition following these assumptions is that value orientations stemming from Islamic conceptions of justice may engender support for democracy among the religious individuals. This chapter tests the effect of Muslim religiosity on individual value orientations and support for democracy. To that end, it conducts statistical analyses of the WVS and reports the results of several regression models.

The theoretical framework presented in this chapter builds on the implications of political and social justice trajectories to explain how religion shapes value orientations and support for democracy via two distinct paths. The first path explains why democracy will be a more acceptable form of government than authoritarian systems to religious Muslims. It is proposed that religious individuals will hold pro-distributive preferences due to Islam's emphasis on charity and egalitarianism. Pious Muslims will be more supportive of democracy because egalitarian distribution is more likely in democracies. A second path concerns the implications of the political justice trajectory in Islam. One legacy of this trajectory emphasizes free will and responsibility as qualities compatible with an individualistic value orientation. Research shows that individualism is conducive to democracy because of promoting individual autonomy, openness to innovation, and critical outlooks, which are foundational for a democratic culture.[4] Therefore, religious individuals holding individualistic value orientations should be more supportive of democracy than those with collectivist orientations. These explanations are grounded in a cultural approach by linking religion to social justice preferences and individualistic value orientations.[5] The empirical analysis tests these propositions using thousands of interviews conducted by the WVS in about two-dozen Muslim-majority countries.

Religion and Support for Democracy

Extant scholarship on Islam and democracy resulted in a theoretical fault line, with one stream of scholarship anticipating the cultural incompatibility between Islamic faith and democracy.[6] Proponents of the other stream argue that principles of faith promote pluralistic ideas, and one can trace the procedural foundations of democracy in conceptions of Islamic legal methodology.[7] The quantitative studies—built on the implications of this fault line—deployed significant empirical evidence to test the incompatibility thesis, focusing on the claim that Muslim religiosity is a source of opposition to democracy.[8]

Despite vigorous research, much ambivalence remains about the relationship between Muslim religiosity and support for democracy. The net contribution of this empirical scholarship is that Muslim religiosity is not necessarily at odds with support for democracy. Studies detecting a negative relationship between piety and democratic attitudes find that the proposed effect is inconsistent or negligible.[9] To account for this ambivalence, some scholars consider the role of context as a significant determinant of democratic preferences.[10] Others link trust and tolerance to support for democracy.[11] A recent study explains Muslim support for democracy with different religious outlooks among the pious, including communitarian, individualistic, and Islamist views.[12] These attempts at resolving the ambivalence in the relationship of Muslim faith and democracy do not point to a conclusive finding to satisfy the academic curiosity about this relationship. One reason for this ambivalence might be a lack of interest in examining the specific mechanisms linking religion to value orientations.

The theoretical framework introduced in previous chapters proposed that Islamic justice discourses have profound implications for the attitudes and behavior of the devout. To recap, justice discourses followed two historical trajectories in the Muslim political experience. The first trajectory is political justice rooted in the early Muslim community's conflicts over political leadership. The second trajectory, social justice, is rooted in Islam's emphasis on charity and welfare provision. These trajectories have implications for pious individuals' attitudes and value orientations because religious individuals presumably follow Islamic faith principles to form their opinions and guide their behavior.

Religion's effect on support for democracy may work through two paths. First, individual religiosity will affect support for democracy, but the direction of this relationship is ambivalent, according to the empirical research noted above. Second, religion will have an indirect effect on support for democracy by two mediating mechanisms: the first path conveys religion's effect on support for democracy via social justice preferences; the second path relies on one implication of the Islamic political justice trajectory concerning free will that might be conducive to individualistic value orientations. The former mediates religion's effect on support for democracy via Islam's doctrinal focus on egalitarian distributive preferences and the notion of maṣlaḥa. The latter path is related to free will and individual responsibility according to an individualistic interpretation of Islam that views man as vicegerent of God. The following sections introduce the theoretical underpinnings of religion's direct and mediated effects on support for democracy.

Social Justice, Egalitarianism, and Support for Democracy

Social justice values provide the first mediation mechanism linking Islamic faith to support for democracy. Charity, giving to the poor, and economic egalitarianism are central elements of Islamic social justice.[13] Scripture encourages the transfer of wealth from the rich to the poor as zakat (obligatory almsgiving), usually amounting to 2.5 percent of the wealth.[14] There are numerous examples from the life of Prophet Muhammad where he asked the believers to pay zakat, give in charity, and help those who are in the most need. In the modern era, Islamist intellectuals introduced economic models that proposed wealth restrictions and made policy recommendations regarding redistribution.[15] For example, Shariati proposed a model where social well-being is achieved by removing class differences and economic inequalities through the voluntary practice of charity and benevolence rather than by wealth accumulation.[16] Islam's emphasis on economic justice resulted in the collection and distribution of zakat by the state administration during the early and modern periods of Islam.[17] Islamist political parties and organizations have expanded their support base by providing welfare services.[18]

The existing social theory provides several insights that could help explain the mediating role of Islamic social justice principles on support for democracy. Davis and Robinson argue that religious individuals should be "disposed toward economic communitarianism, whereby the state should provide for the poor, reduce inequality, and meet the community needs via economic intervention."[19] The Islamic communitarian outlook toward social justice may intersect with democracy's tendency toward distribution. Acemoglu and Robinson argue that democratic government will emerge due to the struggle between the wealthy elites and the poor over the redistribution of a nation's wealth.[20] The masses want democracy because universal suffrage and political accountability give them some sway over the determination of tax rates that affects redistributive policy.[21] One observable implication of this theory is that pious Muslims will favor governance models where it is more likely to implement distributive policy and social justice, such as democracies. At a minimum, regardless of democracy's real success in establishing egalitarian distributive policies, religious individuals would favor democratic institutions as far as their expectations about the redistributive capacity of democratic government are in line with their religiously informed economic preferences.

'Iḥsān (benevolence), a concept closely related to the principles of public interest and goals of sharia, provides additional insights about the connection between Islamic social justice and Muslim attitudes toward democracy. Helping those in need, charity, and working toward economic justice are acts of 'iḥsān compatible with public interest and the goals of sharia. There are many verses in the Koran encouraging *'iḥsān*.[22] One notable piece of advice of Prophet Muhammad that has come to be a maxim of Islamic governance shows the importance of benevolence and kindness toward others: "There should be neither harming nor reciprocating harm (*lā ḍarar wa lā ḍirār*)."[23]

In a system where public deliberation occurs freely and according to civic reason, using An-Náim's terms, democracy will be viewed as the best form of government prone to social justice by the pious.[24] This is because democracy provides the most significant potential among all political systems to perform benevolent acts and achieve the social welfare implied by Islamic law principles. Benevolence is central to the Muslim religious practice because one of the government's primary goals is defined as "provision of good and prevention of vice" (*al-amr bi-l-ma'rūf wa-n-nahy 'ani-l-munkar*). Being a significant pillar of Islamic society, this maxim may be heard every week by pious Muslims during the Friday sermons. The benevolence principle requires a context where individuals who believe in it can freely organize to influence policy toward provision of good and prevention of vice or they can mobilize to implement social justice oriented policies. Just as altruistic behavior is more likely to flourish in civic cultures and political systems promoting trust, solidarity, and tolerance,[25] the benevolence principle can be practically implemented in a system with free deliberation and the civic reason that allows religious Muslims to develop or influence public policy according to their faith's prescriptions.[26] As a result, democracy will be preferable for pious Muslims relative to its alternatives because it presents a comparative advantage in achieving social justice.

Islamist intellectuals also argue that there is compatibility between benevolence, social justice, and democracy. For example, Shariati highlights the importance of *ithar* (love, benevolence) as a founding principle of Islamic society.[27] For Qutb, charitable acts matter a great deal for purifying human conscience and creating social solidarity.[28] Consequently, benevolence geared toward public interest would engender support for democracy among the devout to the extent that democracy is perceived to be a regime that has a comparative advantage in implementing egalitarian distribution according to Islamic social justice values.

Political Justice, Individualism, and Support for Democracy

The second mediating mechanism linking religiosity to support for democracy is individualistic value orientations. According to the collectivist/individualistic cultural framework, cultures have general patterns that shape value orientations.[29] Such cultural frames may explain the differences in political and economic outcomes such as development[30] and democratization.[31] Societies that emphasize individualism engender value orientations compatible with independence, free will, transparency, critical thinking, and individual responsibility. In collectivist societies, attitudes and behaviors align with social conformity, obedience, and maintenance of hierarchical norms.[32] By and large, value orientations align with democratic governance principles in individualistic and nondemocratic political institutions in collectivist societies.[33]

Religion has been a significant factor in the study of individualist/collectivist cultures and democracy. For example, Max Weber famously stated that protestant ethics made economic development possible by emphasizing individual responsibility and hard work.[34] In general, however, religion is seen as inimical to individualism—and, by extension, economic growth, progress, and democracy—due to its emphasis on hierarchy, in-group solidarity, and order. By the same token, scholars argue that Catholicism, Asian values, and Islam are hostile to democracy and good government due to their strict doctrinal principles, prioritizing order over change, tradition over innovation, and hierarchy over autonomy.[35]

In contrast to this scholarship's incompatibility argument, this chapter proposes that one implication of Islam's political justice trajectory may be conducive to individualistic value orientations. To reiterate, the disagreement about selecting a leader after Muhammad's passing created the first political cleavage in the early period of Islamic history. This cleavage spilled over into philosophical and theological spheres over time and resulted in the sectarian division between the Sunni and the Shia, contrasting theologies built on free will and predetermination, and political struggles between the proponents of authoritarian and democratic systems in the modern era.

One important implication of this lineage is the split along the popular sovereignty and obedience axis. The proponents of popular sovereignty include Khawarij, Qadarites, Mu'tazila, Muslim philosophers, and much later rational/modernist Islamist scholars. According to this view, individuals have free will and are responsible for their actions as God's vicegerents. This position's primary implication is that every believer has the duty of fighting injustices, including the deposition of an unjust ruler. The proponents of the obedience axis, in contrast, propagated unconditional submission to political authority based on predestination. Known as the Jabrī school and later consolidated into the Umayyad State's and other Islamic empires' official political ideology, this argument prioritized order over free will and conformity over independence.

The implications of the distinction between free will and predestination neatly overlap with the implications of the individualistic/collectivist frame-

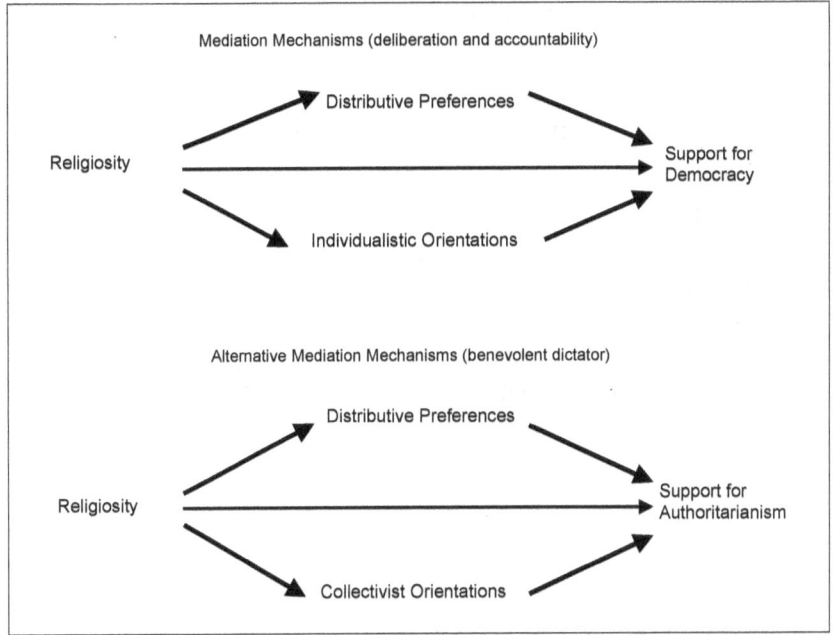

Figure 7.1 Religiosity and support for democracy: Mediating mechanisms.

work. Pious individuals inspired by the idea of man's vicegerent status are likely to hold outlooks cherishing free will and individual responsibility. According to this outlook, man can choose and shape his destiny through independence and hard work. As such, he can take action against injustices and can—or should—rebel against tyranny. Throughout Islamic political history, various intellectual traditions promoted this idea, and many rebellions took place against unjust rulers. In the modern era, this legacy incorporated the conceptions of political sovereignty and democracy as manifested in the modernist tradition, constitutionalist movements of the twentieth century, and mass protests of contemporary times, including the Arab Spring. This legacy of the political justice trajectory is based on individualistic ideals and should engender support for democracy.[36]

Figure 7.1 summarizes this theoretical framework by depicting the mediation mechanisms linking religiosity to support for democracy. Religiosity should engender prodistributive and individualistic value orientations, which will increase support for democracy. However, alternative explanations imply that religiosity will decrease support for state-led distributive preferences and engender collectivist orientations. As a result, religiosity may hamper the positive effect of these values on support for democracy or increase support for authoritarianism. The next section discusses the theoretical mechanisms of these alternative explanations.

Alternative Explanations

Although religious values are likely to generate egalitarian distributive preferences, religious individuals and organizations may not always long for state-led redistribution. Religious belief and participation act as insurance in times of hardships reducing the need for state-led distribution.[37] The highly devout might be less likely to favor state welfare policies than the nonreligious, and, subsequently, the proposed mediating effect of social justice value orientations on support for democracy may be the opposite of what is proposed above (or null). If religious individuals prefer state-led distributive policies due to their adherence to egalitarian principles, they may not care much about the specific system in place. To the extent that a leader can provide public goods, a "benevolent dictatorship" may be preferable to a democratic alternative. Any regime's ability to deliver public goods and provide general welfare according to the goals of sharia may make it a desirable option for the pious despite its nondemocratic character.

It is also likely that the legacies of the political justice trajectory will stimulate collectivist value orientations in some settings. To reiterate, political divisions in the early Muslim community created an intellectual fault line separating a philosophy of predetermination from that of free will and individual choice. Those who accepted the predetermination as a worldview defended the status quo, order, and hierarchy. For them, avoiding fitna and maintaining public order was crucial for the community's well-being. For example, the analysis of the writings in the Turkish Islamist journals from 1960 to 2010 in Chapter 5 revealed that religious groups justified political obedience by invoking public order (kamu düzeni) over anarchy for the sake of public interest. The emphasis on public order is not unique to the Turkish Islamists. Authoritarian leaders in other Muslim-majority countries had conveniently exploited political opportunities arising from civil wars (e.g., Algerian civil war) or international conflict (e.g., Arab-Israeli wars) to justify unconditional obedience, even when the ruler was unjust. This view created various hierarchies, including those between God and man, the religious elite and the masses,[38] and traditional leaders (e.g., father, tribal chief) and their subjects.

Therefore, this second legacy of the political justice trajectory implies collectivist value orientations. Combined with Islam's emphasis on distributive justice, the collectivist implications of the political justice trajectory may engender support for authoritarianism. This is because a benevolent autocrat ensuring social order and general welfare will be viewed favorably by the devout.[39] The bottom panel in Figure 7.1 depicts these alternative mediation mechanisms.

Data and the Model

The WVS contains data suitable for testing the hypotheses concerning the association between religiosity, value orientations, and support for democracy. The six waves of the WVS include twenty-five Muslim-majority countries and 65,191 Muslim-only respondents, providing extensive data for analyzing Muslim political attitudes.[40] The statistical models with all variables of interest contained 26,170 respondents in twenty-four Muslim-majority countries over three waves (4–6).[41] Further robustness analyses relied on smaller samples in select countries with fewer observations. The surveys provide representative samples in a large number of Muslim-majority societies.

Support for democracy is measured by a question asking the respondents whether having a democratic political system is very good, fairly good, fairly bad, or very bad along a four-point scale with higher values representing a positive opinion about a democratic system. In the sample, 57 percent of the respondents believe that having a democratic system is very good, and 34 percent believe it is fairly good. With little variation in these responses, a second measure was used to check the robustness of the results. One survey question asks the respondents whether "people choosing their leaders in free elections" is an essential characteristic of democracy (10) or not (1). Since free and fair elections are among the central elements of democratic systems, this measure should serve as a proxy for evaluating responses about procedural aspects of democracy. About 4 percent of the respondents believe it is not essential, whereas 40 percent think free and fair elections are essential to democracy. Finally, *support for authoritarianism* is obtained using two survey questions. These questions ask whether it is very bad, bad, fairly good, or very good to have a strong leader and army rule. The combined additive index is standardized along a 0–1 scale. About half the respondents voice strong opposition to nondemocratic systems.

Figure 7.2 shows the distribution of mean scores for these three items across the Muslim-majority societies using a 0–1 standardized measure. There is a strong positive correlation between generalized and procedural support for democracy. While average scores are closer to the fitted regression line for most countries, sentiment appears more positive for generalized support than procedural support in Morocco and Nigeria. On the flip side, support for procedural democracy outperforms generalized support in Yemen. As expected, the correlation between generalized support for democracy and the authoritarian system is negative but weak. Notable outliers include Bangladesh, Albania, Burkina Faso, Uzbekistan, and Morocco, lo-

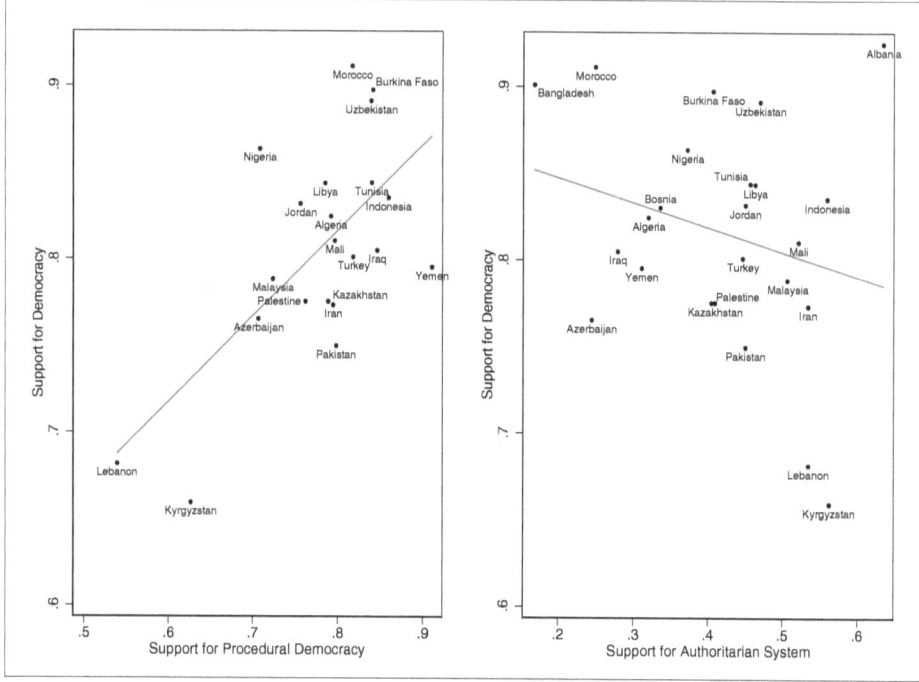

Figure 7.2 Support for democracy and authoritarianism in the Muslim world. The numbers show the mean scores for three different measures of regime support according to a standardized scale of 0–1. *Support for Democracy*: Having a democratic political system is very good, fairly good, fairly bad, or very bad. *Support for Procedural Democracy*: People choosing their leaders in free elections is an essential characteristic of democracy (10) or not (1). *Support for Authoritarian System*: Standardized index of (1) having a strong leader is very bad, bad, fairly good, or very good, and (2) having army rule is very bad, bad, fairly good, or very good. (Source: World Values Survey.)

cated above the fitted line, and Lebanon and Kyrgyzstan, below the line. Overall, this figure shows substantial variation in regime preferences, though support for democracy remains relatively high in the Muslim world.

The WVS also included several survey items that measured *religiosity*, *distributive preferences*, and *individualistic value orientations*. Religiosity is an additive index of four items: religion is important in life (four-point scale), self-reported religiosity (three-point scale), importance of religiosity as a desirable quality in children (dichotomous measure), and the frequency of religious service attendance ranging from 1 (never) to more than once a week (7). These items were standardized to range between 0 and 1 to create an additive index of religious belief with higher values representing more religious individuals.[42] As Figure 7.3 shows, the countries cluster in three

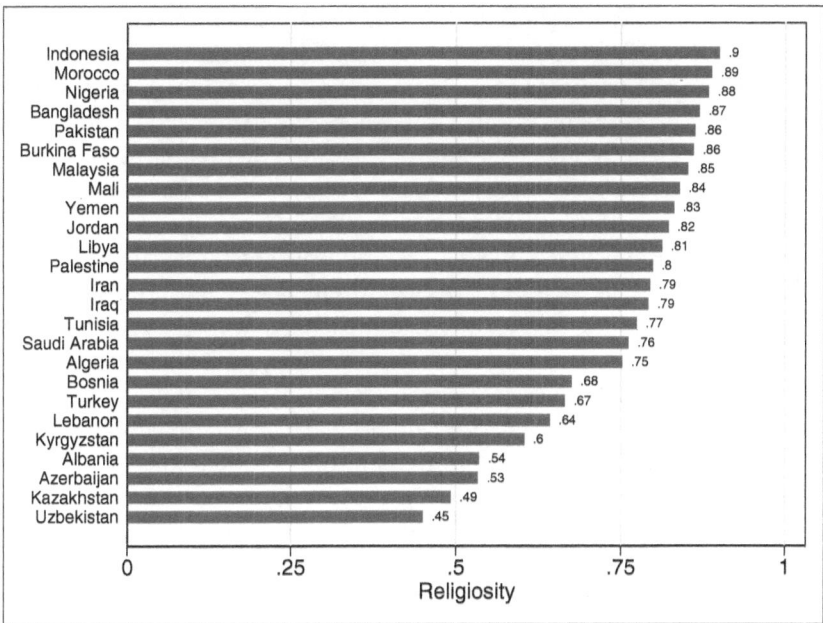

Figure 7.3 Religiosity in the Muslim world. The bars represent the standardized index of four survey questions: Religion is important in life (four-point scale), self-reported religiosity (three-point scale), importance of religiosity as a desirable quality in children (dichotomous measure), and the frequency of religious service attendance (1–7). (Source: World Values Survey, Waves 5 and 6.)

groups of low, medium, and high religiosity levels. Albania, Azerbaijan, Kazakhstan, and Uzbekistan have the lowest levels, with average religiosity scores lower than 0.60. Bosnia, Lebanon, Turkey, and Kyrgyzstan have scores ranging between 0.60 and 0.70. The rest of the sample has relatively high religiosity scores and includes countries from the Arab world, Africa, and South Asia. These figures may also be indicative of cultural differences according to various interpretations of the Islamic faith.

The main mediation mechanisms linking religiosity to support for democracy are distributive preferences (social justice) and individualistic value orientations (political justice). The WVS includes two questions asking the respondents whether they agree with the statement that incomes should be made more equal and whether government (or people) should take more responsibility to provide for people (1–10 scale). The responses to these questions are added to create a standardized index (0–1) representing egalitarian distributive preferences at the higher end. I use Pitlik and Rode's[43] strategy to measure two dimensions of individualistic traits. *Self-direction* evaluates respondents' views about autonomous decision-making and independence. The WVS includes this question: "Here is a list of qualities that children can be encouraged to learn at home. Which, if any, do you consider to be especially important? Please choose up to five." Following Pitlik and Rode, a dichotomous measure was obtained that takes the value of 1 when respondents choose "independence" but not "obedience" and the value of 0 otherwise. As Pitlik and Rode[44] argue, the values of independence and nonobedience imply that individuals disapprove of hierarchical imperatives and coercion in their decisions. This measurement strategy follows the logic of Schwartz's "intellectual autonomy" dimension that encourages people to follow their independent judgment in life.[45] The opposite of independence is obedience, which implies accepting hierarchical relations, unequal values in social life, and conduciveness to authoritarian orientations.

A second measure, *self-determination*, refers to self-efficacy, belief in one's ability to reach success,[46] feeling of control over life outcomes rather than reliance on luck or destiny,[47] or the belief that one can achieve success by working hard.[48] Self-determined individuals will be more likely to question authority and hierarchical order and value hard work and initiative. Pitlik and Rode[49] find that individuals with this orientation are less supportive of economic intervention. By the same logic, self-determined individuals should be critical of authoritarian political systems and lean favorably toward democratic institutions. Self-determination is measured by creating an additive index using two questions from the WVS:

> Some people feel they have completely free choice and control over their lives, while other people feel that what they do has no real effect on what happens to them. Please use this scale [between] "none at all" (1) and . . . "a great deal" (10) to indicate how much freedom of choice and control you feel you have over the way your life turns out.
>
> Now I'd like you to tell me your views on various issues (placing yourself on a continuum). Hard work brings success:
>
> 1 = Hard work doesn't generally bring success, it's more a matter of luck and connections
> 10 = In the long run, hard work usually brings a better life

These questions were added to create a standardized index (0–1) with higher values representing orientations that emphasize individual resolve and control.

The WVS questions used to measure social and political justice orientations are the best measures available to researchers. Distributive preferences measure individuals' devotion to Islam's social justice principles. Self-

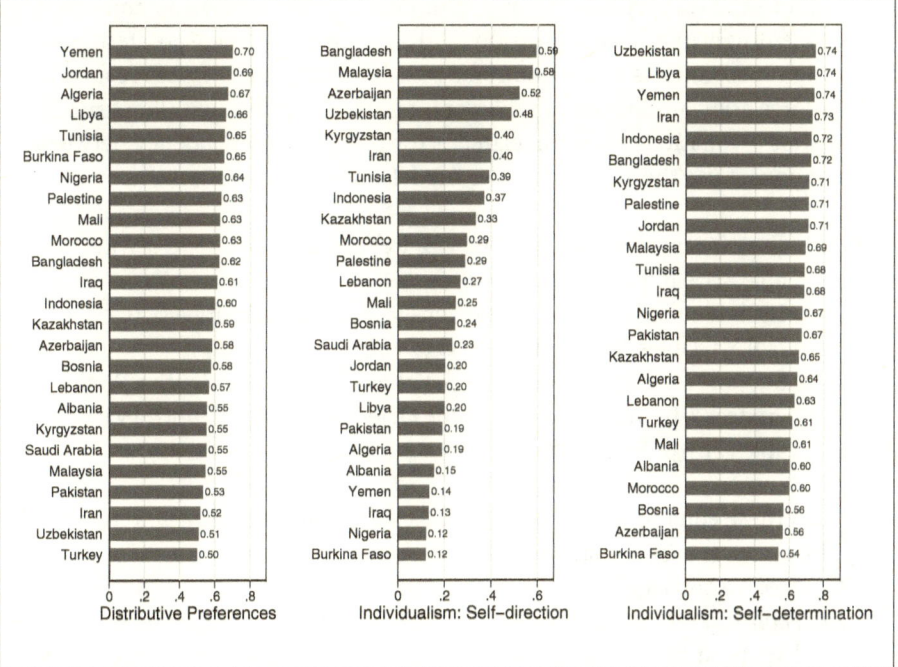

Figure 7.4 Distributive preferences and individualistic orientations in the Muslim world. The bars represent the average scores for each indicator standardized along a 0–1 index. *Distributive Preferences*: Index of (1) incomes should be made more equal (1–10), and (2) government should take more responsibility to provide for people (1–10). *Self-direction*: Individuals who choose "independence" but not "obedience" to the question inquiring about the list of qualities that children can be encouraged to learn at home. *Self-determination*: Index of (1) how much freedom of choice and control you feel you have over the way your life turns out (1–10), and (2) hard work brings success (1–10). (Source: World Values Survey.)

direction and self-determination are proxies for capturing an implication of the political justice trajectory concerning free will and man's responsibility as vicegerent of God. These value orientations should engender support for democracy both directly and by mediating the effect of religiosity. Figure 7.4 provides the summary of these indicators in the Muslim world. Overall, Muslim publics appear to hold egalitarian views and highly self-deterministic orientations. While self-direction measure shows considerable variation, individuals appear to be not very enthusiastic about this trait as a quality to be taught to their children. In general, the sample does not demonstrate a noticeable regional pattern, and the distribution of average opinion appears to be random cross-nationally.

Since the theoretical framework implies parallel mediation analysis, I use seemingly unrelated regression (SUR) estimation to incorporate all mediation mechanisms and account for possible endogeneity issues related to the correlation among the variables of interest. This technique allows simultaneous estimations with correlated error terms and dependency between equations. I use the following three models in SUR estimations.[50]

1. Distributive Preferences = $\propto + \beta_1$ Religiosity + β_2 (Control Variables 1) + β_3 Fixed Effects + ε_1
2. Individualistic Value Orientations = $\propto + \beta_1$ Religiosity + β_2 (Control Variables 1) + β_3 Fixed Effects + ε_2
3. Support for Democracy = $\propto + \beta_1$ Religiosity + β_2 Distributive Preferences + β_3 Individualistic Value Orientations + β_4 (Control variables 2) + β_5 Fixed Effects + ε_3

In these equations, "Control Variables 1" include *age*, *education* (eight-point scale), *gender* (female is the higher score), and *income* (ten-point scale). "Control Variables 2" include the first set of controls along with *personal trust*, *political interest*, and *egalitarian gender beliefs*. Personal trust is measured with an item asking the respondents whether most people can be trusted. Egalitarian gender beliefs are measured with an additive index of three questions: university education is more important for a boy than a girl, men make better political leaders than women, and when jobs are scarce men should have priority in employment. Finally, political interest asks the respondents the degree of their interest in politics on a four-point scale. All of these variables are standardized to a 0–1 scale. Fixed effects include both country and wave dummies where applicable.

Table 7.1 reports the SUR estimation results accounting for parallel mediation mechanisms of distributive preferences and individualistic value orientations. The results corroborate the theoretical expectations. Religiosity is positively related to distributive justice preferences (Equation 1), and these preferences increase support for democracy (Equation 4). Religiosity has a negative effect on self-direction, but this variable is not a statistically significant predictor of support for democracy. Religious individuals are more likely to hold self-determination attitudes and individuals with these attitudes are more likely to support democracy. According to these results, religiosity does not engender individualistic value orientations related to individual autonomy, yet it strengthens one's belief in self-made success and control over destiny (i.e., self-determination). Such a belief, in turn, makes individuals more likely to hold favorable views toward democracy. The differing effect of religiosity on self-direction and self-determination can be explained with the dual nature of Islam's ethical principles as specified in

TABLE 7.1 SEEMINGLY UNRELATED REGRESSION ESTIMATES OF JUSTICE VALUES AND SUPPORT FOR DEMOCRACY

	Equation 1 Distributive Preferences	Equation 2 Self-direction	Equation 3 Self-determination	Equation 4 Support for Democracy
Religiosity	0.046***	−0.270***	0.050***	0.025**
	(0.007)	(0.015)	(0.007)	(0.008)
Social and Political Justice Indicators				
Distributive preferences	—	—	—	0.033***
				(0.007)
Self-direction	—	—	—	−0.001
				(0.003)
Self-determination	—	—	—	0.103***
				(0.007)
Control Variables				
Female	0.003	−0.021***	−0.017***	−0.001
	(0.003)	(0.006)	(0.003)	(0.003)
Age	0.004	−0.031	0.049***	0.025*
	(0.009)	(0.018)	(0.008)	(0.010)
Education	0.015***	0.086***	0.027***	0.039***
	(0.004)	(0.010)	(0.004)	(0.005)
Income	−0.019**	0.002	0.041***	−0.005
	(0.012)	(0.001)	(0.012)	(0.002)
Personal trust	—	—	—	−0.006
				(0.004)
Gender beliefs	—	—	—	−0.025***
				(0.006)
Political interest	—	—	—	0.025***
				(0.005)
Constant	0.529***	0.298***	0.556***	0.828***
	(0.011)	(0.023)	(0.011)	(0.013)
Fixed effects	YES	YES	YES	YES
N	26,170	26,170	26,170	26,170
R^2	0.087	0.112	0.084	0.086

Standard errors are in parentheses. * $p < .05$, ** $p < .01$, *** $p < .001$. Fixed effects are reported in Appendix A, Table A7.1. *Source:* World Values Survey.

the scripture and other religious sources. Several verses and many sayings of the Prophet encourage obedience and kindness to parents.[51] At the same time, Islam encourages hard work, effort, and striving for permissible worldly provision. One notable example is the verse that states, "Surely Allah does not change the condition of a people until they change their own condition" (Koran 13:11). The results might be showing the opposing effects of these religious principles on individuals' value orientations.

The results show a positive and statistically significant relationship between religiosity and support for democracy (Equation 4). Subsequently, controlling for the possible endogeneity issues through mediation mechanisms involving distributive preferences and individualistic value orientations, we can resolve some ambivalence about religiosity's effect on support for democracy. Religiosity increases support for democracy both directly and by increasing distributive preferences and individualistic value orientations, which also predict support for democracy.[52]

Overall, these results support the hypotheses concerning the individual-level implications of political and social justice trajectories in the Muslim world. Table 7.2 reports the direct, indirect, and total effects associated with the mediating mechanisms. Ceteris paribus and accounting for mediation mechanisms of social and political justice values, a large proportion of religiosity's total effect on support for democracy is associated with the direct path (about 79 percent). This is a surprising finding given the lively debate about the ambivalence of religion as a determinant of democratic support. The mediating mechanisms explain the remaining proportion of the total effect (21 percent). The indirect effect of religiosity via distributive prefer-

TABLE 7.2 DIRECT AND INDIRECT EFFECTS OF RELIGIOSITY ON SUPPORT FOR DEMOCRACY

Effect	As Percentage of Total Effect of Religiosity on Support for Democracy
Religiosity → Support for Democracy (Direct)	78.83%
Religiosity → Distributive Preferences → Support for Democracy	4.60%
Religiosity → Self-direction → Support for Democracy[a]	0.45%
Religiosity → Self-determination → Support for Democracy	16.11%
Total indirect effect via individualistic orientations	16.56%
Total indirect effect	21.17%

[a] This path is not statistically significant.
The effects are calculated from the estimation presented in Table 7.1. *Source:* World Values Survey.

ences accounts for 4.60 percent, whereas the indirect effect via self-determination path accounts for 16.11 percent. Since religiosity decreases self-direction orientation and because self-direction is not a statistically significant predictor of support for democracy, the net effect for this on the support for democracy path is substantively negligible.

Overall, these results show that religious individuals are more likely to hold economically egalitarian preferences and specific type of individualistic value orientations, which increase support for democracy. Of the individualistic value orientations, self-direction (independence in decision-making) does not significantly affect support for democracy. Meanwhile, religious individuals tend to be less independent and more conformist, both of which are value orientations emphasizing acceptance of a hierarchical social order. In contrast, religious individuals are more likely to hold value orientations that emphasize initiative, hard work, self-made success, and belief in control over their life choices (self-determination). This self-deterministic outlook increases support for democracy.

Several additional models are estimated to test the implications of alternative explanations and check the robustness of the results. Table 7.3 reports alternative specification results using *support for procedural democracy* and *authoritarianism* (Models 1 and 2, respectively). Using the alternative measure for support for procedural democracy as a dependent variable is a necessary robustness check because it may help alleviate concerns about the minimum variation observed in support for democracy. The estimation results with this alternative dependent variable remain unchanged (Model 1 in Table 7.3). The coefficients for religiosity, distributive preferences, and self-determination are positive and statistically significant, showing the same links to procedural support as they did to overt democratic support. Self-direction values do not have a meaningful effect on support for procedural democracy.

The bottom panel of Table 7.3 runs the same SUR model on support for authoritarianism (Model 2). Support for authoritarian systems is measured with an index combining responses to two questions about the desirability of army rule and a strong leader who does not bother with parliament and elections with higher values showing authoritarian support. Religiosity is a statistically significant and positive correlate of support for authoritarianism in these estimations. However, the signs for the coefficients of distributive preferences and self-determination in relation to support for authoritarianism are negative and statistically significant. These results imply that religiosity may also engender support for an authoritarian system. However, self-deterministic value orientations and distributive preferences decrease support for authoritarianism. Since *religion* has a positive effect on these correlates, it indirectly reduces support for an authoritarian regime.

TABLE 7.3 SEEMINGLY UNRELATED REGRESSION ESTIMATES OF JUSTICE VALUES AND SUPPORT FOR PROCEDURAL DEMOCRACY AND AUTHORITARIANISM

Model 1

	Equation 1 Distributive Preferences	Equation 2 Self-direction	Equation 3 Self-determination	Equation 4 Support for Procedural Democracy
Religiosity	0.035***	−0.261***	0.072***	0.035***
	(0.008)	(0.018)	(0.008)	(0.010)
Distributive preferences	—	—	—	0.062***
				(0.009)
Self-direction	—	—	—	−0.003
				(0.004)
Self-determination	—	—	—	0.170***
				(0.009)
Constant	0.653***	0.394***	0.534***	0.617***
	(0.012)	(0.028)	(0.012)	(0.018)
Fixed effects and controls	YES	YES	YES	YES
N	21,063	21,063	21,063	21,063
R^2	0.095	0.090	0.074	0.091

Model 2

	Equation 1 Distributive Preferences	Equation 2 Self-direction	Equation 3 Self-determination	Equation 4 Support for Authoritarianism
Religiosity	0.046***	−0.270***	0.048***	0.020*
	(0.007)	(0.016)	(0.007)	(0.009)
Distributive preferences	—	—	—	−0.061***
				(0.008)
Self-direction	—	—	—	0.002
				(0.003)
Self-determination	—	—	—	−0.039***
				(0.008)
Constant	0.525***	0.268***	0.564***	0.655***
	(0.011)	(0.024)	(0.011)	(0.015)
Fixed effects and controls	YES	YES	YES	YES
N	24,687	24,687	24,687	24,687
R^2	0.087	0.112	0.081	0.187

Standard errors are in parentheses. * $p < .05$, ** $p < .01$, *** $p < .001$. Full results are reported in Appendix A, Table A7.2 for Model 1 and Table A7.3 for Model 2. *Source:* World Values Survey.

Religious Outlooks, Value Orientations, and Support for Democracy

The analysis up to this point explained religion's effect on support for democracy via social justice preferences and cultural value orientations. While the link between religion and social and political justice orientations allowed partly overcoming the ambivalence surrounding the effect of a "catch-all" category of religiosity on support for democracy, the analysis remains inconclusive due to the positive correlation between religiosity and support for authoritarianism. The latter finding undermines confidence in the statistical robustness of religion's positive effect on support for democracy. Religion's indirect effect on support for democracy works through distributive preferences and individualistic/collectivist value orientations. This effect may be due to religious outlooks that are more conducive to specific preferences and value orientations. Students of religion and politics have correctly voiced their skepticism about using a unidimensional measure of religiosity in quantitative studies and argued that the devout may hold many different outlooks that vary contextually.[53] Religious individuals may hold communitarian or individualistic value orientations,[54] or piety may be defined along a modernist/orthodox continuum.[55] These religious outlooks likely shape distributive preferences and individualistic/collectivist orientations as well as support for democracy.

Although the mediation mechanisms, presented above, account for Islam's impact on support for democracy via social and political justice orientations, the measure of religiosity used here is not suitable for capturing the effects of different religious outlooks. In other words, if we could show that the effect of religious outlooks, rather than a general measure of religiosity, indirectly increase support for democracy (or authoritarianism) via distributive preferences and individualistic value orientations, we could have more confidence about the positive correlation between religiosity and support for democracy. Fortunately, the WVS included the following questions that could partially remedy this shortcoming. One question evaluates the respondents' opinion about the importance of government's implementation of sharia along a five-point scale of (1) not important to (5) very important. Another question asks the respondents if they strongly agree, agree, disagree, or strongly disagree with the statement, "Whenever science and religion conflict, religion is always right" (four-point scale with higher values showing agreement with the statement).

In their study examining the association between religious orthodoxy and distributive preferences in several Muslim-majority societies, Davis and Robinson used the first question.[56] They found that theological communitarianism of the religiously orthodox engenders egalitarian economic outlooks and authoritarian social preferences. In contrast, the theological individualism of modernists leads to support for liberal economic policies and individualistic value orientations.[57] Davis and Robinson use the question about sharia implementation as a proxy for communitarian outlooks, with more support for sharia representing the religiously orthodox individuals' theological communitarianism. Stark and Finke find that religious individuals with the modernist outlook are more likely to emphasize independent thinking and self-direction than obedience as a value to be taught to children in the American context.[58] Similarly, Davis and Robinson argue that individuals with a modernist outlook put a premium on free will and individual choice.[59]

Following Davis and Robinson, I use the question asking about preferences for sharia implementation as a proxy for measuring communitarian outlook. Individuals who support government's implementation of sharia presumably hold religiously orthodox and communitarian outlooks. These individuals should be more likely to hold collectivist orientations and should be less supportive of democracy.

The second survey item captures individual preferences concerning the contrast between scientific thinking and religious doctrine. This variable is a good proxy for measuring whether individuals prefer a scientific worldview to rigid religious authority. The political justice trajectory's legacy involves a similar division between those who cherish the rational approach over unquestioned religious authority. Individuals who prefer religion to science should be less supportive of democracy.

The first variable capturing views about the government's role in sharia implementation is asked only in the fourth wave of the surveys (1999–2004) and in Algeria, Bangladesh, Egypt, Indonesia, Iraq, Jordan, Nigeria, Pakistan, and Saudi Arabia.[60] According to the data, 5 percent of the respondents believe that the implementation of sharia is not important, whereas 42 percent say it is very important. The proportion of respondents who believe that the implementation of sharia is important or very important is 79 percent. Not surprisingly, highly religious individuals are more likely to view the government's role in sharia implementation as very important. The second question is asked in the sixth wave (2010–2014) and is available in seventeen countries from across the Muslim world.[61] According to the survey results, 21 percent of the respondents in the sample strongly disagree or disagree with the statement favoring religion over science, whereas 79 percent agree or strongly prefer religion over science. Not surprisingly, highly religious individuals generally believe that religion is always right when it conflicts with science.

Figure 7.5 shows the mean score for religiosity with 95 percent confidence bars over different categories of the questions measuring views about

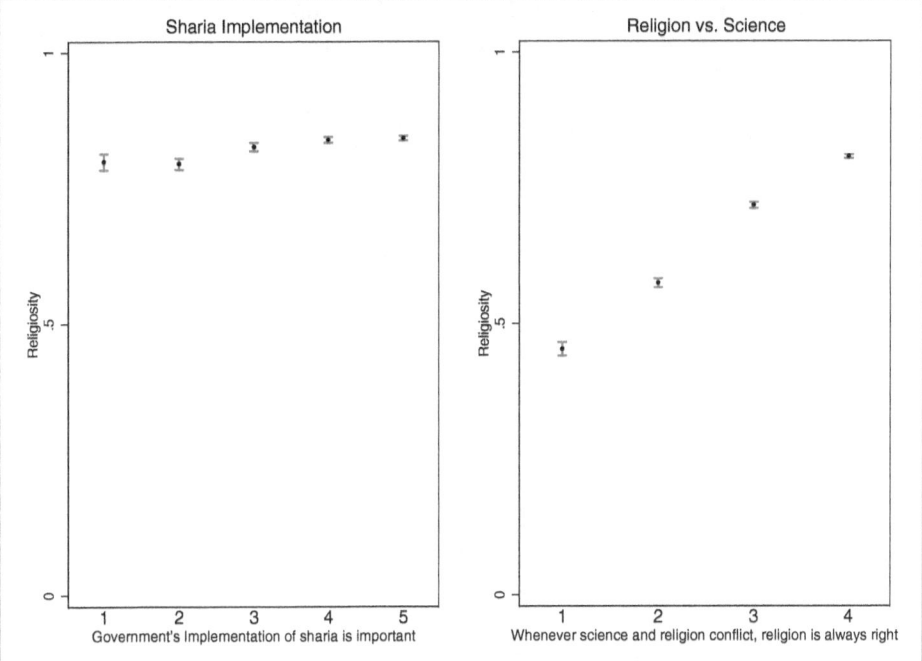

Figure 7.5 Religiosity and religious outlooks in the Muslim world. The circles show the average score for religiosity with the 95 percent confidence interval over different categories of the questions measuring opinion about government implementation of sharia and preferences about the religion/science binary. *Sharia Implementation*: I would like to know your views about a good government. Which of these traits is (1) very important, (2) important, (3) somewhat important, (4) least important, or (5) not important for a good government to have? It should implement only the laws of the sharia. *Religion vs. Science*: Please tell us if you strongly agree, agree, disagree, or strongly disagree with the following statements: Whenever science and religion conflict, religion is always right. (Source: World Values Survey.)

sharia implementation and preferences about the religion/science binary. The extent of average religiosity does not widely vary across different responses to the first question, indicating high levels of religiosity in the sample, and it should be noted that the question on sharia implementation was asked in countries with a higher average religiosity, including Bangladesh, Indonesia, Nigeria, and Pakistan, as depicted in Figure 7.3. Nevertheless, the differences between some responses to this item remain statistically significant. The question inquiring about preference between religion and science demonstrates larger variation indicating significant variation at different levels of this religious outlook.

Table 7.4 reports the results from the SUR estimations using the same mediation mechanisms of distributive preferences and individualistic value orientations. The only difference relative to the original models is that instead of religiosity, the models use two indicators of religious outlooks. As Model 1 in Table 7.4 shows, individuals who strongly favor the implementation of sharia (religiously orthodox) are less likely to emphasize independent decision-making (self-direction). The questions measuring self-deterministic attitudes are not available in the sample in hand, so the first model cannot test this particular mediation mechanism.

Meanwhile, religious orthodoxy (sharia implementation) engenders distributive preferences, which is in line with the findings of previous studies.[62] The results in the third equation demonstrate a negative correlation between sharia implementation and support for democracy. The effect of self-direction on support for democracy is negative and statistically significant. In the original models presented in Table 7.1, religiosity had a negative effect on self-direction, but the latter had no significant effect on support for democracy. In the current model, self-direction has a negative and significant effect on support for democracy.

Model 2 in Table 7.4 uses the question asking about a preference for religion or science. The estimation results are consistent with the original model (Table 7.1). As discussed previously, Islam emphasizes both hard work and family values encouraging obedience to parents. The latter might be the reason for the negative correlation between religiosity and self-direction value orientations. Individuals who have strict doctrinal outlooks by way of preferring religion to science are less likely to hold self-direction and more likely to hold self-determination value orientations. When the model controls for both indicators of individualistic value orientations, self-direction is no longer statistically significant in the fourth equation. Meanwhile, a strict religious outlook preferring religious authority over science increases self-determination and support for democracy.

Overall, these results have several implications. First, controlling for the mediating mechanisms of distributive preferences, religiosity increases support for democracy. This result holds whether religiosity is operationalized as a general tendency or as a religious outlook. Second, Muslim religiosity does not necessarily inhibit individualistic value orientations. While religion inhibits self-direction values, it increases the self-determination orientations. This result is not surprising given the simultaneous emphasis on obedience to parents and hard work and achievement in the Islamic faith. Finally, there appears to be a robust correlation between religiosity and distributive preferences in a positive direction. At the same time, distributive preferences consistently increase support for democracy.

TABLE 7.4 SEEMINGLY UNRELATED REGRESSION ESTIMATES OF RELIGIOUS OUTLOOKS, JUSTICE ORIENTATIONS, AND SUPPORT FOR DEMOCRACY

Model 1

	Equation 1 Distributive Preferences	Equation 2 Self-direction	Equation 3 Support for Democracy
Sharia	0.033***	0.030	−0.023*
	(0.008)	(0.017)	(0.010)
Distributive preferences	—	—	−0.018
			(0.016)
Self-direction	—	—	−0.016*
			(0.008)
Constant	0.618***	0.090***	0.888***
	(0.013)	(0.026)	(0.020)
Fixed effects and controls	YES	YES	YES
N	5,500	5,500	5,500
R^2	0.082	0.193	0.030

Model 2

	Equation 1 Distributive Preferences	Equation 2 Self-direction	Equation 3 Self-determination	Equation 4 Support for Democracy
Religion vs. science	0.049***	−0.072***	0.039***	0.036***
	(0.007)	(0.015)	(0.007)	(0.008)
Distributive preferences				0.052***
	—	—	—	(0.010)
Self-determination				0.125***
	—	—	—	(0.010)
Self-direction				0.004
	—	—	—	(0.005)
Constant	0.631***	0.299***	0.561***	0.652***
	(0.011)	(0.024)	(0.011)	(0.016)
Fixed effects and controls	YES	YES	YES	YES
N	15,106	15,106	15,106	15,106
R^2	0.094	0.080	0.071	0.085

Standard errors are in parentheses. * $p < .05$, ** $p < .01$, *** $p < .001$. Full results are reported in Appendix A, Table A7.4 for Model 1 and Table A7.5 for Model 2. *Source:* World Values Survey.

Conclusion

This chapter employed a novel explanation about the microfoundations of Muslim support for democracy—Islamic justice values have significant sway over Muslim distributive preferences and cultural value orientations. The analysis of extensive survey data from two dozen Muslim-majority countries revealed a statistically significant correlation between religiosity and support for democracy. Simultaneously, distributive preferences predict and mediate the effect of religion on support for democracy. This result is robust to different model specifications and the use of alternative measures of religiosity. Furthermore, distributive preferences decrease support for authoritarianism. However, religiosity increases support for authoritarianism, and this is compatible with the implications of the social justice trajectory that Islam may engender both democratic and authoritarian attitudes. However, the net effect of religion on regime preferences through the mediation of the distributive preferences decreases overall support for authoritarianism.

The results of the statistical analysis revealed an interesting pattern about individualistic value orientations. According to the estimation results, religiosity increases the likelihood of self-determination but decreases the likelihood of self-direction. Self-determination is a significant predictor of support for democracy, and self-direction has no meaningful effect on democratic orientations in most models. This is a significant finding showing that the common assumption that certain religions are incompatible with individualistic culture and, hence, are inimical to democratization lacks an empirical basis. Islam simultaneously encourages obedience to familial authority and self-efficacy and hard work, which shows up in the diverging effects of religiosity on self-determination and self-direction. On average, religious Muslims are less likely to hold self-directional attitudes, but they are inclined toward self-determination. This difference is relevant to the extent that self-determination increases support for democracy, whereas self-direction does not. Thus, the positive effect of religiosity on support for democracy is amplified through the mediation of self-determination. Muslim piety, therefore, is not necessarily hostile to individualism. Islam may boost certain aspects of individualistic value orientations and engender support for democracy.

8

Constitutionalist Movements, Arab Spring, and Justice

Aish, ḥuriyya, karama insaniyya (Bread, freedom, and human dignity).

—Arab Spring chant

On a nice Sudanese evening in Khartoum on April 8, 2019, a twenty-two-year-old female engineering student Alaa Saleh stood atop a car wearing a traditional white Sudanese gown with her right index finger pointing to the sky. Surrounded by other protesters, Saleh was protesting the authoritarian regime. For many months, protesters took to the streets demanding the resignation of long-reigning president Omar al-Bashir. Amid the protests, Saleh was compared to the ancient Nubian queens, *kandake*, known for their power and the sacrifices they made for their country.[1] Saleh's iconic image, invoking comparisons with the Statue of Liberty, was shared by millions on social media. That year, hundreds of thousands chanted for freedom, justice, and peace in Sudan. In the end, al-Bashir resigned, and protesters signed a pact with the military leaders to initiate Sudan's transition to democracy.

To the north of Sudan, the inefficient waste management services sparked massive protests in Lebanon during the summer of 2015. The "You Stink" movement quickly spread as a campaign against corruption and inefficient government and turned into a massive plea for political accountability. To the west of Lebanon, Algerian citizens took to the streets against the candidacy of President Abdelaziz Bouteflika. Also known as the *Revolution of Smiles* or *Ḥirāk*, these peaceful protests mark one of the longest-lasting mass mobilization campaigns against an authoritarian regime. Whether the protesters were taking to the streets against repression, corruption, or declining economic fortunes, their primary motivation was justice. These demonstrations echoed the earlier mass uprisings in the Arab region that took many by surprise in 2011. Bouazizi of Tunisia unleashed a popular wave on December 17, 2010, when he set himself on fire protesting the repression and corruption in his country. The spark in Tunisia quickly led to mass mobilization campaigns in the streets and squares of the Arab-majority countries. People were chanting for freedom, the fall of the regime, and justice.

The first wave of the Arab Spring and the last protests taking place in Lebanon, Sudan, and Algeria are extraordinary for a region that has been characterized with an infamous democracy gap—that is, the persistent lack of democratic government in the Middle East.[2] These protests provided unequivocal evidence that people of the region want democracy.[3] Protesters also attached several other demands to this wish, such as ending economic decline and corruption.[4] However, these extraordinary upheavals were hardly new to the region as the history of the Middle East and North Africa (MENA) is replete with mass protests since the nineteenth century.[5] The region, just as other parts of the globe,[6] witnessed many protests in the name of constitutionalism, nationalism, socialism, and Islamism throughout the nineteenth and twentieth centuries.

Many scholars have already studied the causes and consequences of these protests in MENA.[7] This chapter employs a different approach and examines the attitudes and behaviors of the protesters rather than the structural underpinnings of contentious politics in the region. It focuses on the protesters' perceptions about the violation of social and political justice in the Arab Spring using evidence from the second and third waves of the Arab Barometer (2011 and 2013).

For a more informative picture, I provide a brief account of constitutionalist movements during the nineteenth and early twentieth centuries in the Middle East before reporting the findings from the survey data analysis. Of many revolts taking place in Islamic history, the period of constitutionalist movements during the late nineteenth and early twentieth centuries can be viewed as a critical juncture because it represents Muslim encounters with the Western powers that created important social and political transformations. However, in most cases these changes were not solely motivated by colonialism, because domestic political decay was also viewed as a significant source of social problems. Constitutional government was the primary instrument for solving the prevailing social and political injustices. The demands put forth by the leaders of these constitutionalist movements resemble the chants of the Arab Spring protesters.

We lack the microlevel data to compare the perceptions of people in the nineteenth century to those during the Arab uprisings. Luckily, an examination of the discourses of the constitutionalist movements provides many clues about conceptions of justice and democracy in the elites and the public's imagination a century earlier than the Arab Spring. If we had public opinion surveys carried out in Istanbul during the first and second constitutional governments (1876 and 1908), in Tehran during the age of revolutions (1905–1911), or in Cairo during the Urabi Revolt (1879–1882), we would have probably found that people demanded good government, an end to corruption, and social justice. This is exactly what citizens demanded in the Arab Spring, according to the evidence found in the Arab Barometer surveys.[8]

This chapter builds on insights derived from the study of the nineteenth- and twentieth-century constitutionalist movements in the Middle East to better understand contemporary public opinion and, especially, perceptions about violations of political and social justice. The analysis focuses on rhetoric and perceptions of injustice as the main drivers of political participation for religious individuals.

Culture, Justice, and Democracy

Students of comparative political history argue that there is a unique path leading to democracy in the West involving a complex set of institutions facilitating the transition from feudalism to democracy.[9] Some of these institutions include protection from arbitrary rule, the institutionalization of economic contracts, ruler longevity, and the right of resistance. In his *Social Origins of Dictatorship and Democracy*, Barrington Moore Jr. states, "This complex arose only in Western Europe. Only there did that delicate balance occur between too much and too little royal power which provided an important motivation for switching to parliamentary democracy."[10] This approach does not necessarily capture the whole picture to the extent that cultural factors were also instrumental in the emergence of democratic government. The argument about Western exceptionalism, thus, may be too narrowly focused.

Moore and others[11] have primarily focused on institutional development and executive accountability. Although such institutional development did not entirely occur in the Muslim world, the cultural and contentious roots of democracy were present. In effect, the history of contentious politics in the Muslim world contains examples pointing to many possibilities for a transition from the ancien régime to democracy. The constitutionalist movements in the Ottoman and Qajar Empires, the nationalist independence movements throughout the twentieth century, labor movements, and widespread protests demonstrate the potential for democratization in MENA societies.[12] Furthermore, the idea of rebellion against tyranny—a common theme in Muslim politics since the early periods of Islam—can be seen as a cultural attribute of democratic thinking.

Islamic conceptions of justice constitute another noninstitutional element that could engender support for democracy among Muslims. For example, the notion of the circle of justice has been a central feature of government in the Middle East.[13] Thompson and Darling trace reincarnations of traditional conceptions of justice in modernist Islam, the Iranian Revolution, and various protest waves including the Arab Spring.[14] The language of democracy and justice has been visible in the constitutionalist movements and the Arab Spring. The study of these events is likely to shed light on the underlying continuities of Islamic justice discourses in the Middle East.[15] Elizabeth Thompson, for example, argues that at the dawn of the twenty-first century, the Middle East is once again witnessing the reincarnation of the constitutional justice model that first appeared in the late nineteenth and early twentieth centuries.[16] In Thompson's words, "Constitutionalism has returned as the dominant model of justice in the Middle East. Turks elected an opposition government that has eased the military out of politics. In Iran, the Green movement rose up in 2009 against religious elites' control of government. Two years later, the Arab Spring broke out against the petty and pervasive tyranny of governments in Tunisia, Libya, Egypt, Syria, Yemen, and Bahrain."[17]

A note of caution is in order before the two revolutionary periods are examined. This study does not assume that Islam or religiously inspired justice values have been the only causes of constitutionalist movements or the Arab Spring. Rather, it traces the presence of Islamic justice values in the rhetoric of the constitutionalist movements and the attitudes of the Arab Spring protesters. Overall, this chapter undertakes a difficult task demonstrating historical continuities and rifts in justice discourses, then linking them to the popular demands in the Arab Spring, and, finally, bringing empirical evidence about perceptions of political and social injustices from the public opinion surveys to explain political behavior. Surveys do not directly measure values, but they include questions allowing us to empirically evaluate perceptions of justice such as those concerning violations of justice norms. As the following analysis shows, we can trace the implications of Islamic justice trajectories in the rhetoric of the constitutionalist intellectuals and of the protesters chanting in the Arab Spring. The analysis will show that these implications are consequential for political behavior.

Islam, Constitutionalism, and Justice Discourses

Bernard Lewis views the reformism in the nineteenth-century Ottoman Empire as a reaction of the elites to the West's ascendance.[18] As the Ottoman elite became increasingly aware of the economic and political decline vis-à-vis the rising status of Europe, they started to view various reforms as the only solution for saving the state. An essential aspect of these reforms was the installation of a constitutional government. Diplomats and students who traveled to European countries believed that freedom and a constitutional government would be a cure-all to the ills of the Ottoman Empire. Initial reforms were top down, and they did not question the authority of the sultan. However, increasingly, the intellectuals of the age, the Young Ottomans, proposed political strategies inspired by Western political models and the notion of popular sovereignty.[19]

There were several top-down attempts at constitutional government in the Ottoman capital and the periphery, including the *Tanzimat* reforms, the convening of an elected parliament by the khedive of Egypt, and the declaration of a constitution by the Tunisian ruler, Hayreddin Pasha (A.D. 1861). More significant in paving the way for future popular mobilization was the Ottoman constitutionalist movement that was inspired by the concepts of popular sovereignty and executive accountability despite being confined to a small group of elites.[20] This movement eventually gave way to a short-lived constitutional monarchy, *Meşrutiyet*, in 1876. Notably, Ottoman reformism inspired similar movements in the other parts of the Middle East, especially the Iranian constitutionalist movement of 1905–1911.

The transformation of constitutional revolutions from being an elite business to a grassroots movement—abetted by justice rhetoric—is a highly significant development in the twentieth-century Middle East. For example, the Urabi Revolt in Egypt was initially carried out by some military officers against the government, but it later inspired the ordinary people and motivated their engagement in contentious politics. In Iran, a coalition of religious scholars, merchants, and professional class had been instrumental in carrying out the constitutional revolution of 1905. The leaders of these groups managed to mobilize the masses utilizing the language of Islamic justice and building on an anti-imperialist ideology.[21] For example, the anger against the concessions given to the imperial powers during the Tobacco Protest (1890–1891) in Iran[22] or the Ottoman intellectuals' protest of financial imperialism were significant rallying points for the constitutional movements of the age. Other factors leading to public mobilization included anger against the corrupt governments, declining economic conditions, and prevailing injustices. Religious scholars, including Iranian Muhammad Husayn Tabataba'i and Egyptian Muhammad Abduh, have taken leadership roles in these revolutions.[23]

The success of these constitutionalist movements greatly depended on their leaders' ability to mobilize the public toward their political ideals. In turn, this ability stemmed from their success in framing constitutionalism and freedom within the discourse of traditional ideologies, especially the Islamic conceptions of just government. Thus, these movements conveyed that popular sovereignty, freedom, and constitutional government are not foreign to Islam but elements of Islamic government. In other words, popular support for constitutionalism that gave way to widespread mobilization in the first constitutionalist movements of the Middle East was a product of a creative intellectual strategy that justified such notions as accountability, executive constraints, and freedom with religion.

Modernists like Afghānī and Iqbal argued that belief in science, progress, and democracy was intrinsic to Islam.[24] A similar tendency was observed much earlier in the ideas of the revivalist intellectuals of South Asia.[25] Justice has been a central problematic in Islamic political philosophy. As such, the language of modernizing reforms and constitutionalism involved frequent references to justice. However, more interestingly, these modernist accounts provide specific solutions related to good government, efficient administration, and political accountability. To be echoed in Tahrir Square and the streets of various Tunisian cities more than a century later, ordinary people were motivated by the same issues to establish systems conforming to the principles of justice in the Muslim lands.

A brief account of the ideas of Namık Kemal (1840–1888), a famous poet, playwright, and ardent supporter of Ottoman constitutionalism, will help demonstrate this point. In an influential essay titled, "And Seek Their Council in the Matter," Kemal tried to reconcile Western political theory with Islamic law to prevent the Ottoman Empire's decline.[26] He blamed the decay on the lack of democratic institutions such as popular sovereignty and executive constraints. His main argument was that God created man free as his representative on earth. This is significant because of its accordance with one of the legacies of the Islamic political justice trajectory that views man as an agent with free will in the capacity of God's vicegerent. The public, thus, should have a say in political matters, especially those safeguarding individual freedoms. As Kemal states, "Therefore, just as all individuals have the natural right to exercise their own power, so too conjoined powers naturally belong to all individuals as a whole, and consequently, in every society, the right to sovereignty belongs to the public."[27]

In traditional Islamic political theology, sovereignty belongs to the umma—the worldwide community of Muslims. However, for practical necessities, the public should choose an imam but retain the right to hold the leader accountable and depose him if the need arises.[28] According to Kemal, power should not be given to an absolute ruler who has no constraint on his power and may conduct injustices.[29] To ensure that the state will abide by justice principles, Kemal proposed that state's executive and administrative duties be open and subject to scrutiny and that the legislative function be given to an elected, representative body. The essay also discusses causes of state's decay, including inefficient government, corruption, and failing economic policies. These problems could be addressed in a constitutional regime that relies on the principles of executive accountability and popular sovereignty.[30] In sum, Kemal justified a democratic system through principles of Islamic law and also addressed the practical ills of the state as impediments to implementing justice.

Kemal's political theory exemplifies an intellectual strategy also seen in Egypt during the Urabi Revolt and in Iran during the constitutional revolution. During the age of constitutionalist movements, it was essential to convince the public about Western political government's compatibility with Islam. Intellectuals could have related religious values and the circle of justice to explain this proposition to the public. However, a second element was needed for the success of grassroots mobilization. The leaders of the constitutionalist movements had to inspire the masses by linking these abstract ideas to real-life problems to make them comprehensible. As a result, they discussed corruption, inefficient government, poverty, economic decline, lack of freedom, and inequality and linked these notions to Islamic justice. In other words, the constitutionalist movements necessitated leaders who would use traditional language familiar to the public to motivate the masses. These leaders emerged throughout the twentieth century in the various uprisings, including such names as Ahmad Urabi in Egypt, Nazem Islam al-Kermani in Iran, and Halide Edip in Turkey.[31]

The constitutionalist movements employed a strategy that linked the social and political problems of the day to the decline of the circle of justice. As Thompson and Darling argue, the circle of justice lost its prominence as a political idea in modern times, however, the underlying principles about public goods provision, security, and legitimacy continued to thrive in the nationalist, liberal, socialist, and Islamist ideologies in the twentieth century.[32] As the Middle East descended into authoritarianism in the aftermath of World War II, the ideals stemming from the Islamic justice trajectories continued to survive in popular usage. These ideals included good governance, lack of corruption, freedom, human dignity, and general welfare. Arab Spring is the latest example of mass protests where these ideas thrived once again in the chants and demands of the protesters. The next section traces the continuities of these ideas in these extraordinary upheavals.

Arab Spring and Perceptions of Injustice

The Arab Spring took many by surprise. The protests started in Tunisia and quickly spread to Egypt, Syria, Bahrain, Yemen, and other corners of the Arab region. However, the initial wave of enthusiasm about political reform has mostly vanished, leaving the scene to sectarian conflict, repressive regimes, and civil wars.[33] Except in Tunisia, no lasting democratic transition took place in the region. Egypt fell back to military dictatorship, and Syria, Libya, and Yemen descended into civil war. In the Gulf region, a combination of economic incentives and repression policies quelled the protests.

Despite this grim picture, a second wave of protests has been underway in Algeria, Iraq, Lebanon, and Sudan since 2015. In both waves, the protesters rallied against the corrupt regimes that have broken their social contracts with their respective societies.[34] In Tunisia, Mohamed Bouazizi and millions of young protesters had suffered from a feeling of disempowerment caused by corrupt authoritarian regimes. As discussed earlier, Alaa Saleh led the chants with similar motives in Sudan. Once again, the region might be at a critical juncture, akin to the turning point at the end of the nineteenth century. Just as declining economic conditions, international intervention, and authoritarian regimes led to popular mobilization against injustices at the dawn of the constitutionalist revolutions, corruption, poverty, repression, lack of opportunities for the youth, and inefficient government are currently breeding a strong desire for change through mass engagement in MENA.

In the nineteenth and twentieth centuries, the leaders of the constitutionalist movements infused modern ideas into the traditional conceptions of justice. Arab Spring similarly witnessed the emergence of new interpretations of traditional justice ideas in a new context. Freedom and equality were the slogans of constitutionalists in Istanbul, Tehran, and Cairo a century ago. The protesters in the Arab Spring were also chanting for democracy, but they had other demands most precisely captured in the slogan, *aish, ḥuriyya, karama insaniyya*, that is, bread, freedom, and human dignity. The protesters in the Arab Spring wanted political and social justice against corrupt and inefficient governments. Implementing political justice would end the corruption and hold the authoritarian leaders accountable. The protesters also called for social justice to end the unemployment, poverty, and other problems especially pertinent to the youth.

Although dissatisfaction with the existing political systems and social justice demands were the main drivers of the Arab uprisings, most studies about these extraordinary events have generally focused on the determinants of regime stability, repression, and dynamics of mass mobilization.[35] The subsequent analysis attempts to expand the current focus of scholarship by examining the perceptions of injustices in the Arab Spring. To that end, it presents an empirical analysis of conceptions of justice using the Arab Barometer data. The Arab Barometer surveys are based on probability samples of citizens—older than eighteen—and are conducted via face-to-face interviews with an error margin of 3 percent. As of 2020, there are six waves including about sixty national surveys and more than seventy thousand observations in fifteen countries.[36] The first wave of the Arab Barometer took place in 2006–2009 and the second wave in 2010–2011. Since then, three more waves of surveys were implemented.

The surveys include many questions that may help in assessing perceptions about political and social justice issues. The survey items do not directly measure justice values or value commitments, but they include questions evaluating government practices, economic conditions, and social problems that could be proxies for measuring perceptions about injustices. Unfortunately, the questions used to gauge perceptions about violations of political and social justice norms are not asked in all waves. Therefore, the analysis relied on the second and third waves of the surveys in which these questions were asked. The second wave took place in Algeria, Egypt, Iraq, Jordan, Lebanon, Palestine, Saudi Arabia, Sudan, Tunisia, and Yemen. The third wave dropped Saudi Arabia from the sample but added Kuwait, Libya, and Morocco to the surveys. Together, the two waves include twenty-two national surveys from thirteen countries and a highly representative sample of the Arab region.

Although these data are not conducive to evaluating the causal effect of religion on values, the surveys are useful for examining the perceptions of political and social injustices and their relation to piety. Protesters joining the Arab uprisings came from all corners of life and included men, women, young, old, liberal, Islamist, religious, and nonreligious.[37] As was the case during the constitutionalist revolutions at the turn of the past century, Islamic values had a powerful presence in the Arab Spring protests.

Arab Barometer includes several questions evaluating individual religiosity and perceptions of injustices. In the following analyses, perceptions about violation of justice are summarized under political and social justice dimensions, following the distinction in the developmental trajectories of justice as explained in earlier chapters. Citizens' views about violations of political justice are measured using survey questions about the state of democracy and human rights, corruption, access to public services, and political trust. Survey questions about the state of economic conditions and distributive preferences are used to measure individual perceptions about social injustice. Self-reported employment status is also used as a proxy to include a personal account of perceived social injustice. The expectation is that unemployed individuals would be more likely to have grievances and take action against perceived injustices.

Economic injustices and the resulting social justice demands were particularly important in the Arab Spring.[38] Table 8.1 reports the proportion of respondents who specify different issues as the most or the second most important problem facing the nation across the five waves of the surveys (2006–2019). Since 2006, citizens in the Arab-majority countries view economic issues such as poverty and unemployment as the most pressing problems

TABLE 8.1 MOST IMPORTANT CHALLENGES FACING THE NATION

	AB Wave 1	AB Wave 2	AB Wave 3	AB Wave 4	AB Wave 5
Economic situation (poverty, unemployment, etc.)	47	63	68	59	36
Financial and administrative corruption	21	15	18	18	17
Authoritarianism/strengthening democracy	5	2	3	2	2
Other (stability, security, Palestine, etc.)	27	21	12	21	45
Number of respondents	7,328	12,782	14,809	8,400	26,779

The numbers show the total percentage of respondents who specify that a corresponding issue is the most or the second most important problem. *Source:* Arab Barometer, Waves 1–5.

with a slight increase in the percentage of respondents after the Arab Spring protests. In the second wave (2010–2011), 63 percent of the respondents see economic issues as the most important problem facing the nation. This number jumps to 68 percent two years later in the third wave of the surveys. Despite a decline in the later waves—especially the fifth wave—the proportion of Arab citizens who view economic issues as the most significant problem remains very high.

Corruption is seen as the most important problem by one out of every five respondents. Finally, only a small proportion of individuals view authoritarianism and the need for strengthening democracy as the most significant challenge. While the desire for democracy has always been high in the Middle East, many people view the political regimes in light of declining economic conditions, corruption, and inefficient government. The chants in the Arab streets certainly invoked freedom as an ideal, but perceived injustices, inefficient government, and corruption also mattered a great deal in the protests.

For all four indicators of political justice perceptions, public opinion is on the negative side as depicted in Figure 8.1. Despite persistent authoritarianism,[39] empirical studies show that citizens in Arab-majority countries overwhelmingly support democracy.[40] Figure 8.1 shows that more than 30 percent of the respondents have negative perceptions about the state of democracy and human rights in their country. This implies that Arab citizens are sensitive to the lack of democracy and human rights and, presumably, about the political injustices in their country. About half of the respondents are distrustful of the government in both waves. The proportion of citizens reporting difficulty accessing public officials for their complaints has increased from 46 percent to 55 percent from the second to the third wave of the surveys.

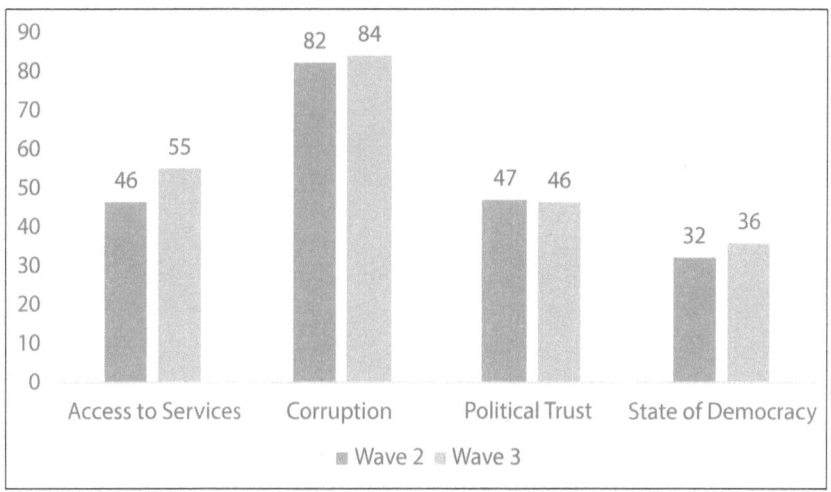

Figure 8.1 Perceptions of political injustice in the Arab world. *State of Democracy*: Percentage of survey participants responding state of democracy is "bad" or "very bad." *Political Trust*: Percentage of survey participants responding "trust government to a limited extent" or "absolutely do not trust." *Access to Services*: Percentage of survey participants responding "difficult" or "very difficult" to reach an official to file a complaint. *Corruption*: Percentage responding "yes, there is corruption in the state institutions." (Source: Arab Barometer, Waves 2 and 3.)

An overwhelming proportion of the survey respondents believe that there is widespread corruption in state institutions. Petty corruption, bribery, and, especially, *wasta* (connections) are endemic problems in the Arab region.[41] According to Transparency International's 2018 Corruption Perceptions Index, the Middle East is behind the Americas and the Asia Pacific region in the fight against corruption, but it is slightly better than Central Asia and Eastern Europe.[42] While countries like the United Arab Emirates appear to be less corrupt according to this index, Yemen and Syria are in the bottom five on a global scale. In 2019, Syria was ranked 178th, Algeria 168th, Iraq 162nd, and Egypt 106th out of 198 countries. Public perceptions about corruption agree with these figures in the Arab-majority societies. In the thirteen countries included in the second and third waves of the Arab Barometer surveys, 82 percent and 84 percent, respectively, of the respondents reported that they believe there is widespread corruption in state institutions. The prevalence of corruption, lack of trust in government, and difficulty accessing state officials for complaints are signs of state weakness because they indicate that the state is failing in public goods provision and is not capable of impartially and efficiently delivering services.[43] Corruption and abuse of power by government officials creates a feeling of impartiality

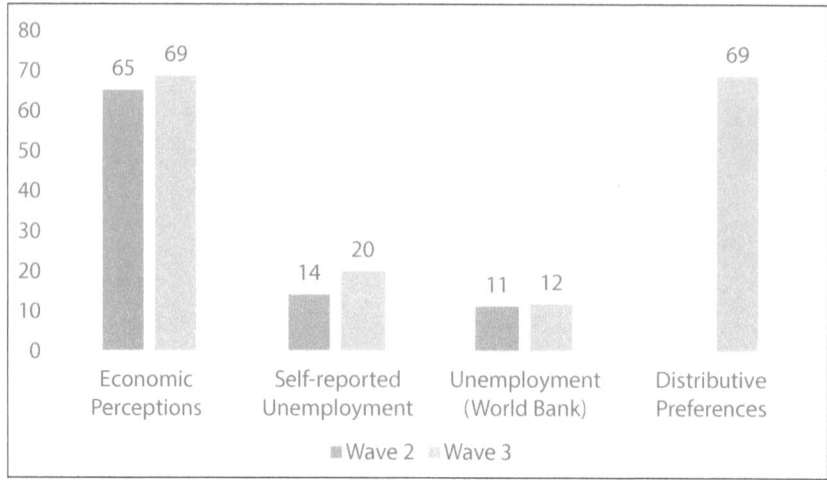

Figure 8.2 Perceptions of social injustice in the Arab world. *Economic Perceptions*: Percentage of survey participants responding that economic condition in the country is "bad" or "very bad." *Unemployment*: Survey-based and World Bank (available at https://data.worldbank.org) unemployment rates. *Distributive Preferences*: Preference on a scale where 0 means that the government should impose higher taxes on the rich to generate resources to spend on the poor, and where 10 means that the rich already create job opportunities and economic growth and that the government shall lessen the taxes they pay and allow them to retain more of their net worth. (Source: Arab Barometer, Waves 2 and 3.)

among the citizens and such practices also prevents the efficient delivery of public goods.[44] Combined with the considerable dissatisfaction with the state of democracy and human rights in the respondents' country, these figures confirm that respondents are cognizant of prevailing political injustices.

Figure 8.2 reports the distribution of responses to the questions related to the perceived social injustices and unemployment status. Although the Arab Barometer does not consistently ask questions capturing distributive preferences and perceptions of economic injustices, it includes several items that could be good proxies such as evaluation of economic conditions and support for egalitarian distributive policy. Evaluation of economic conditions is an indicator of economic grievances linked to social injustices. Egalitarian distributive preferences, on the other hand, may represent individuals' desire to establish social justice in their society. In both surveys, most citizens believe that current economic conditions in their country are bad or very bad. One source of this pessimistic outlook could be the high unemployment rates, especially among the youth. According to the survey responses, the unemployment rate was 14 percent in 2011 and increased to 20 percent in 2013. The self-reported unemployment rate is slightly higher than the official numbers, which is expected. According to the World Bank indicators, youth unemployment in MENA is the highest globally, reaching 30 percent in some years. Youth unemployment can fuel grievances to increase demands for social justice during social crises.[45] Finally, Figure 8.2 reports the proportion of respondents who lean favorably toward egalitarian distributive policies from the third wave of the surveys—69 percent of the survey participants prefer increasing taxes so that the state can help the poor. This result implies a strong desire for social justice in the Arab region.

Together, these indicators show that citizens in the Arab region are very concerned about political and social injustices. The protesters' grievances and their demands in the Arab Spring arose from reactions to the incompetent governments, failing states, widespread corruption, unemployment, and lack of economic opportunities. Just as corruption and decline in state institutions were significant issues before the constitutionalist revolutions of the nineteenth and twentieth centuries, today, they continue to be pressing social problems in Arab-majority countries. In the late nineteenth century, the Ottoman intellectual Namık Kemal proposed that popular sovereignty and a constitutional government would facilitate domestic reform and prevent the decline of the Ottoman state.[46] Protesters in the Arab street also called for freedom, but they attached their demands of justice to their desire for an efficient state, public services, and democracy.

Correlates of Protest Behavior in the Arab World

After providing a summary of responses to these questions, I proceed to the multivariate analysis to test the effects of perceptions of political and social injustices on protest participation. It is especially crucial to test whether perceptions of social injustices affect the decision to engage in protests against the state for understanding the effects of these perceptions on political behavior.

Mass protests have complicated reasons related to structural inequalities, repression, economic grievances, psychological factors, and modernization.[47] Religion may also play a role in the decision to participate in protests. Religion's influence on protest behavior may stem from communal religious participation that builds civil skills and networks, which, in turn, increase the likelihood of mobilization.[48] A second mechanism through which religion may motivate protest participation is the influence of norms and related values. The proponents of this view argue that the world's major faiths promote justice, which may motivate individuals to change the world around them according to their faith principles.[49] A third mechanism is related to grievances. Individual grievances may stem from political injustices as much as they are linked to social injustices. Religious values may inform grievances by shaping perceptions of injustices. Religious networks may build on these values and grievances to shape members' attitudes and behavior.[50] This chapter focuses on overall religiosity and perceptions of injustices to explain protest behavior.

The following analysis focuses on religion's mobilizing capacity in the Arab Spring and tests the effects of both political and social justice perceptions on the likelihood of protest participation. There have been recurring waves of mass protests in the Middle East since the nineteenth century in reaction to various injustices. People protested against corrupt and inefficient governments, repression, and economic decline.[51] Prevailing economic and social injustices presumably played an important role also in the Arab Spring. Social justice demands in these protests were about lack of employment opportunities, poverty, and declining economic conditions.

Hoffman and Jamal found that social justice mattered a great deal in the Arab Spring, especially among the pious who engage with the scripture daily.[52] In their article, they do not provide a direct test of social justice values on protest behavior but present social justice values as a mechanism that links piety to protest participation in the cases of Egypt and Tunisia. Building on these insights, I argue that grievances about the lack of social justice related to an individual's unemployment status will make protest participation more likely. This relationship should be especially strong for the most devout individuals due to Islam's emphasis on social justice values. Evidence supporting this hypothesis will imply that the Islamic social justice trajectory continues to inform contemporary political preferences.

Although the religion–social justice nexus is important, we also need to consider individuals' perceptions about political injustices to understand better how religion can motivate political behavior. Corruption, weak government, inefficient public goods provision, and lack of freedom were among the primary political demands of the protesters in the Arab Spring.[53] These demands represent people's outcry against the political injustices in their societies. Therefore, individuals who distrust the government, those who believe that there is widespread corruption, individuals who find it difficult to access public officials, and those who are unhappy with the state of democracy and human rights in their country will be more likely to participate in protests. Moreover, the effect of perceived political injustice on protest participation will be more substantial for highly religious individuals, given Islam's doctrinal emphasis on removing injustices and assigning a duty on the faithful to fight against tyranny.

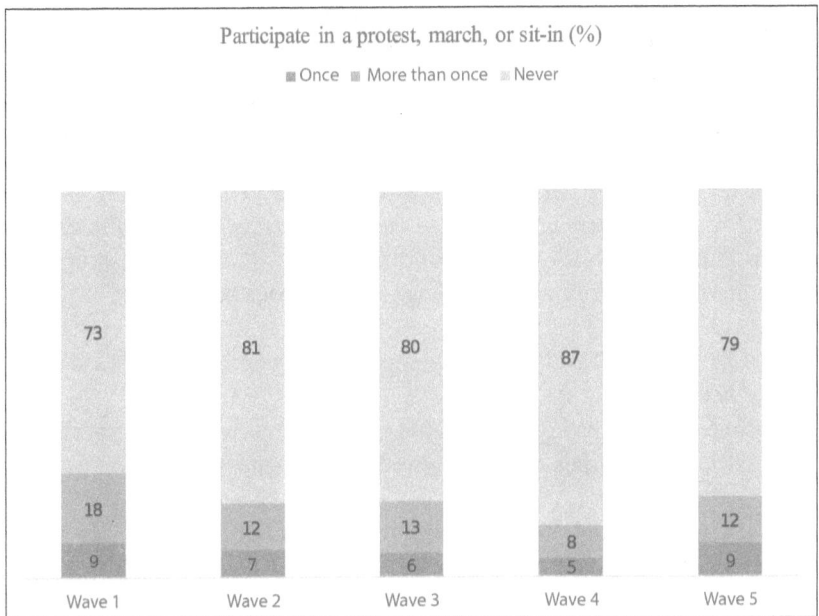

Figure 8.3 Protest participation in the Arab world. Sample sizes vary in each wave. The numbers show the average proportions for the protest participation in the full sample. (Source: Arab Barometer, Waves 1–5.)

A series of multivariate statistical estimations were conducted to test these hypotheses. The analysis used the second and third waves of the Arab Barometer surveys based on the timing of the survey fieldwork and the availability of the necessary survey items. The multivariate model estimations used full samples, interaction effects with religiosity, split samples for each wave of the surveys, and a reduced sample of devout individuals. Different estimation strategies allow for testing the robustness of the results and the effect of justice perceptions on protest behavior conditional on religiosity. The analysis is also replicated for Egypt and Tunisia—the two most prominent cases of the Arab Spring—using the survey data collected during the Arab Spring (Wave 2).

The dependent variable, *protest participation*, is measured with a question asking the respondents whether they participated in a protest, march, or sit-in during the past three years. This item has a slightly different wording in the second wave for the Egyptian and Tunisian samples where the respondents were asked whether they participated in a protest in the last several months. Figure 8.3 shows the trends in protest participation between (2006–2019) in fifteen Arab-majority countries and about sixty country surveys. In general, the proportion of people who attend protests, marches, or sit-ins is stable over time but there are fluctuations between different survey waves. Most people report that they have never participated in any protest (range from 73 percent to 87 percent). Those who participated in a protest once or more are about 20 percent of the survey participants. Reported protest participation is especially high in the first wave (2006) and the lowest (13 percent) in the fourth wave (2016–2017).

The main independent variables measure perceptions of political and social injustices. Additionally, an additive index of religiosity is obtained using the two questions about self-reported religious behavior:[54]

> Q6101: Do you pray daily always, most of the time, sometimes, rarely or never? (*prayer*)
>
> Q6106: Do you read or listen to the *Qur'an* daily always, most of the time, sometimes, rarely or never? (*Koran readership*)

Both items strongly correlate, and the factor analysis confirms a single dimension of religiosity. Responses to both questions are highly skewed with over 70 percent of the respondents falling at the high end of self-reported religious behavior. This is not an unexpected finding for the Arab-majority countries as religion is a formidable social force with a majority of people reporting to be pious. The following models also include controls for respondents' age, educational attainment, household income, gender (female), and fixed effects.[55]

Since the dependent variable, *protest*, is dichotomous, I use logistic regression as shown in Table 8.2. Model 1 runs the estimation based on the full sample of the respondents from the two waves, whereas Models 2 and 3 use the second and third waves, respectively. Model 4 adds the variable measuring distributive preferences, which is available only in the third wave, and Model 5 uses the two components of the *religiosity index*. The models show that perceived political injustices affect protest. *Distrust in government* (Models 1, 2, and 5) and *difficulty accessing state officials* (Models 1, 3, 4, and 5) significantly increase protest behavior. Perceptions of social injustice exert a more pronounced effect on the likelihood of protest attendance. Individuals with *pessimistic economic outlooks* (Models 1, 2, and 5) and those who are unemployed (Models 1, 3–5) are more likely to protest. Egalitarian distributive preferences also make protest behavior more likely (Model 4).

Pious individuals are less likely to engage in protests when the samples from the two waves are combined for the statistical estimation. It appears that the sample from the third wave might be driving this result because this variable is statistically significant in the estimations using the third wave ($p < .05$), but it has no statistically significant effect on protest in the second wave. Interestingly, the less frequently individuals pray, the more

TABLE 8.2 LOGISTIC REGRESSION ESTIMATES OF PROTEST PARTICIPATION IN THE ARAB WORLD

	Model 1 Waves 2 and 3	Model 2 Wave 2	Model 3 Wave 3	Model 4 Distributive Preferences	Model 5 Prayer and Koran Reader
Perceptions of Political Injustice					
State of democracy	−0.0313	−0.0195	−0.0482*	−0.0447	−0.0315
	(0.020)	(0.031)	(0.027)	(0.028)	(0.020)
Distrust in government	0.0379*	0.106***	−0.00945	0.00216	0.0374*
	(0.022)	(0.033)	(0.030)	(0.031)	(0.022)
Access to state	0.0450***	0.0331	0.0419*	0.0420*	0.0451***
	(0.017)	(0.025)	(0.022)	(0.023)	(0.017)
Perception of corruption	−0.0809	−0.144	−0.00984	−0.0365	−0.0775
	(0.057)	(0.089)	(0.077)	(0.078)	(0.057)
Perceptions of Economic Injustice					
Evaluation of economic situation	0.0810***	0.232***	−0.0420	−0.0411	0.0816***
	(0.027)	(0.041)	(0.036)	(0.037)	(0.027)
Unemployed	0.155**	−0.100	0.357***	0.346***	0.153**
	(0.061)	(0.110)	(0.077)	(0.079)	(0.061)
Distributive preferences	—	—	—	0.0284***	—
				(0.008)	
Religiosity					
Religiosity index	−0.0231**	0.0114	−0.0325**	−0.0335**	—
	(0.011)	(0.015)	(0.016)	(0.016)	
Daily prayer	—	—	—	—	−0.0591***
					(0.021)
Koran readership	—	—	—	—	0.00418
					(0.018)
Control Variables					
Age	−0.0116***	−0.0102***	−0.0134***	−0.0139***	−0.0115***
	(0.002)	(0.002)	(0.002)	(0.002)	(0.002)
Female	−0.716***	−0.670***	−0.762***	−0.753***	−0.711***
	(0.038)	(0.058)	(0.052)	(0.053)	(0.038)

(Continued)

TABLE 8.2 (Continued)

	Model 1 Waves 2 and 3	Model 2 Wave 2	Model 3 Wave 3	Model 4 Distributive Preferences	Model 5 Prayer and Koran Reader
Education	0.157***	0.152***	0.197***	0.195***	0.156***
	(0.012)	(0.018)	(0.017)	(0.017)	(0.012)
Income	0.139***	0.0911***	0.115***	0.114***	0.139***
	(0.021)	(0.032)	(0.029)	(0.030)	(0.021)
Constant	−2.226***	−2.569***	−2.255***	−2.408***	−2.123***
	(0.164)	(0.243)	(0.240)	(0.251)	(0.172)
Observations	20,941	9,464	11,477	10,954	20,941

Standard errors in parentheses. Fixed effects are reported in Appendix A, Table A8.3. * $p < .1$, ** $p < .05$, *** $p < .01$. Source: Arab Barometer.

likely they are to take part in protests. This result differs from the findings of Hoffman and Jamal's study that used the second wave of the Arab Barometer in the Egyptian and Tunisian samples. Although the survey data did not allow them to determine causal effects, Hoffman and Jamal found evidence supporting the hypothesis that Koran readership informs perceptions of injustices, including distrust in government, views of state impartiality, and support for democracy.[56] The analysis presented here uses a multidimensional measure of religiosity and specifies the exact political and social justice perceptions to test their effects on protest behavior.

When a more suitable measure, distributive preferences, is used in Model 4, religiosity decreases protest participation and only difficulty accessing state officials has a meaningful effect on protest behavior. The explanatory power of distributive preferences as a measure of social justice orientation cancels out the statistical effects of different perceptions of political injustice and even the negative effect of the *evaluation of economic situation*.

While the samples in the second and third waves of the surveys include countries where protest activity had been significant, such as Egypt and Tunisia, in most countries, protest activity did not reach the levels seen in these two countries. In cases like Algeria, Sudan, Kuwait, and Saudi Arabia, either the protesters did not press too hard or the regime managed to suppress the protests. Therefore, the sample in hand is not ideal for testing the effect of religiosity on protest behavior. I employed two strategies to alleviate the concerns that come with this limitation. First, I ran a separate model using the interaction terms between religiosity and all indicators of perceptions of political and social injustices. This strategy tests the conditioning

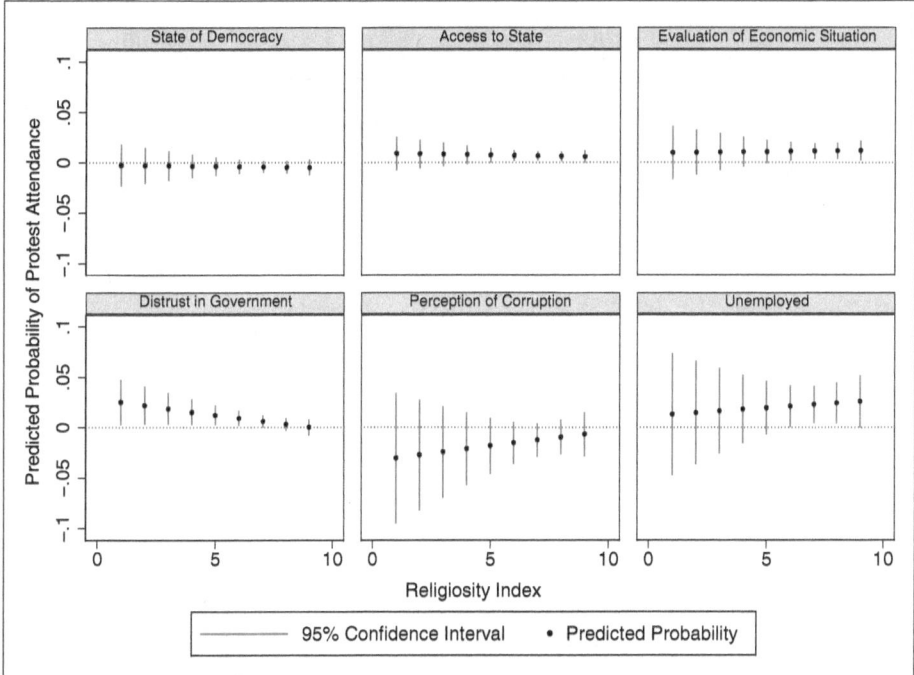

Figure 8.4 Religion, perceptions of injustice, and protest behavior.
Each panel shows the change in predicted probability of protest behavior associated with different indicators measuring perceptions of political and social injustice at different levels of religiosity (interaction effects). The circles represent the predicted probability, and the bars show the 95 percent confidence interval. Full estimation results are presented in Appendix A, Table A8.4. (Source: Arab Barometer, Waves 2 and 3.)

effect of religiosity index on predictors of protest behavior. Second, Tunisia and Egypt are closely examined to provide a more conclusive account of interactions concerning religiosity and perceptions of injustices on protest participation. Figure 8.4 shows the average effects of each indicator of perceived injustices at different levels of religiosity based on interaction terms.[57]

The substantive effects associated with perceptions of political and social injustices are not very large. However, the predicted probability of protest participation is attenuated by the degree of religiosity, especially for evaluation of the economic situation and unemployment status—two measures of perceived social injustices or grievances. At the same time, the confidence bounds get narrower at high levels of piety. Therefore, religiosity makes a substantive difference in the likelihood of protest attendance for unemployed individuals and those with pessimistic economic views, especially for the most pious. A similar effect is also observed for the difficulty

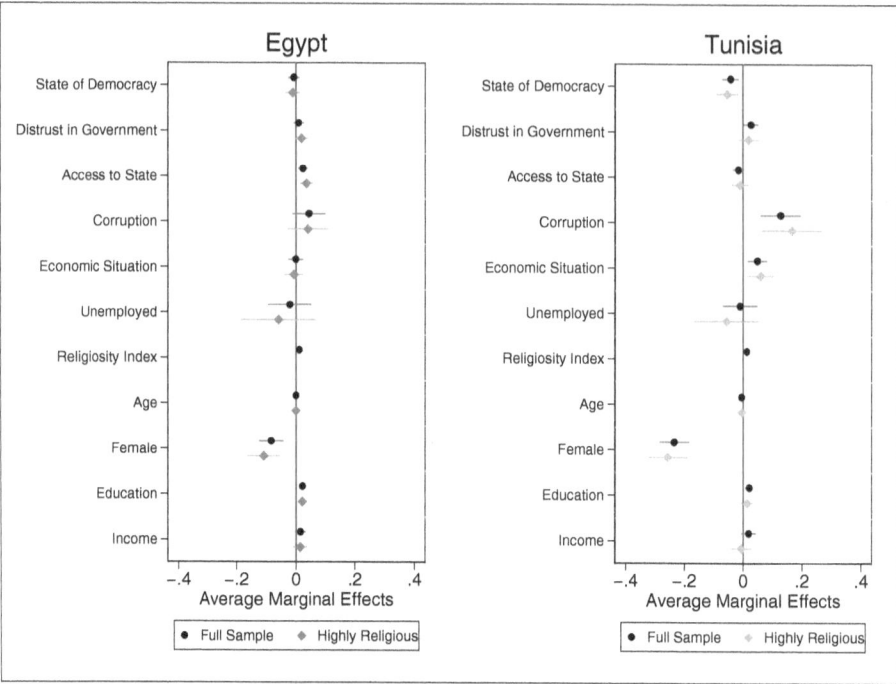

Figure 8.5 Determinants of protest participation. The circles show the average predicted probability of protest participation in the full sample and the diamonds in the highly religious sample. The horizontal lines show the 95 percent confidence interval. Full estimation results are presented in Appendix A, Table A8.5. (Source: Arab Barometer, Wave 2.)

accessing state officials. Religious individuals are more likely to protest if they are not satisfied with the ease of access to officials for filing a complaint. Interestingly, at increased levels of religiosity, individuals become less likely to protest when they are not happy with the state of democracy in their country or distrust the government. Evidently, perceptions of political injustices and the conditioning effect of religiosity on their impact are less pronounced than the perceptions of social injustices. This result confirms the viability of grievance-based explanations related to the perceived violations of social justice.[58]

Additionally, logistic regressions of protest behavior were estimated for Egypt and Tunisia using the second wave of the Arab Barometer. Figure 8.5 shows the average marginal effects from these estimations for the full and the highly religious samples for each country.[59] In Egypt, only difficulty accessing state officials increases the likelihood of protest. Religiosity increases protest participation, and this effect amplifies the impact of distrust in government and difficulty accessing state officials. In Tunisia, individuals who perceive widespread corruption and distrust the government are more likely to participate in protest (this latter effect disappears in the highly religious sample). Of social justice indicators, pessimistic economic outlook also increases the protest attendance. The impact of these indicators on protest participation is larger among the highly religious, and religiosity itself increases protest behavior.

These results show that piety motivates people to take action against an authoritarian regime. The analysis identifies the specific mechanisms that link religious doctrine to protest participation. These mechanisms include perceived injustices when it is difficult to file complaints with the state officials and individuals hold pessimistic outlooks about the economic situation. As the theoretical framework suggested, Islam's doctrinal emphasis on rebellion against tyranny and social justice may result in prodemocratic behavior (i.e., protest participation against the authoritarian government). Although the data in hand are not conducive to dissecting the causal pathways, the findings of past studies and this chapter point to grievances about the state and economic injustice as a possible explanatory factor, at least in the two most prominent cases of the Arab Spring.

Conclusion

The Arab Spring marks one of the most significant junctures in the history of Middle Eastern democratization. People taking to the streets during these extraordinary protests were fighting against social and political injustices. These protests took many by surprise, but observers of the region pointed to ordinary people's democratic aspirations for an explanation.[60] This chapter took a similar approach to empirically evaluate people's demands in the Arab Spring. The analysis implied continuity in the discourse of the contemporary protest movements and the constitutionalist revolutions in the Middle East in the nineteenth and twentieth centuries. Both movements represented grievances against social and political injustices, but they were mostly targeting the corrupt, inefficient, and declining states. While the elite championing the constitutionalist regimes called for implementing popular sovereignty and executive constraints, the people in the Arab streets chanted for freedom, human dignity, and social justice. Religion played a significant role in these events as a reference frame. For example, constitutionalists justified the Western political models with traditional ideas including the scriptural principle of consultation and man's responsibility as the vicegerent of God. Although Arab Spring protesters were not exclusively religious, the language of these protests involved many Islamic symbols represented in a post-Islamist outlook, implying that devotion and support for political rights are compatible.[61]

According to the Arab Barometer data, economic issues are among the most significant problems for Arab citizens. The data also revealed that corruption, difficulty accessing state services, and political distrust are important indicators of political injustices. The results showed that political and social injustices played a role in motivating protest participation in the Arab Spring. A closer examination of the two most significant cases of the Arab Spring, Egypt and Tunisia, demonstrated that religion mattered in these countries. Highly devout individuals protested due to perceived political injustices related to corruption and lack of access to state services or perceived social injustices measured by the pessimistic economic outlook.

By and large, the results are far from being conclusive. The analysis cannot pinpoint the causal pathways linking religion, justice perceptions, and protest behavior. However, even with less than ideal data, it can be reasonably concluded that perceptions of social and political injustices mattered, especially for the religious individuals in their decision to attend the protests. State decay, corruption, and distrust of government along with perceptions of economic decline and the lack of opportunities were important factors driving the upheaval in the Arab world. The appeal of various Islamist parties in the aftermath was indicative of support for a religiously informed path to solving the mounting problems in these societies. However, the disillusionment came rather quickly in Egypt. For now, the success story appears to be Tunisia, where the Islamist Ennahda movement continues to play an instrumental role in Tunisian democratization. It is important to note that Islamic justice plays a significant role in the ideology of Ennahda as defined by its founder, Rāshid al-Ghannūshī. A closer examination of Islamist party ideologies and determinants of support for these parties will, perhaps, reveal additional mechanisms through which religion, Islamic justice, and political engagement are connected.

9

Conclusion

> If religion does not work before death, it certainly will not work after it.
> —'Alī Shariati, "Eslam-Shenasi (Islamology)"

The resilience of ordinary people taking to the streets in the Arab Spring and their strong desire for democracy is extraordinary for a region known for robust authoritarianism. These protests also reflected a longing for justice, Islamic faith's primary value. Many observers discredited the role of religion in the Arab Spring. Like its predecessors, the protests in various squares and corners of the Arab world were not religious revolutions, but religion did play a significant role in these uprisings. This is because Islam has always been a formidable social force shaping values, attitudes, and behavior over centuries. Justice was the most significant value in the discourses of the Arab Spring protesters. Ironically, the counterdiscourse against the Arab Spring also used religious conceptions of justice to undermine the protests. How can Islamic justice simultaneously be a source for democratic and authoritarian discourses?

Two years after the Arab uprisings, participation of some Islamist groups in the Gezi Park protests against an Islamist party with the word "justice" in its name, in Turkey, was quite puzzling. These groups' discourses of freedom heavily relied on Islamic conceptions of justice. However, AKP also used the Islamic justice conception to undermine the legitimacy of Gezi protests. From Cairo to Istanbul, both people's quest for democracy and the repression of these demands were justified by the Islamic conceptions of justice. This book is about "Islam and democracy," a significant puzzle that kept many intellectuals, scholars, and pundits busy for many years. It argues that justice discourses are the substance of this puzzle, stimulating rival legitimacy claims about governance. This volume tried to understand these discourses and their relation to democracy by examining the implications of conceptions of justice in Muslim agency's attitudes and behavior.

This book's main contention is that conceptions of justice are the primary cultural determinants of democracy in Islam. Because justice is the most significant notion in Islam's ethicopolitical system, this relationship should be most clearly visible in Muslim political experience. It is this perspective that sets this book apart from many other studies on Islam and democracy. Rather than delving into endless debates about macro or structural determinants of democracy in Islam, this volume primarily focused on Muslims and democracy. As such, the central question guiding this volume is not whether Islam and democracy are compatible. Instead, the motivating questions concern what kind of democracy religious Muslims want and would accept, and to what extent Islamic justice values inform support for democracy by pious Muslim men and women. This approach puts a premium on understanding ordinary people's attitudes and value orientations instead of focusing on institutional and structural roots of democracy. To that end, previous chapters explored what Muslim agency thinks and does about democracy from past to present and in various contexts.

The volume does not propose a deterministic link between culture and democracy. Democratization occurs when specific constellations of political, economic, and cultural factors give way to institutions aligned with popular sovereignty, accountability, and mass participation. Given this complicated process, democracy is a phenomenon that may or may not occur within a favorable cultural framework. However, if culture plays a role in the masses accepting democracy as a desirable government system, this book demonstrated that Islam may provide such a basis because of its emphasis on justice and this central concept's potential in engendering outlooks conducive to democracy.[1] The volume employed a *longue durée* perspective about the legacy of justice discourses and their capacity in shaping political preferences, attitudes, and behavior to elaborate on this point.

The legacies of Islamic justice engender rival legitimacy claims about governance. While Islamic justice values and the related preferences and orientations may provide a cultural foundation for democratic thinking, the same forces may also justify authoritarianism. In fact, Islamic conceptions of justice are also used to legitimize the authoritarian rule, which has been the prevailing governance model for much of Islamic history. This outcome resulted from many factors, including the alliance of political and religious elites[2] and the monopoly of legal tradition as a truth-claim controlling the social, religious, and political spheres against the philosophical and mystic alternatives.[3] While acknowledging that there might be a path to authoritarian rule passing through Islamic discourses of obedience and order, this volume did not deal with this complicated history, leaving it to future studies as a fruitful research endeavor. However, the book made a case for the role Islamic conceptions of justice can play in stimulating mass democratic tendencies in Muslim democratization.

This conclusion about Islam's potential to engender democratization relies on two interrelated trends within the Islamic tradition. First, starting from the doctrine that man is God's vicegerent, one Islamic worldview gave way to critical thinking, flexible interpretations of religion, and a political stance against injustice—all implied by a specific understanding of Islamic justice.[4] Second, throughout Islamic history, this worldview became the basis of numerous uprisings, rebellions, and revolutions—most prominently in the modern age and with respect to democracy.[5]

Previous chapters deployed evidence from Islamist texts, public opinion surveys, and ethnographic research to demonstrate that Islamic conceptions of justice shape prodemocratic attitudes and value orientations among ordinary men and women in the Muslim world. Based on this evidence, a critical implication of this study is that devout Muslims support and want democracy because of their preferences and orientations originating from Islamic conceptions of justice. Two caveats should be mentioned. First, the Muslim agency's support for democracy is contingent on the perception of democracy as a regime with a comparative advantage in implementing social and political justice by most religious citizens in a given polity. Such perception is related to the central role of justice in Islam and democracy's capacity in generating public deliberation according to rational-civic reason, allowing the realization and enactment of Islamic justice.[6] Second, despite favorable opinion and numerous waves of mass mobilization to bring democracy to the Muslim lands, domestic and international forces prevented the realization of this goal.[7] The centripetal force of masses toward democratization has been countered by the centrifugal force of domestic dictators and their international collaborators, resulting in authoritarian, corrupt, and inefficient governments in Muslim-majority societies.[8] This volume did not explore these centrifugal forces in detail, which, among other strategies, use security and order-oriented discourses of justice to maintain authoritarian political systems in the Muslim world. Exploring the linkages between Islam, justice discourses, and these centrifugal forces will be a fertile research subject for future studies.

This book's explanatory framework relied on a stylistic distinction between social and political justice. Islamic conceptions of justice originate from two critical junctures that gave way to lasting legacies in Muslim politics. Significant political events accompanied by conceptual, theological, and ideological debates marked these moments. The first critical juncture came about after Muhammad's passing. Succession to the Prophet and the leadership question divided the first Muslim community, seen as a perfect society despite simmering disagreement in the background. Such disagreement resulted in the first civil war between 'Ali and Mu'āwiya's supporters and other groups who did not affiliate with them. These parties claimed to uphold justice and came up with justifications about their entitlement to rule the Muslim community. Their inspiration was the same, Koran and Muhammad. Nevertheless, they reached contrasting opinions about what justice is and how it should be implemented in a community of supposedly pure believers. It was all political in the beginning, and the debates concentrated on such issues as the right to rule, legitimacy, and a wise ruler's morals. Political rhetoric spilled over into the doctrinal/legal sphere, and the latter eventually came to shape the former over time as the initial divisions repeated with different actors creating new traumas over time.

This first communal division and the resulting differences in doctrine, law, and Islamic interpretations are the foundations of various political theories building on conceptions of justice. Two legacies followed this first critical juncture. Some believed in free will, individual choice, and man's responsibility as God's vicegerent to represent a principled opposition and mobilization against tyranny for establishing political justice. A second position started from the necessity of bringing order and security to the community long-marred with fitna and conflict. Thus, it was unethical and against God's justice to rebel against a ruler, even if unjust. These two positions left a lasting imprint on Muslim political experience to shape values, preferences, and attitudes over centuries. The first position culminated in democratic and the latter authoritarian orientations. At the turn of the twentieth century, the first constitutionalist movements built on these legacies to develop democratic solutions to the state decline and prevent foreign intervention. Discourses of Islamic justice were instrumental in reaching masses and mobilizing them for this cause. Coating modern political ideas with Islamic justice has been the primary strategy in independence movements, labor mobilization, and popular uprisings since the nineteenth century. Arab Spring is the latest example of this approach as observed in the contentious acts demanding justice and freedom in MENA. On the flip side, traditional political forces similarly built on the authoritarian implications of the political justice trajectory. Their justifications for a type of enlightened despotism relied on discourses of predetermination, order and security, rulers' wisdom, and forbearance. Despite favorable public opinion and widespread mass action for a democratic system, various domestic and external forces prevented democracy from taking root in Muslim-majority societies. The main conclusion of this book, nonetheless, remains—religious Muslims long for democracy and periodically take action to bring it home.

A second critical juncture came about when the Muslim world faced disintegration and suffered under the Mongol invasion. While political justice discourses still mattered regarding rulers' qualities and executive constraints imposed by Islamic law's imperatives, it was the imminent danger to society that concerned the scholars most. In the face of weakening political authority, the primary issue became the protection of society: The state should protect life, property, religion, and progeny to ensure order and security. Welfare and public interest were the primary concerns of the scholars at that time. To prevent the abuse of power and implement social justice, scholars aimed to keep the rulers in check according to the end goals of sharia.[9] In reality, however, this political arrangement gave more power to the rulers and resulted in the co-optation of scholars.[10] A new social justice paradigm legitimized the authoritarian rule to the extent that an abstract notion of public interest took precedence over individual well-being and human dignity. Justice discourses of order, security, and public interest strengthened the hand of "benevolent dictators." To the extent that a ruler provided security, order, and public goods or protected the religion, the benefits of obedience to him would outweigh the cost of rebellion for freedom and justice. In a sense, a particular lineage of social justice trumps the freedom-oriented lineage of political justice to legitimize authoritarianism.

This stylistic distinction helps us better evaluate the implications of Islamic political and social justice trajectories in contemporary politics. In reality, the picture is much more complicated than this simplified version. There is significant synergy between political and social justice discourses. For example, the notion of human dignity resulting from man's vicegerent status implies a preference for egalitarian distribution, an important social justice goal. This emancipative approach provides an alternative to the medieval social justice model by putting human agency and dignity to the center of social order rather than prioritizing communal benefit. Because the former is more likely to occur in democracies, the path to social justice goals through one legacy of political justice will engender support for democracy among the pious. This book presented some empirical evidence supporting this hypothesis by using surveys conducted in the Muslim world.

There also appears to be an inherent tension between the implications of political and social justice. For example, many authoritarian leaders in the Middle East supported the Palestinian cause as a rallying point for social justice. From Nasser to Saddam Hussein, many leaders used Islamic justice discourses to push for the Palestinian statehood, presumably for political gains. However, domestically, they repressed social movements or ethnic/religious groups demanding their rights. In that, these leaders used fear of fitna and necessity of order to legitimize their unjust acts.

A similar dynamic is also in play in the programs and policies of Islamist political parties. Most Islamist parties use the word "justice" in their names, and their programs emphasize welfare provision. This tendency becomes visible when these parties gain political power giving them an Islamist economic advantage.[11] The primary example for an Islamist party government, AKP in Turkey, demonstrates that Islamists exploit this advantage. Social service provision has been an important rallying point for voter recruitment for AKP, and it became the main instrument of maintaining electoral support once the party came to power. However, as the party consolidated its power into the third term, the ability to continue to provide these services allowed the party leaders to buy off loyalty against democratic backsliding. AKP leaders repeatedly mentioned the difficulty of maintaining distributive policies and public interest when the social order was threatened. According to this approach, a benevolent but strong leader who does not have to bother with democratic institutions could ensure public interest. In the Turkish context, discourses of order and public interest can be traced back to the 1960s when Islamist intellectuals took issue with communism and put the needs of the society over the individual and the idea of social order over equality. This is a familiar dynamic also seen in rentier monarchies of the Middle East, where the price of loyalty is security, protection of religion, and welfare provision. Discourses of order and benevolence are crucial elements in this political strategy.

Social and political justice discourses have considerable sway over the attitudes and value orientations of the pious. The statistical analysis of public opinion surveys provided significant support for this proposition. Religious individuals are more likely to support democracy because they hold egalitarian distributive preferences and value orientations that are conducive to individual autonomy. The analysis of protest behavior in the Arab Spring showed that perceived social and political justice violations are among the leading causes of protest participation. Therefore, perceptions and orientations of social and political justice values greatly influence pious men and women's attitudes and behaviors.

There is a longing for democracy and justice in Muslim-majority societies. Democracy lacks in these societies, but most people seem to have a strong desire to bring it home. Simultaneously, grievances due to perceived injustices have resulted in widespread protests in the Muslim world. These two notions are inherently connected insofar as justice demands appear alongside a longing for democracy, and democracy is viewed as the political system more conducive to justice. As stated previously, the Arab Spring protests took many by surprise, but protests inspired by the ideals of justice have frequently occurred in these societies. Before the Arab Spring, people took to the streets against colonialism, domestic dictators, and corruption on many occasions. They demanded freedom, constitutional government, independence, and social justice. Justice has always been the primary value shaping contention and politics in the Muslim world. Since the age of constitutional revolutions more than a century ago, Islamic justice demands repeatedly appeared alongside the calls for democracy in the Muslim world.

Justice is the substance of Islamic political discourse. Its origins contain a liberation ideology. In Mecca, Prophet Muhammad preached political and social justice to emancipate man from the social and economic shackles of his time. From the prophetic community to contemporary society, justice values have shaped Muslim agency's attitudes and behaviors, frequently according to this liberation ideology. However, over time, Islamic conceptions of justice have taken various forms attaching themselves to discourses of obedience and conformist ideologies. For example, medieval ulema seeking to constrain the executive for the sake of social justice defined justice as order and security.

In contrast, Islamic justice discourses took an anti-imperialist tone against colonialism and legitimized rebellion against foreign powers at the turn of the twentieth century. Muslims saw justice as the opposite of tyranny and protested the corrupt despots. The opposition groups of Islamist and secular types operating within authoritarian regimes have been using the discourse of opposition to tyranny for a long time to justify rebellion against political authority. In short, Islamic justice discourses have always been present in Muslim politics. That Muslim agency is free, responsible, and has control over her destiny is the cornerstone of much-desired justice and democracy within the Muslim political experience.

This book brought significant evidence about the attitudes and behaviors of Muslim agency. For example, Qutb and Shariati's justice theories rely on the idea of man being a free agent striving for dignity, only serving God. They argue that social justice practices can emancipate the man leading him to rebel against injustices. There is a revolutionary and democratic quality to this approach. In practice, however, the same conceptions can also legitimize authoritarian government for the sake of harmony, solidarity, and communal order.

The dual nature of justice discourses swinging between democratic and authoritarian preferences is easily visible in the development of Turkish Islamist ideology. In a relatively short period (1960–2010), mainstream Turkish Islamism went full circle from defending obedience to political authority for the sake of social justice and public order, to fierce opposition to the hegemonic world order against political injustices targeting Muslim communities, and back to the legitimization of Turkey's descent into a competitive authoritarian regime using the same justice-oriented discourses. This book aimed to explain these different outcomes. To that end, it presented the first systematic account of political implications of justice discourses from an agency-centered perspective by bringing evidence from diverse settings and putting individual attitudes and value orientations at the center of its exploration.

Since Islam has substantial sway over individual attitudes, value orientations, and behaviors, and justice is the central concept of Islamic political discourse, it is essential to conduct further studies examining the relationship of Islam and democracy through the discourses and rhetoric of justice. As one of the first volumes taking this direction, *Islam, Justice, and Democracy* explored the synergies between religion and support for democracy from the perspective of intellectuals, social activists, and, most prominently, ordinary people whose common denominator is piety.

The effect of religiosity on support for democracy is rarely clear-cut. This book employed two approaches to clarify this ambivalence. First, it cast a wide net and employed a *longue durée* perspective to capture continuities in conceptions of justice from the beginnings of Islam to contemporary contentious politics. It explored the interplay of justice and democracy in contemporary Islamist thought and journals. It examined the mass contentious acts from the nineteenth century to the Arab Spring as sites of justice and democracy demands. This approach proved to be fruitful for demonstrating the complex nature of this relationship.

Second, *Islam, Justice, and Democracy* examined the specific mechanisms that link religion to democracy. Statistical analysis of survey data demonstrated how social and political justice values shape distributive preferences and value orientations, which affect support for democracy. The analyses in Chapters 6, 7, and 8 revealed that religion informs social and political justice orientations, and these orientations mediate the effect of piety on support for democracy. A surprising finding concerned the divergent effects of individualistic value orientations. Islam encourages obedience to parents and religious authority, but, at the same time, it cherishes hard work and individual success. Religious individuals are less likely to encourage independent thinking as a quality to teach children, but they also value hard work and believe one can control her destiny. Overall, individualistic value orientations can swing between implications of free will and predetermination axes to create opposing views about democracy.

According to these extensive analyses, we can confidently say that Muslim religiosity increases support for democracy by generating prodistributive preferences and certain types of individualistic value orientations. This conclusion, however, is contingent on the nature of religious outlooks. Because religiously inspired justice values may engender democratic and authoritarian attitudes, religion's positive effect on support for democracy will be conditional on prodistributive social justice preferences and individualistic value orientations cherishing belief in the power of Muslim agency as the shaper of her destiny. Religion may also inspire collectivist value orientations favoring social harmony and order. Individuals holding such religious communitarian outlooks are more likely to support obedience to authority in social relations and, thus, authoritarian systems.[12]

This book did not propose that religious values, as a cultural foundation for democracy, will democratize Muslim-majority societies. However, the analyses showed that culture matters, and religion as the leading determinant of culture in Muslim-majority societies can be conducive to democracy. There is significant potential for legitimizing democracy through Islamic values that are familiar to religious Muslims. Islamic justice values are, essentially, this component, arguably the missing link in converting supporters of democracy to practitioners of democracy.

Islamic justice values are necessary but not sufficient for making democracy the only game in the Muslim world. Democratization is a complex process shaped by social and economic forces. Despite widespread support for democracy, neither elite-led nor mass movements managed to bring democracy to a good portion of the Muslim world. One can blame the international powers, which crushed democratic rebellions, orchestrated numerous coups, and supported authoritarian governments for economic gains. This would be a necessary but an insufficient condition for explaining the lack of democracy in Muslim-majority societies. There needs to be a conscious effort to build a democratic culture according to Islamic values. Just as authoritarian leaders employ religious scholars to justify their rules with Islamic values, democracy supporters need to use the same values to point to Islam's liberating potential.

The critical element is man's vicegerent status that implies free will, individual choice, and responsibility to correct injustices. There is considerable evidence that citizens in the Muslim world have employed this element over different periods. Numerous uprisings, rebellions, and revolutions seeking justice and democracy unfolded in the past century in all corners of the Muslim world. The discourses of order and security and Islam's authoritarian interpretations were instrumental in crushing these democratic rebellions.

We need to closely examine the discourses of freedom and better understand how religion shapes Muslim political attitudes. An important question that could be explored in future studies is why the liberation discourse did not succeed, whereas discourses of order and obedience prevailed. One answer to this question concerns the naive assumption about forbearance. That is, for so long, pious Muslims assumed that just for declaring to be a believer, by obtaining the blessing of religious scholars, or paying lip service to Islamic principles, a ruler would constrain himself and avoid tyranny. In reality, rulers have rarely followed forbearance norms, except for some exceptional figures like Muhammad, 'Umar, and 'Ali. It is crucial to understand these dynamics and related perceptions in the Muslim world. Examining the synergies between discourses of justice and ideological and structural conditions inhibiting their democratic potential will provide valuable new insights about the democracy question in the Muslim world.

In conclusion, if we define culture as the total sum of individual values, orientations, preferences, and attitudes, it should be clear that Islamic justice values provide great potential for democracy's acceptability and implementation. This is not to argue that only pious individuals make up the citizenry of Muslim-majority societies. Quite the contrary, there are both pious and less religious individuals in Muslim-majority societies as well as atheists and adherents of other faiths as in any society. Notwithstanding the differences in piety and faith of communities among the citizenry in the Muslim world, Islam is a formidable social force, even among the less religious. Its presence is felt in every corner of life, including the political sphere. Thus, Muslim democratization will have to pass through the gate of Islam to survive.[13] Islamic justice discourses will be the primary key to unlocking this gate with their impressive presence and long-lasting legacies.

Appendix A

TABLE A5.1 LIST OF JOURNALS ARCHIVED IN İLEM (1960–2010)

Journal	Publication Dates	Volumes
1960–1980		
Yeniden Milli Mücadele	1970–1980	528
Büyük Doğu	1943–1978	512
Diriliş	1960–1992	396
Hilal	1958–1993	367
Sebil	1976–1992	269
İslamın İlk Emri Oku	1961–1979	209
Hareket	1939–1982	187
Edebiyat	1969–1984	157
İlahi Işık	1966–1973	135
Tohum	1963–1979	115
İslam	1956–1976	108
Sönmez	1964–1972	77
Selamet	1962–1963	67
Fedai	1963–1979	64
Milli Gençlik	1963–1979	56
Kriter	1976–1984	48
Nesil	1976–1980	48

(*Continued*)

TABLE A5.1 (*Continued*)

Journal	Publication Dates	Volumes
İslam Medeniyeti	1967–1982	44
Şura	1978	41
Tevhid	1978–1979	32
Vesika	1975–1977	31
Çatı	1975–1978	30
Gölge	1976–1978	14
Akıncılar	1979–1980	12
Zülfikar	1964	11
Sancak	1967–1968	10
Özlem	1961–?	9
Uhuvvet	1964	9
Şule	1962–1963	8
1980–2010		
Kudüs	2003–2005	7
Bilgi ve Hikmet	1993–1995	12
Bilgi ve Düşünce	2002–2003	14
Yeni Zemin	1993–1994	18
Yeni Yeryüzü	1993–1995	20
İnsan	1985–2000	33
Bilge Adamlar/Adamlar	2002–present	44
Vahdet	1996–2000	48
Değişim	1993–1999	61
Anlayış	2003–2010	84
Özgün İrade	2004–present	152
Umran	1991–present	280
Haksöz	1991–present	320
İktibas	1981–present	464

Source: İLEM Archives.

TABLE A6.1 CHARACTERISTICS OF THE INTERVIEWEES

Interview Number	Nickname	Gender	Age	Occupation	Member of Islamist Organization
1	Cüneyt	Male	25	Medical doctor	NO
2	Türkan	Female	34	Graduate student/Dorm manager	NO

(*Continued*)

TABLE A6.1 (Continued)					
Interview Number	Nickname	Gender	Age	Occupation	Member of Islamist Organization
3	Fatma	Female	22	Undergraduate student	NO
4	Tarık	Male	27	Graduate student/ Research assistant	YES
5	Kadir	Male	29	Graduate student/ Research assistant	YES
6	Kemal	Male	20s	Graduate student	YES
7	Şener	Male	20s	Graduate student	YES
8	Filiz	Female	37	Unemployed	YES
9	Engin	Male	50	Worker	YES
10	Murat	Male	24	Graduate student	NO
11	Kartal	Male	34	Worker	YES
12	Ayşen	Female	22	Student	NO
13	Ferit	Male	20s	Worker	YES
14	Ayhan	Male	24	Doctor	NO
15	Talat	Male	19	Student	YES
16	Hale	Female	20s	Student/Part-time work	YES
17	Ferdi	Male	34	Worker	YES
18	Mesut	Male	32	Small business owner	YES
19	Ali	Male	24	Graduate student	NO
20	Ediz	Male	20s	Public employee	NO

Note: Interviewees' names are changed for confidentiality purposes.

TABLE A7.1 FIXED EFFECTS FOR TABLE 7.1				
	Equation 1 Distributive Preferences	Equation 2 Self-direction	Equation 3 Self-determination	Equation 4 Support for Democracy
Algeria	0.122***	0.041	−0.022	−0.116***
	(0.013)	(0.028)	(0.013)	(0.015)
Azerbaijan	0.020	0.315***	−0.081***	−0.170***
	(0.011)	(0.023)	(0.011)	(0.012)
Bangladesh	0.061***	0.441***	0.088***	−0.045***
	(0.012)	(0.025)	(0.012)	(0.013)
Bosnia	0.009	0.075*	−0.062***	−0.088***
	(0.016)	(0.034)	(0.016)	(0.018)

(*Continued*)

TABLE A7.1 (Continued)

	Equation 1 Distributive Preferences	Equation 2 Self-direction	Equation 3 Self-determination	Equation 4 Support for Democracy
Palestine	0.084***	0.097***	0.046***	−0.160***
	(0.013)	(0.028)	(0.013)	(0.015)
Indonesia	0.023	0.196***	0.041**	−0.116***
	(0.013)	(0.029)	(0.013)	(0.015)
Iran	−0.057***	0.253***	0.073***	−0.189***
	(0.012)	(0.027)	(0.012)	(0.014)
Iraq	0.093***	−0.015	0.032*	−0.135***
	(0.013)	(0.027)	(0.013)	(0.014)
Kazakhstan	0.047***	0.058*	−0.001	−0.158***
	(0.013)	(0.027)	(0.013)	(0.014)
Jordan	0.140***	0.099***	0.024	−0.139***
	(0.012)	(0.027)	(0.012)	(0.014)
Kyrgyzstan	0.009	0.167***	0.051***	−0.297***
	(0.012)	(0.026)	(0.012)	(0.014)
Lebanon	0.037*	0.083**	−0.025	−0.226***
	(0.015)	(0.031)	(0.015)	(0.016)
Libya	0.113***	0.021	0.083***	−0.105***
	(0.012)	(0.026)	(0.012)	(0.014)
Malaysia	−0.014	0.403***	0.020	−0.160***
	(0.012)	(0.026)	(0.012)	(0.014)
Mali	0.067***	0.021	−0.028	−0.098***
	(0.016)	(0.034)	(0.016)	(0.018)
Morocco	0.058***	0.199***	−0.078***	−0.017
	(0.016)	(0.034)	(0.016)	(0.018)
Nigeria	0.072***	0.013	0.023*	−0.093***
	(0.011)	(0.023)	(0.011)	(0.012)
Pakistan	0.027*	0.130***	0.012	−0.241***
	(0.013)	(0.027)	(0.013)	(0.014)
Tunisia	0.102***	0.227***	0.042**	−0.076***
	(0.013)	(0.028)	(0.013)	(0.015)
Turkey	−0.055***	0.066**	−0.020	−0.135***
	(0.010)	(0.022)	(0.010)	(0.012)
Burkina Faso	0.076***	−0.059	−0.132***	−0.020
	(0.017)	(0.037)	(0.017)	(0.020)

(Continued)

Appendix A / 165

TABLE A7.1 (*Continued*)

	Equation 1 Distributive Preferences	Equation 2 Self-direction	Equation 3 Self-determination	Equation 4 Support for Democracy
Uzbekistan	−0.035**	0.243***	0.103***	−0.040**
	(0.012)	(0.026)	(0.012)	(0.014)
Yemen	0.163***	−0.023	0.114***	−0.113***
	(0.014)	(0.031)	(0.014)	(0.016)
Wave 5	0.006	0.084***	0.033***	0.004
	(0.007)	(0.015)	(0.007)	(0.008)
Wave 6	−0.015**	0.068***	0.031***	−0.020***
	(0.005)	(0.010)	(0.005)	(0.005)
N	26,170	26,170	26,170	26,170
R^2	9%	11%	8.40%	9%

Standard errors are in parentheses. * $p < .05$, ** $p < .01$, *** $p < .001$. *Source:* World Values Survey.

TABLE A7.2 FULL RESULTS FOR TABLE 7.3 (MODEL 1)

	Equation 1 Distributive Preferences	Equation 2 Self-direction	Equation 3 Self-determination	Equation 4 Support for Procedural Democracy
Religiosity	0.035***	−0.261***	0.072***	0.035***
	(0.008)	(0.018)	(0.008)	(0.010)
Distributive preferences	—	—	—	0.062***
				(0.009)
Self-direction	—	—	—	−0.003
				(0.004)
Self-determination	—	—	—	0.170***
				(0.009)
Female	0.007**	−0.022***	−0.015***	−0.008*
	(0.003)	(0.006)	(0.003)	(0.004)
Age	−0.005	−0.015	0.048***	0.029*
	(0.009)	(0.021)	(0.009)	(0.012)
Education	0.011*	0.082***	0.028***	0.036***
	(0.005)	(0.011)	(0.005)	(0.006)
Income	−0.032***	0.004	0.038***	−0.043***
	(0.006)	(0.014)	(0.006)	(0.008)

(*Continued*)

TABLE A7.2 (Continued)

	Equation 1 Distributive Preferences	Equation 2 Self-direction	Equation 3 Self-determination	Equation 4 Support for Procedural Democracy
Personal trust	—	—	—	−0.005
				(0.005)
Egalitarian gender beliefs	—	—	—	−0.017*
				(0.008)
Political interest	—	—	—	−0.001
				(0.006)
Azerbaijan	−0.114***	0.240***	−0.096***	−0.060***
	(0.010)	(0.024)	(0.010)	(0.014)
Palestine	−0.028**	0.066**	0.052***	−0.039**
	(0.010)	(0.024)	(0.010)	(0.014)
Indonesia	−0.076***	0.182***	0.078***	0.058***
	(0.012)	(0.026)	(0.012)	(0.015)
Iran	−0.158***	0.238***	0.111***	0.011
	(0.011)	(0.025)	(0.011)	(0.014)
Iraq	−0.020*	−0.041	0.039***	0.007
	(0.010)	(0.023)	(0.010)	(0.013)
Kazakhstan	−0.067***	0.037	0.012	−0.001
	(0.011)	(0.024)	(0.011)	(0.014)
Jordan	0.029**	0.070**	0.029**	−0.122***
	(0.010)	(0.022)	(0.010)	(0.013)
Kyrgyzstan	−0.103***	0.144***	0.062***	−0.168***
	(0.010)	(0.022)	(0.010)	(0.013)
Lebanon	−0.078***	0.054	−0.014	−0.214***
	(0.012)	(0.028)	(0.012)	(0.016)
Libya	0.003	−0.002	0.090***	−0.029*
	(0.009)	(0.021)	(0.009)	(0.012)
Malaysia	−0.119***	0.379***	0.040***	−0.066***
	(0.010)	(0.022)	(0.010)	(0.013)
Mali	−0.034*	−0.002	0.008	0.030
	(0.014)	(0.032)	(0.014)	(0.019)
Morocco	−0.040**	0.180***	−0.045**	0.040*
	(0.014)	(0.032)	(0.014)	(0.019)

(Continued)

TABLE A7.2 (Continued)				
	Equation 1 Distributive Preferences	Equation 2 Self-direction	Equation 3 Self-determination	Equation 4 Support for Procedural Democracy
Nigeria	−0.040***	0.005	0.003	−0.092***
	(0.009)	(0.021)	(0.009)	(0.012)
Pakistan	−0.085***	0.119***	0.014	0.021
	(0.010)	(0.023)	(0.010)	(0.013)
Tunisia	−0.011	0.200***	0.052***	0.040**
	(0.011)	(0.024)	(0.011)	(0.014)
Turkey	−0.156***	0.044*	0.032***	0.035**
	(0.009)	(0.021)	(0.009)	(0.012)
Burkina Faso	−0.027	−0.080*	−0.096***	0.085***
	(0.016)	(0.036)	(0.016)	(0.021)
Uzbekistan	−0.148***	0.214***	0.110***	0.046***
	(0.010)	(0.023)	(0.010)	(0.013)
Yemen	0.050***	−0.052	0.121***	0.111***
	(0.012)	(0.027)	(0.012)	(0.016)
Wave 6	−0.011	−0.011	0.029***	0.012
	(0.006)	(0.015)	(0.007)	(0.009)
Constant	0.653***	0.394***	0.534***	0.617***
	(0.012)	(0.028)	(0.012)	(0.018)
N	21,063	21,063	21,063	21,063
R^2	0.095	0.090	0.074	0.091

Standard errors are in parentheses. * $p < .05$, ** $p < .01$, *** $p < .001$. *Source:* World Values Survey.

TABLE A7.3 FULL RESULTS FOR TABLE 7.3 (MODEL 2)				
	Equation 1 Distributive Preferences	Equation 2 Self-direction	Equation 3 Self-determination	Equation 4 Support for Authoritarianism
Religiosity	0.046***	−0.270***	0.048***	0.020*
	(0.007)	(0.016)	(0.007)	(0.009)
Distributive preferences	—	—	—	−0.061***
				(0.008)
Self-direction	—	—	—	0.002
				(0.003)

(Continued)

TABLE A7.3 (Continued)

	Equation 1 Distributive Preferences	Equation 2 Self-direction	Equation 3 Self-determination	Equation 4 Support for Authoritarianism
Self-determination	—	—	—	−0.039***
				(0.008)
Female	0.005	−0.020***	−0.016***	0.016***
	(0.003)	(0.006)	(0.003)	(0.003)
Age	0.005	−0.028	0.047***	−0.057***
	(0.009)	(0.019)	(0.009)	(0.010)
Education	0.015**	0.085***	0.029***	−0.059***
	(0.005)	(0.010)	(0.005)	(0.005)
Income	−0.021***	0.004	0.039***	0.038***
	(0.006)	(0.013)	(0.006)	(0.007)
Personal trust	—	—	—	0.011*
				(0.004)
Egalitarian gender beliefs	—	—	—	0.095***
				(0.006)
Political interest	—	—	—	0.008
				(0.005)
Algeria	0.144***	0.079*	−0.021	−0.465***
	(0.014)	(0.031)	(0.014)	(0.017)
Azerbaijan	0.022	0.340***	−0.090***	−0.432***
	(0.012)	(0.025)	(0.011)	(0.014)
Bangladesh	0.070***	0.486***	0.069***	−0.540***
	(0.013)	(0.028)	(0.013)	(0.015)
Bosnia	0.012	0.107**	−0.054***	−0.249***
	(0.017)	(0.035)	(0.016)	(0.019)
Palestine	0.090***	0.129***	0.043**	−0.332***
	(0.014)	(0.030)	(0.014)	(0.016)
Indonesia	0.026	0.218***	0.038**	−0.213***
	(0.014)	(0.030)	(0.014)	(0.017)
Iran	−0.055***	0.278***	0.070***	−0.300***
	(0.013)	(0.028)	(0.013)	(0.016)
Iraq	0.098***	0.017	0.028*	−0.374***
	(0.013)	(0.029)	(0.013)	(0.016)

(Continued)

TABLE A7.3 (Continued)

	Equation 1 Distributive Preferences	Equation 2 Self-direction	Equation 3 Self-determination	Equation 4 Support for Authoritarianism
Kazakhstan	0.053***	0.089**	−0.006	−0.312***
	(0.013)	(0.029)	(0.013)	(0.016)
Jordan	0.143***	0.136***	0.017	−0.351***
	(0.013)	(0.028)	(0.013)	(0.016)
Kyrgyzstan	0.015	0.199***	0.047***	−0.130***
	(0.013)	(0.027)	(0.013)	(0.015)
Lebanon	0.030*	0.110***	−0.033*	−0.198***
	(0.015)	(0.033)	(0.015)	(0.018)
Libya	0.117***	0.050	0.080***	−0.280***
	(0.013)	(0.027)	(0.013)	(0.015)
Malaysia	−0.009	0.430***	0.017	−0.263***
	(0.013)	(0.027)	(0.013)	(0.015)
Mali	0.073***	0.046	−0.036*	−0.350***
	(0.017)	(0.035)	(0.016)	(0.020)
Morocco	0.063***	0.220***	−0.085***	−0.516***
	(0.017)	(0.035)	(0.017)	(0.020)
Nigeria	0.076***	0.043	0.019	−0.329***
	(0.011)	(0.024)	(0.011)	(0.013)
Pakistan	0.033*	0.165***	0.008	−0.264***
	(0.013)	(0.029)	(0.013)	(0.016)
Tunisia	0.112***	0.268***	0.040**	−0.300***
	(0.014)	(0.030)	(0.014)	(0.016)
Turkey	−0.051***	0.099***	−0.026*	−0.293***
	(0.011)	(0.024)	(0.011)	(0.013)
Burkina Faso	0.084***	−0.043	−0.127***	−0.407***
	(0.018)	(0.039)	(0.018)	(0.021)
Uzbekistan	−0.028*	0.275***	0.097***	−0.260***
	(0.013)	(0.028)	(0.013)	(0.016)
Yemen	0.172***	0.016	0.110***	−0.466***
	(0.015)	(0.033)	(0.015)	(0.018)
Wave 5	0.006	0.089***	0.031***	0.133***
	(0.007)	(0.015)	(0.007)	(0.008)
Wave 6	−0.018***	0.066***	0.029***	0.088***
	(0.005)	(0.010)	(0.005)	(0.006)

(Continued)

TABLE A7.3 (Continued)

	Equation 1 Distributive Preferences	Equation 2 Self-direction	Equation 3 Self-determination	Equation 4 Support for Authoritarianism
Constant	0.525***	0.268***	0.564***	0.655***
	(0.011)	(0.024)	(0.011)	(0.015)
N	24,687	24,687	24,687	24,687
R^2	0.087	0.112	0.081	0.187

Standard errors are in parentheses. * $p < .05$, ** $p < .01$, *** $p < .001$. *Source:* World Values Survey.

TABLE A7.4 FULL ESTIMATION RESULTS FOR TABLE 7.4 (MODEL 1)

	Equation 1 Distributive Preferences	Equation 2 Self-direction	Equation 3 Support for Democracy
Sharia	0.033***	0.030	−0.023*
	(0.008)	(0.017)	(0.010)
Distributive preferences	—	—	−0.018
			(0.016)
Self-direction	—	—	−0.016*
			(0.008)
Personal trust	—	—	0.002
			(0.007)
Egalitarian gender beliefs	—	—	−0.063***
			(0.013)
Political interest	—	—	0.040***
			(0.010)
Female	0.007	0.003	−0.014*
	(0.005)	(0.011)	(0.006)
Age	0.061**	−0.010	0.026
	(0.019)	(0.038)	(0.022)
Education	0.046***	0.047**	0.009
	(0.008)	(0.017)	(0.010)
Income	−0.006	0.054*	−0.006
	(0.013)	(0.026)	(0.015)
Bangladesh	−0.077***	0.525***	0.064***
	(0.010)	(0.021)	(0.013)

(*Continued*)

TABLE A7.4 (Continued)

	Equation 1 Distributive Preferences	Equation 2 Self-direction	Equation 3 Support for Democracy
Indonesia	−0.088***	0.150***	−0.059***
	(0.011)	(0.023)	(0.013)
Iraq	−0.068***	0.004	−0.014
	(0.009)	(0.018)	(0.011)
Jordan	0.001	−0.003	−0.014
	(0.010)	(0.020)	(0.011)
Nigeria	−0.014	0.028	0.020
	(0.012)	(0.025)	(0.015)
Pakistan	−0.184***	−0.043	−0.033*
	(0.012)	(0.023)	(0.014)
Constant	0.618***	0.090***	0.888***
	(0.013)	(0.026)	(0.020)
N	5,500	5,500	5,500
R^2	0.082	0.193	0.030

Standard errors are in parentheses. * $p < .05$, ** $p < .01$, *** $p < .001$. Source: World Values Survey.

TABLE A7.5 FULL ESTIMATION RESULTS FOR TABLE 7.4 (MODEL 2)

	Equation 1 Distributive Preferences	Equation 2 Self-direction	Equation 3 Self-determination	Equation 4 Support for Democracy
Religion vs. science	0.049***	−0.072***	0.039***	0.036***
	(0.007)	(0.015)	(0.007)	(0.008)
Distributive preferences	—	—	—	0.052***
				(0.010)
Self-direction	—	—	—	0.004
				(0.005)
Self-determination	—	—	—	0.125***
				(0.010)
Personal trust	—	—	—	−0.017**
				(0.005)
Egalitarian gender beliefs	—	—	—	−0.003
				(0.009)

(Continued)

TABLE A7.5 (Continued)

	Equation 1 Distributive Preferences	Equation 2 Self-direction	Equation 3 Self-determination	Equation 4 Support for Democracy
Political interest	—	—	—	0.022**
				(0.007)
Female	0.003	−0.014	−0.024***	0.008
	(0.003)	(0.007)	(0.003)	(0.004)
Age	0.004	−0.048*	0.074***	0.024
	(0.011)	(0.024)	(0.011)	(0.013)
Education	0.025***	0.038**	0.027***	0.031***
	(0.006)	(0.013)	(0.006)	(0.007)
Income	−0.044***	0.009	0.053***	−0.006
	(0.008)	(0.017)	(0.008)	(0.010)
Azerbaijan	−0.020*	−0.085***	0.059***	−0.028*
	(0.010)	(0.022)	(0.010)	(0.012)
Palestine	0.020*	0.032	0.046***	−0.038**
	(0.010)	(0.021)	(0.010)	(0.012)
Iraq	−0.041***	−0.058**	0.027**	0.023*
	(0.009)	(0.020)	(0.009)	(0.011)
Kazakhstan	−0.089***	0.061**	0.035***	−0.134***
	(0.010)	(0.022)	(0.010)	(0.012)
Jordan	−0.107***	0.281***	−0.088***	−0.080***
	(0.011)	(0.024)	(0.011)	(0.013)
Kyrgyzstan	−0.036***	0.041	0.070***	−0.051***
	(0.010)	(0.023)	(0.010)	(0.013)
Lebanon	−0.070***	0.037	0.020	−0.042**
	(0.011)	(0.025)	(0.011)	(0.014)
Libya	−0.103***	0.141***	0.075***	−0.178***
	(0.010)	(0.021)	(0.010)	(0.012)
Malaysia	−0.077***	0.028	0.000	−0.120***
	(0.012)	(0.027)	(0.012)	(0.015)
Morocco	−0.006	−0.049*	0.103***	−0.005
	(0.009)	(0.020)	(0.009)	(0.011)
Nigeria	−0.127***	0.315***	0.086***	−0.035**
	(0.010)	(0.023)	(0.010)	(0.013)

(Continued)

TABLE A7.5 (Continued)

	Equation 1 Distributive Preferences	Equation 2 Self-direction	Equation 3 Self-determination	Equation 4 Support for Democracy
Pakistan	−0.071***	0.204***	0.039**	0.113***
	(0.013)	(0.029)	(0.013)	(0.016)
Tunisia	−0.016	0.168***	0.059***	0.021
	(0.010)	(0.023)	(0.010)	(0.013)
Turkey	−0.151***	0.047*	0.033***	−0.017
	(0.009)	(0.021)	(0.009)	(0.012)
Uzbekistan	−0.140***	0.249***	0.124***	0.071***
	(0.010)	(0.023)	(0.010)	(0.013)
Yemen	0.035**	−0.094***	0.139***	−0.005
	(0.012)	(0.026)	(0.012)	(0.014)
Constant	0.631***	0.299***	0.561***	0.652***
	(0.011)	(0.024)	(0.011)	(0.016)
N	15,106	15,106	15,106	15,106
R^2	0.094	0.080	0.071	0.085

Standard errors are in parentheses. * $p < .05$, ** $p < .01$, *** $p < .001$. *Source:* World Values Survey.

TABLE A8.1 SURVEY INDICATORS OF POLITICAL AND SOCIAL JUSTICE

Perceptions of Political Justice

State of democracy	Q 504 If you were to evaluate the state of democracy and human rights in your country today, would you say that they are … ?	Very good (1) to very bad (5)
Political trust	Q201 I will name a number of institutions, and I would like you to tell me to what extent you trust each of them: Government	Not at all (1) to a great extent (4)
Access to public officials	Q205 Based on your actual experience, how difficult or easy is it to obtain access to an official to file a complaint when you feel that your rights are violated?	Very easy (1) to very difficult (5)*
Corruption	Q210 Do you think that there is corruption within the state's institutions and agencies?	Yes (1), no (0)

Perceptions of Social Justice

Economic condition	Q101 How would you evaluate the current economic situation in your country?	Very good (1) to very bad (4)

(*Continued*)

TABLE A8.1 (Continued)

Perceptions of Social Justice

Employment status	Q.1005 Are you employed/unemployed/self-employed/etc.?	Unemployed (1), other (0)
Distributive preferences**	Q 240 Where would you put yourself on a scale where 0 means that the government should impose higher taxes on the rich to generate resources to spend on the poor, and where 10 means that the rich already create job opportunities and economic growth, and that the government shall lessen the taxes they pay and allow them to retain more of their net worth?	Lessen the tax burden (1), impose higher taxes (11)*

* Scale reversed or modified from the original coding. ** Only asked in Wave 3. *Source:* Arab Barometer, Waves 2 and 3.

TABLE A8.2 DESCRIPTIVE STATISTICS OF THE VARIABLES IN THE MODELS

Variable	Obs.	Mean	Std. Dev.	Min	Max	Description
Protest participation	25,668	0.19	0.39	0	1	1 Yes / 0 No
State of democracy	24,851	3.04	1.10	1	5	1 Very good / 5 Very bad
Distrust in government	25,447	2.59	1.10	1	4	1 A great extent / 4 Not at all
Access to officials	25,617	3.45	1.22	1	5	1 Very easy / 5 Very difficult
Corruption perception	24,353	0.85	0.36	0	1	1 Yes / 0 No
Economic condition	25,857	2.84	0.88	1	4	1 Very good / 4 Very bad
Unemployed	26,183	0.10	0.30	0	1	1 Yes / 0 No
Prayer frequency	25,762	4.56	0.92	1	5	1 Never / 5 Daily
Koran readership	25,632	3.72	1.19	1	5	1 Never / 5 Daily
Religiosity index	25,561	7.29	1.74	1	9	1 Not Religious / 9 Very Religious
Age	26,185	37.28	13.50	18	89	Self-reported age

(*Continued*)

TABLE A8.2 (Continued)

Variable	Obs.	Mean	Std. Dev.	Min	Max	Description
Female	26,238	0.49	0.50	0	1	1 Female 0 Male
Education	26,149	3.66	1.71	1	7	1 No education 7 Advanced degree
Household income	25,549	2.24	0.95	1	4	1 Income not sufficient 4 Can Save

TABLE A8.3 FIXED EFFECTS FOR TABLE 8.2

	Model 1 Waves 2 and 3	Model 2 Wave 2	Model 3 Wave 3	Model 4 Distributive Preferences	Model 5 Prayer and Koran Reader
Egypt	−0.259**	−0.791***	0.610***	0.571***	−0.290***
	(0.105)	(0.150)	(0.170)	(0.178)	(0.106)
Iraq	0.256***	−0.0328	0.773***	0.749***	0.239***
	(0.092)	(0.119)	(0.157)	(0.164)	(0.093)
Jordan	−0.926***	−0.965***	−0.573***	−0.618***	−0.955***
	(0.111)	(0.153)	(0.176)	(0.184)	(0.112)
Kuwait	0.402***	—	0.828***	0.851***	0.383***
	(0.116)		(0.157)	(0.164)	(0.116)
Lebanon	0.575***	0.0595	1.326***	1.259***	0.539***
	(0.098)	(0.128)	(0.165)	(0.172)	(0.099)
Libya	0.938***	—	1.593***	1.580***	0.920***
	(0.104)		(0.153)	(0.161)	(0.104)
Morocco	0.321***	—	0.953***	0.891***	0.303**
	(0.120)		(0.162)	(0.170)	(0.121)
Palestine	0.906***	0.436***	1.588***	1.564***	0.874***
	(0.090)	(0.120)	(0.150)	(0.158)	(0.091)
Saudi Arabia	−2.515***	−2.732***	—	—	−2.526***
	(0.280)	(0.287)			(0.281)
Sudan	0.825***	0.599***	1.241***	1.197***	0.807***
	(0.089)	(0.114)	(0.157)	(0.165)	(0.089)
Tunisia	0.222**	0.0960	0.711***	0.682***	0.175*
	(0.098)	(0.125)	(0.168)	(0.176)	(0.101)

(Continued)

TABLE A8.3 (Continued)

	Model 1 Waves 2 and 3	Model 2 Wave 2	Model 3 Wave 3	Model 4 Distributive Preferences	Model 5 Prayer and Koran Reader
Yemen	1.720***	0.734***	2.898***	2.892***	1.708***
	(0.087)	(0.118)	(0.149)	(0.157)	(0.087)
Wave 3	0.0982**	—	—	—	0.0924**
	(0.041)				(0.041)

* $p < .1$, ** $p < .05$, *** $p < .01$. *Source:* Arab Barometer, Waves 2 and 3.

TABLE A8.4 INTERACTION EFFECTS (LOGISTIC REGRESSION)

Variables	Coefficients
State of democracy	−0.0145
	(0.080)
Distrust in government	0.190**
	(0.088)
Access to state	0.0618
	(0.065)
Perception of corruption	−0.216
	(0.240)
Evaluation of economic situation	0.0642
	(0.103)
Unemployed	0.0750
	(0.230)
Religiosity index	0.0282
Interactions with Religiosity	
State of democracy	−0.00221
	(0.011)
Distrust in government	−0.0209*
	(0.012)
Access to state	−0.00232
	(0.009)
Perception of corruption	0.0185
	(0.032)
Evaluation of economic situation	0.00221
	(0.014)
Unemployed	0.0113
	(0.032)

(Continued)

TABLE A8.4 (Continued)

Variables	Coefficients
Age	−0.0115***
	(0.002)
Female	−0.715***
	(0.038)
Education	0.157***
	(0.012)
Income	0.139***
Constant	−2.601***
	(0.376)
FIXED EFFECTS	YES
Observations	20,941

Standard errors in parentheses. * $p < .1$, ** $p < .05$, *** $p < .01$. This table is the basis for Figure 8.4. *Source:* Arab Barometer.

TABLE A8.5 LOGISTIC REGRESSION ESTIMATES FOR PROTEST PARTICIPATION (EGYPT AND TUNISIA)

	Model 1 Egypt, Full Sample	Model 2 Egypt, Highly Religious	Model 3 Tunisia, Full Sample	Model 4 Tunisia, Highly Religious
State of democracy	−0.0990	−0.130	−0.351***	−0.453**
	(0.134)	(0.152)	(0.126)	(0.185)
Distrust in government	0.125	0.230*	0.235**	0.238
	(0.125)	(0.137)	(0.105)	(0.160)
Access to state	0.332***	0.442***	−0.129	−0.0837
	(0.115)	(0.133)	(0.083)	(0.135)
Corruption	0.603	0.499	1.054***	1.209***
	(0.396)	(0.432)	(0.290)	(0.444)
Economic situation	−0.0171	−0.0867	0.413***	0.515**
	(0.173)	(0.196)	(0.143)	(0.222)
Unemployed	−0.289	−0.719	−0.0834	−0.702
	(0.513)	(0.790)	(0.257)	(0.496)
Religiosity index	0.151*	—	0.113**	—
	(0.090)		(0.045)	
Age	−0.0114	−0.00657	−0.0405***	−0.0337***
	(0.010)	(0.010)	(0.008)	(0.012)
Female	0.292***	0.259***	0.178***	0.159*
	(0.074)	(0.083)	(0.059)	(0.094)

(*Continued*)

TABLE A8.5 (*Continued*)

	Model 1 Egypt, Full Sample	Model 2 Egypt, Highly Religious	Model 3 Tunisia, Full Sample	Model 4 Tunisia, Highly Religious
Education	0.199	0.167	0.160	−0.0570
	(0.128)	(0.146)	(0.110)	(0.163)
Income	−1.154***	−1.320***	−1.934***	−2.308***
	(0.281)	(0.330)	(0.236)	(0.359)
Constant	−5.876***	−4.728***	−2.142***	−1.088
	(1.102)	(1.088)	(0.791)	(1.212)
Observations	1,034	701	884	400

Standard errors in parentheses. * $p < .1$, ** $p < .05$, *** $p < .01$. This table is the basis for Figure 8.5. *Source:* Arab Barometer, Wave 2.

Appendix B

Note: This fieldwork is supported by Global Religion Research Initiative at Notre Dame University (Award #BG5225). University Research Compliance Office at Kansas State University has reviewed the field proposal and approved it (IRB approval #8776).

INTERVIEW QUESTIONS

Note: The interviews were nonstructured. Therefore, some variation in the question wording was introduced and some additional questions were asked during the interviews.

1. Nowadays, people talk about justice a lot. Do you also find yourself talking about justice lately?
2. How do you define justice and social justice?
3. Does this definition include an economic dimension or a political dimension? Can you explain?
4. Do you ever feel that justice is violated in your workplace? In social life? Among your friends? In politics? Can you talk about these instances?
5. Do you think religious people are always just?
6. Does Islam as a religious system promote justice? What kind? Can you provide any examples from Koran or Islamic History?
7. Is social justice more likely in an Islamic state? Why, can you explain?
8. Assume that you are presented with two choices. In each option, the leaders will implement social justice policies to help the poor, reduce poverty and inequality, and create impartial courts. Which one would you prefer: (1) An authoritarian regime ruled by religious leaders who want to rule according

to the Islamic principles. (2) A democracy but secular regime where religion plays a lesser role in government.
9. Can there be a Muslim democracy? If yes, do you think this regime will be better in establishing social, economic, and political justice?
10. Do you consider yourself a religious person? What does this involve as a practice and identity? Can you elaborate?
11. Some people talk about a Damascus model while others refer to the Medina model in terms of political formulas in Muslim history. Are you familiar with this debate? If not, here is a description. The Damascus model refers to establishing power and order at the expense of social justice and Islamic ethics whereas the Medina model refers to Islam's ethical values. Which position do you find yourself closer to? Can you explain?
12. Do you think social justice policies are more likely to be successful in secular democracies or in Muslim democracies? Can you explain?
13. Would you rather support a benevolent dictator than a nonreligious democrat if the benevolent dictator rules the country according to Islamic principles?
14. Do you feel responsibility for removing a religious but nondemocratic leader from power if this ruler is religious in the name of justice? Why or why not? What would you do?

Notes

CHAPTER 1

1. A detailed review of studies in this field are presented in Chapter 2. Here, I present only the main contours of the debate.

2. Lewis, "Islam and Liberal Democracy: Historical Overview"; Kedourie, *Democracy and Arab Political Culture*; Huntington, "Clash of Civilizations."

3. This view is largely informed by the nineteenth-century Islamists, including al-Afghānī, Namık Kemal, Muhammad Iqbal, Mehmed Akif, and Muhammad Abduh. Contemporary scholars use insights from the works of these pioneers to make the case for religious democracy through flexible interpretations of religious texts or religious notions of freedom and rationality, public interest, or justice. Some of the influential scholars in this vein include Rāshid al-Ghannūshī, Mohammed Arkoun, Abdolkarim Soroush, and Nurcholish Madjid. See Ayoob, *Many Faces of Political Islam*, for an account of modernist Islam, and Kurzman, *Liberal Islam*, for the original writings of these intellectuals.

4. Ciftci, Wuthrich, and Shamaileh, "Islam, Religious Outlooks, and Support."

5. For notable exceptions, see Thompson, *Justice Interrupted*; Tessler, *Islam and Politics*.

6. Statistical studies of Muslim political attitudes engage in this endeavor, but their main focus is on religiosity and political attitudes. See Tessler, *Islam and Politics*, for an overview of these studies. There are some studies that look at values and support for democracy in the Arab region (Ciftci, "Secular-Islamist Cleavage, Values, and Support"; Berger, "Sharī'a, Islamism and Arab Support").

7. El Fadl, *Islam and the Challenge of Democracy*; Sachedina, *Islamic Roots of Democratic Pluralism*; An-Náim, *Islam and the Secular State*; Filali-Ansary, "Muslims and Democracy"; Hashemi, *Islam, Secularism, and Liberal Democracy*.

8. El Fadl, *Islam and the Challenge of Democracy*.

9. March, *Caliphate of Man.*
10. March, *Caliphate of Man.*
11. An-Náim, *Islam and the Secular State.*
12. Khanani, "Contemporary Islamism and the Sacralization of Democracy."
13. Hashemi, *Islam, Secularism, and Liberal Democracy.*
14. Menchik, *Islam and Democracy in Indonesia.*
15. El Fadl, *Islam and the Challenge of Democracy.*
16. I use the term *Muslim political practice* in its broadest sense to include social, economic, and political acts of Muslims throughout centuries including its contemporary displays in protest movements and political organizations.
17. El Fadl, *Islam and the Challenge of Democracy.*
18. As noted above, there are numerous studies that deal with theological and conceptual foundations of Islamic justice including but not limited to An-Náim, *Islam and the Secular State*; Hashemi, *Islam, Secularism, and Liberal Democracy*; Khanani, "Contemporary Islamism and the Sacralization of Democracy"; Menchik, *Islam and Democracy in Indonesia.*
19. Abdelkader, *Social Justice in Islam.* Also see Khadduri, *Islamic Conception of Justice*; Harvey, *Qur'an and the Just Society*; Mirakhor and Askari, *Conceptions of Justice.*
20. Abdelkader, *Social Justice in Islam.* Scholars like El Fadl (*Islam and the Challenge of Democracy*) and Shahab Ahmed (*What Is Islam?*) also emphasize the importance of maṣlaḥa as a legal principle that has far-reaching implications in the political realm.
21. Darling, *Social Justice and Political Power.*
22. The idea behind the circle of justice is expressed succinctly in the following words: "No power without troops, / No troops without money, / No money without prosperity, / No prosperity without justice and good administration" (Darling, *Social Justice and Political Power*).
23. Darling, *Social Justice and Political Power.*
24. Thompson, *Justice Interrupted.*
25. Nader Hashemi's work partly addresses this shortcoming by providing a theoretical account of the association between religiously informed struggles and democracy. However, Islamic justice is not Hashemi's main scholarly concern; rather, he is interested in understanding the role of religious mobilization and struggles in constructing an important condition for democracy, namely, secularism.
26. Maguire, "Religious Influences on Justice Theory."
27. Lorenz, "Emergence of Social Justice."
28. Smith, *Emergence of Liberation Theology*; Goizueta, "Liberation Theology 1."
29. Rawls, *Theory of Justice.*
30. Crone, *God's Rule*; Lapidus, *History of Islamic Societies.*
31. Fitna is an Arabic word that means distress or trial. It is more commonly translated as anarchy or civil strife.
32. Khadduri, *Islamic Conception of Justice*, 5.
33. Enayat, *Modern Islamic Political Thought.*
34. Thompson, *Justice Interrupted.*
35. Abrahamian, *Iran between Two Revolutions.*
36. The notion of 'iḥsān is also treated as the foundation of good governance and public policies by Muqtedar Khan (*Islam and Good Governance*).
37. Ciftci, "Islam, Social Justice, and Democracy."
38. Khadduri, *Islamic Conception of Justice.*
39. This term can be defined as governance according to Islamic law or legal politics.

40. Filali-Ansary, "Muslims and Democracy."
41. Kuru, *Islam, Authoritarianism, and Underdevelopment*.
42. Acemoglu and Robinson, *Economic Origins of Dictatorship and Democracy*.
43. El Fadl, *Islam and the Challenge of Democracy*.
44. Kuru, *Islam, Authoritarianism, and Underdevelopment*.
45. An-Náim, *Islam and the Secular State*.
46. Levitsky and Ziblatt, *How Democracies Die*, 106.
47. Levitsky and Ziblatt, *How Democracies Die*, 106.
48. Levitsky and Ziblatt, *How Democracies Die*, 106–107.
49. Abdelkader, *Social Justice in Islam*.
50. Braudel, "Histoire et Sciences Sociales."

CHAPTER 2

1. Schmitter and Karl, "What Democracy Is," 75.
2. Amaeshi, "Decolonizing African Scholarship," para. 6.
3. Amaeshi, "Decolonizing African Scholarship."
4. Said, *Orientalism*.
5. Khanani, "Contemporary Islamism and the Sacralization of Democracy," 16.
6. Chakrabarty, "Provincializing Europe," 28–29.
7. Sen, *Idea of Justice*.
8. Israel, *Radical Enlightenment*.
9. Bourdeau, "Auguste Comte."
10. Said, *Orientalism*.
11. Renan, "Islamism and Science."
12. Keddie, *Islamic Response to Imperialism*.
13. Weber, *The Protestant Ethic and the Spirit of Capitalism*.
14. Gellner, *Muslim Society*; Kedourie, *Democracy and Arab Political Culture*; Huntington, "Clash of Civilizations"; Lewis, "Islam and Liberal Democracy."
15. Huntington, "Clash of Civilizations."
16. Kedourie, *Democracy and Arab Political Culture*, 5–6.
17. Gellner, *Muslim Society*, 1.
18. Lewis, "Islam and Liberal Democracy," sec. 4, para. 7.
19. Gellner, "Islam and Marxism."
20. Gellner, "Islam and Marxism," 5.
21. Gellner, *Muslim Society*; Gellner, "Islam and Marxism."
22. Ahmed uses this term to describe the vast geographic spread of the Islamic civilization (Ahmed, *What Is Islam?*).
23. Kedourie, *Democracy and Arab Political Culture*, 10.
24. Kedourie, *Democracy and Arab Political Culture*, 13.
25. Lewis, "Islam and Liberal Democracy."
26. Lewis, "Freedom and Justice," 39.
27. Lewis, "Freedom and Justice," 40.
28. Lewis, "Islam and Liberal Democracy"; Lewis, "Freedom and Justice."
29. Lewis, "Islam and Liberal Democracy."
30. Lewis, "Islam and Liberal Democracy"; Lewis, "Freedom and Justice."
31. Lewis, "Islam and Liberal Democracy"; Lewis, "Freedom and Justice."
32. Kuru, *Islam, Authoritarianism, and Underdevelopment*.
33. Lewis, "Islam and Liberal Democracy"; Lewis, "Freedom and Justice."

34. Lewis, "Islam and Liberal Democracy"; Lewis, "Freedom and Justice."
35. Lewis, "Islam and Liberal Democracy"; Lewis, "Freedom and Justice."
36. El Fadl, *Islam and the Challenge of Democracy*; Esposito and Voll, *Islam and Democracy*; Filali-Ansary, "Muslims and Democracy."
37. Esposito and Voll, *Islam and Democracy*; Ramadan, *Islam, the West and Challenges of Modernity*; Sachedina, *Islamic Roots of Democratic Pluralism*; El Fadl, *Islam and the Challenge of Democracy*; Hashemi, *Islam, Secularism, and Liberal Democracy*.
38. Esposito and Voll, *Islam and Democracy*; Moaddel, *Islamic Modernism, Nationalism, and Fundamentalism*; March, *Caliphate of Man*.
39. Ramadan, *Islam, the West and Challenges of Modernity*; Sachedina, *Islamic Roots of Democratic Pluralism*; El Fadl, *Islam and the Challenge of Democracy*; Hashemi, *Islam, Secularism, and Liberal Democracy*.
40. Filali-Ansary, "Muslims and Democracy," 30.
41. Esposito and Voll, *Islam and Democracy*.
42. Ayoob, "Political Islam."
43. Iqbal, *Reconstruction of Religious Thought in Islam*, as cited in, Esposito and Voll, *Islam and Democracy*, 29.
44. Esposito and Voll, *Islam and Democracy*, 30.
45. Schmitter and Karl, "What Democracy Is," 78.
46. Acemoglu and Robinson, *Economic Origins of Dictatorship and Democracy*; Tilly, *Contention and Democracy in Europe*.
47. Crone, *God's Rule*; Lapidus, "Separation of State and Religion."
48. Lapidus, "Separation of State and Religion."
49. Thompson, *Justice Interrupted*.
50. An-Náim, *Islam and the Secular State*; El Fadl, *Islam and the Challenge of Democracy*; Hashemi, *Islam, Secularism, and Liberal Democracy*.
51. An-Náim, *Islam and the Secular State*.
52. An-Náim, *Islam and the Secular State*.
53. An-Náim, *Islam and the Secular State*, 284.
54. An-Náim, *Islam and the Secular State*.
55. Hashemi, *Islam, Secularism, and Liberal Democracy*.
56. Hashemi, *Islam, Secularism, and Liberal Democracy*.
57. Hashemi, *Islam, Secularism, and Liberal Democracy*, 2.
58. Hashemi, *Islam, Secularism, and Liberal Democracy*, 34.
59. Filali-Ansary, "Muslims and Democracy."
60. Hashemi, *Islam, Secularism, and Liberal Democracy*, 67.
61. Hashemi, *Islam, Secularism, and Liberal Democracy*, 63.
62. El Fadl, *Islam and the Challenge of Democracy*. This section largely draws from El Fadl's essay. Citations are reserved for specific arguments taken from this essay and direct quotes.
63. El Fadl, *Islam and the Challenge of Democracy*, 4.
64. El Fadl, *Islam and the Challenge of Democracy*, 4–5.
65. El Fadl, *Islam and the Challenge of Democracy*, 5.
66. El Fadl, *Islam and the Challenge of Democracy*, 5–6.
67. El Fadl, *Islam and the Challenge of Democracy*, 6.
68. El Fadl, *Islam and the Challenge of Democracy*, 7.
69. El Fadl, *Islam and the Challenge of Democracy*, 13.
70. El Fadl, *Islam and the Challenge of Democracy*, 13–15; see also Abdelkader, *Social Justice in Islam*.

71. Esposito and Voll, *Islam and Democracy*.
72. Rahman, "Principle of 'Shūrā' and Role of Umma."
73. Al-Sadr, "Introduction to Islamic Political System."
74. El Fadl, *Islam and the Challenge of Democracy*, 18. El Fadl uses similar reasoning for mercy as a religious value. In the Koranic discourse, mercy means being just to oneself and the others by giving everyone their due. Mercy, thus, is related to a sincere perception of others, recognizing their diversity and being tolerant to one another. Like justice, mercy is a foundational principle of democracy that is more significant than procedural antecedents like *ijmā'*.
75. El Fadl, *Islam and the Challenge of Democracy*, 18.
76. Sachedina, *Islamic Roots of Democratic Pluralism*; El Fadl, *Islam and the Challenge of Democracy*.
77. Weber, *The Protestant Ethic and the Spirit of Capitalism*; Renan, "Islamism and Science"; Kedourie, *Democracy and Arab Political Culture*; Lewis, "Islam and Liberal Democracy"; Gellner, *Muslim Society*; Huntington, "Clash of Civilizations."
78. Iqbal, *Reconstruction of Religious Thought in Islam*; Rahman, "Principle of 'Shūrā' and Role of Umma"; for an overview see Esposito and Voll, *Islam and Democracy*.
79. Hashemi, *Islam, Secularism, and Liberal Democracy*.
80. An-Náim, *Islam and the Secular State*.
81. Ramadan, *Islam, the West and Challenges of Modernity*.
82. Sachedina, *Islamic Roots of Democratic Pluralism*.
83. El Fadl, *Islam and the Challenge of Democracy*.
84. Tessler, "Islam and Democracy"; Jamal, "Reassessing Support for Islam and Democracy"; Ciftci, "Modernization, Islam, or Social Capital"; Tessler, Jamal, and Robbins, "New Findings on Arabs and Democracy"; Spierings, "Influence of Islamic Orientations"; Driessen, "Sources of Muslim Democracy."

CHAPTER 3

1. Reported in Balcı, "'Umar (r.a)," accessed on June 22, 2020, available at https://www.lastprophet.info/Umar-r-a-a-leader-crowned-with-truth-and-justice.
2. Crone, *God's Rule*; Lapidus, "Separation of State and Religion."
3. Abdelkader, *Social Justice in Islam*; El Fadl, *Islam and the Challenge of Democracy*; Ahmed, *What Is Islam?*
4. Abdelkader, *Social Justice in Islam*; El Fadl, *Islam and the Challenge of Democracy*.
5. For a detailed account of this proposition, see Ahmed, *What Is Islam?*
6. Kemal, "And Seek Their Council"; Keddie, *Islamic Response to Imperialism*; Khadduri, *Islamic Conception of Justice*.
7. Thompson, *Justice Interrupted*.
8. Qutb, *Social Justice in Islam*; Shariati, "Man and Islam."
9. El-Affendi, *Who Needs an Islamic State?*
10. Khadduri, *Islamic Conception of Justice*.
11. Khadduri has provided a detailed account of the history of conceptions of justice and ideas in his masterpiece, *Islamic Conception of Justice*. The literal, interpretative, and hermeneutical analysis of justice as a central value is usually done in the context of broad questions such as the meaning of Islam (Ahmed, *What Is Islam?*), human rights and democracy (Karagiannis, *New Political Islam*), or Islamist activism (Abdelkader, *Social Justice in Islam*). For notable studies in the semantic analysis of justice in relation to the hermeneutical study of the Koran, see Izutsu, *Ethico-Religious Concepts in the*

Qur'an. Recently, Abbas Mirakhor and Hossein Askari (*Conceptions of Justice*) provided a conceptual evolution of justice from the early period of Islam to the modern age and, in comparison, to the Western conceptions of justice.

12. Ahmed, *What Is Islam?*

13. There is a voluminous literature on religion and politics supporting this statement. Some recent examples include Fish, *Are Muslims Distinctive?* Bloom, Arikan, and Courtemanche, "Religious Social Identity"; Grzymała-Busse, *Nations under God*; Djupe and Claassen, *Evangelical Crackup?* Ciftci, Wuthrich, and Shamaileh, "Islam, Religious Outlooks, and Support."

14. Philpott, "Political Ambivalence of Religion."

15. Al-Mawdudi, "Islam in Transition"; Qutb, *Social Justice in Islam*; Abdelkader, *Social Justice in Islam*; Ahmed, *What Is Islam?* March, *Caliphate of Man*.

16. Khadduri, *Islamic Conception of Justice*.

17. Ahmed, *What Is Islam?*

18. Khadduri, *Islamic Conception of Justice*; Moaddel, *Islamic Modernism, Nationalism, and Fundamentalism*; Ayoob, "Challenging Hegemony."

19. Khadduri, *Islamic Conception of Justice*, 6.

20. Khadduri, *Islamic Conception of Justice*, 6; Mirakhor and Askari, *Conceptions of Justice*, 182–185.

21. Khadduri, *Islamic Conception of Justice*, 6.

22. Some examples include, "Allah witnesses that there is no deity except Him, and [so do] the angels and those of knowledge—[that He is] maintaining [creation] in justice. There is no deity except Him, the Exalted in Might, the Wise" (3:18); "O you who have believed, be persistently standing firm for Allah, witnesses in justice, and do not let the hatred of a people prevent you from being just. Be just; that is nearer to righteousness. And fear Allah; indeed, Allah is Acquainted with what you do" (5:8); "Indeed, Allah orders justice and good conduct and giving to relatives and forbids immorality and bad conduct and oppression. He admonishes you that perhaps you will be reminded" (16:90); "Indeed, Allah commands you to render trusts to whom they are due and when you judge between people to judge with justice" (4:58). The translations of the verses are taken from Saheeh International, available at http://www.quran.com.

23. Khadduri views this debate as dialectical, where usually two parties struggle to establish a paradigm of justice and, eventually, a new synthesis is reached. This intellectual synthesis becomes a source of new disagreement among scholars until its resolution. My theory about the duality of political and social justice, and the implications of this distinction, is greatly inspired by this perspective (Khadduri, *Islamic Conception of Justice*, 1–3).

24. I use the time frame "early period of Islam" to refer to the period extending from the preaching of Muhammad in Mecca and *hijra* (the migration of Prophet from Mecca to Medina in A.D. 622) to the end of the Abbasid Golden Age (A.D. 861).

25. The accompanying intellectual debates taking place around the notion of justice came to prevalence over time. For example, during the age of constitutional revolutions in the Middle East in the nineteenth and twentieth centuries, the social and political injustices were attributed to domestic tyranny and foreign intervention. Intellectuals proposed popular sovereignty and constitutional government as two instruments for establishing justice.

26. Crone, *God's Rule*.

27. Ayoob, "Political Islam."

28. Crone, *God's Rule*; Lapidus, "Separation of State and Religion"; Lapidus, *History of Islamic Societies*; Hodgson, *Venture of Islam*.

29. March, "Genealogies of Sovereignty."

30. The discussion in this section makes gross generalizations for the sake of simplicity and for stylistically developing the argument presented in this chapter. The Shia and Sunni theories of imamate involved deeper discussions and took centuries to consolidate (see Hodgson, *Venture of Islam*; Enayat, *Modern Islamic Political Thought*).

31. Enayat, *Modern Islamic Political Thought*.

32. Khadduri, *Islamic Conception of Justice*, 19. This argument has led some contemporary political theorists to define the political theology of Islam in terms of popular sovereignty (March, *Caliphate of Man*).

33. This section largely draws on the historical account provided by Majid Khadduri (*Islamic Conception of Justice*).

34. Khadduri, *Islamic Conception of Justice*, 23.

35. Kalam (Islamic scholastic theology) is the field where most of these debates unfolded. See Fakhry, *History of Islamic Philosophy*, for an excellent treatment about the development of this field.

36. To demonstrate this position, Majid Khadduri cites a letter written by the Umayyad caliph al-Walīd II to his governors explaining his decision to appoint two of his sons as his successors. In this letter, al-Walīd presents the caliphate as a divine institution that ensures the implementation of order and justice and argues that obedience to the caliph is necessary, because God predetermined everything and those who rebel will earn the displeasure of God (Khadduri, *Islamic Conception of Justice*, 25–26).

37. For example, the rationalist Mu'tazila and traditional/legalist Hanbali School found themselves at the center of a political crisis in the early ninth century during the reign of Abbasid caliph al-Ma'mūn. The disagreement concerned religious doctrine, but it was tied to the political ideologies of the time. This event is important, because it signifies the separation of religious and political authority and the power of the former to hold the latter accountable in the name of justice and religious principles (Lapidus, "Separation of State and Religion").

38. El-Affendi, *Who Needs an Islamic State?*

39. El-Affendi, *Who Needs an Islamic State?* 170–183.

40. This term was first used by Hodgson to refer to the religious community that refused to endorse any particular claim about the caliphate and accepted the doctrine of Rashidun caliphs. They relied on traditional interpretations of Koran and hadith and came to form the Sunni sect (Hodgson, *Venture of Islam*).

41. Hodgson, *Venture of Islam*, 241.

42. Hodgson, *Venture of Islam*, 248.

43. Hodgson, *Venture of Islam*, 250.

44. Hodgson, *Venture of Islam*; Lapidus, "Separation of State and Religion"; Crone, *God's Rule*.

45. Hodgson, *Venture of Islam*.

46. El-Affendi, *Who Needs an Islamic State?*

47. Khadduri, *Islamic Conception of Justice*.

48. Ahmed, *What Is Islam?*

49. Harris, "Martyrs' Welfare State and Its Contradictions."

50. Beblawi and Luciani, *Rentier State*.

51. Murphy, "Saudi King Unveils Massive Spending Package."

52. Quisay and Parker, "Thought, On the Theology of Obedience." Bin Bayyah is a traditional scholar of Mauritanian origin with significant credentials in the field of *'uṣūl al-fiqh*. He has close ties to the monarchs in Saudi Arabia and the United Arab Emirates.
53. Khadduri, *Islamic Conception of Justice*, 174–177.
54. Darling, *Social Justice and Political Power*.
55. Abdelkader, *Social Justice in Islam*.
56. Ahmed, *What Is Islam?* 471.
57. Khadduri, *Islamic Conception of Justice*; Abdelkader, *Social Justice in Islam*; Ahmed, *What Is Islam?*
58. Khadduri, *Islamic Conception of Justice*, 174–177.
59. Danışman, *Koçi Bey Risalesi*.
60. *Tanzimat* refers to the series of educational, political, military, and economic reforms that were carried to reverse the decline of the state between 1840 and 1870.
61. Khadduri, *Islamic Conception of Justice*, 177–182.
62. Ahmed, *What Is Islam?* 453–463.
63. N. Feldman, *Fall and Rise of the Islamic State*; Filali-Ansary, "Muslims and Democracy."
64. Kuru, *Islam, Authoritarianism, and Underdevelopment*. Kuru's theory differs from that of Noah Feldman (*Fall and Rise of the Islamic State*), who argues that ulema plays a critical role in constraining the ruler. Feldman's argument is similar to Filali-Ansary's notion of the "medieval compromise" (Filali-Ansary, "Muslims and Democracy," 27–28) that refers to an implicit agreement between the rulers and the subjects. In the classical medieval Islamic state, implementation of sharia in social, economic, and political realms ensured a just social order alongside political legitimacy. In this setting, ulema played a central role and viewed themselves as "the guardians of prophetic tradition."
65. Farabi, *On the Perfect State*.
66. Farabi, *On the Perfect State*.
67. Ahmed, *What Is Islam?* 463.
68. El Fadl, *Islam and the Challenge of Democracy*.
69. Khadduri, *Islamic Conception of Justice*, chap. 8.
70. Khadduri, *Islamic Conception of Justice*, 179–180.
71. Levitsky and Ziblatt, *How Democracies Die*.
72. Kuru, *Islam, Authoritarianism, and Underdevelopment*.
73. Kuru, *Islam, Authoritarianism, and Underdevelopment*.
74. Yavuz, "Turkey: Islam without Shari'a?"
75. Gellner, "Islam and Marxism."
76. Some scholars employ modern ideas to reconstruct a political theology of obedience based on the classical Islamic state. A notable example includes the Mauritanian scholar who has been advising the ruling family in the United Arab Emirates (Quisay and Parker, "Thought, On the Theology of Obedience"). State-controlled religious organizations such as Turkey's Directorate of Religious Affairs play a similar role.
77. Kedourie, *Democracy and Arab Political Culture*; Quisay and Parker, "Thought, On the Theology of Obedience."
78. Keddie, *Islamic Response to Imperialism*; Kemal, "And Seek Their Council"; Ayoob, "Challenging Hegemony"; Iqbal, *Reconstruction of Religious Thought in Islam*; Moaddel, *Islamic Modernism, Nationalism, and Fundamentalism*.
79. Khadduri, *Islamic Conception of Justice*, 197–198.
80. Keddie, *Islamic Response to Imperialism*; Sedgwick, *Muhammad Abduh*; Kemal, "And Seek Their Council."

81. De Mesquita et al., *Logic of Political Survival*; Svolik, *Politics of Authoritarian Rule*; Ciftci, "Self-Expression Values."
82. Ciftci, Wuthrich, and Shamaileh, "Islam, Religious Outlooks, and Support."
83. Clark, *Islam, Charity and Activism*; Grewal et al., "Poverty and Divine Rewards."
84. Khadduri, *Islamic Conception of Justice*; Ahmed, *What Is Islam?*
85. Acemoglu and Robinson, *Economic Origins of Dictatorship and Democracy*.
86. Boix, *Democracy and Redistribution*.
87. Acemoglu and Robinson, *Economic Origins of Dictatorship and Democracy*.
88. Levitsky and Ziblatt, *How Democracies Die*.
89. Kuru, *Islam, Authoritarianism, and Underdevelopment*.
90. An-Náim, *Islam and the Secular State*.
91. El Fadl, *Islam and the Challenge of Democracy*.
92. Tessler, "Islam and Democracy"; Ciftci, "Modernization, Islam, or Social Capital"; Menchik, *Islam and Democracy in Indonesia*; Ciftci, Wuthrich, and Shamaileh, "Islam, Religious Outlooks, and Support"; Spierings, "Influence of Islamic Orientations."
93. Ramadan, *Western Muslims and the Future of Islam*.
94. Jamal and Robbins, "Social Justice and the Arab Uprisings."

CHAPTER 4

1. Abdelkader, *Social Justice in Islam*; Hashemi, *Islam, Secularism, and Liberal Democracy*; Bayat, "Revolution without Movement."
2. Masoud, *Counting Islam*.
3. Praxis is defined as a "practical-critical" activity, a combination of practice and theory in a Marxist sense (Marx, "Theses on Feuerbach [1845]"). My attempt to unfold the linkages between Islamic theory and the struggle for justice in Qutb's and Shariati's philosophy follows Frankfurt School's and especially Horkheimer's approach to praxis (Horkheimer, *Critical Theory*).
4. This term is brought to prominence by Lyotard (*Postmodern Condition*) in his discussion of modernism (Ciftci, "Modernden Postmoderne Iktidar").
5. This sentence, and the remainder of this paragraph, draws heavily on Ahmed, *What Is Islam?* chap. 3, esp. pp. 177–197.
6. Ahmed, *What Is Islam?* 209.
7. Lorenz, "Emergence of Social Justice"; Rawls, *Theory of Justice*.
8. March, *Caliphate of Man*; Tamimi, *Rachid Ghannouchi*.
9. An-Náim, *Muslims and Global Justice*, 1.
10. March, "Taking People as They Are."
11. Much earlier than Qutb and Shariati, Muhammad Abduh used tawhid as a fundamental principle organizing social, economic, and political life. Abduh combines the tawhid principle with such concepts as free will, obedience to God, and rationality of the scriptures as foundations of perfect Islamic society (Sedgwick, *Muhammad Abduh*).
12. The following discussion builds on Qutb's *Social Justice in Islam* and Shariati's multiple works. I sparingly use citations for the direct quotes and when a discussion heavily relies on the terminology of the texts.
13. Qutb, *Social Justice in Islam*.
14. Qutb, *Social Justice in Islam*, 41.
15. Qutb, *Social Justice in Islam*; Qutb, *Milestones*.
16. Qutb, *Social Justice in Islam*, 44.
17. Qutb, *Social Justice in Islam*, 45.

18. Qutb, *Social Justice in Islam*, 47–48.
19. Qutb, *Social Justice in Islam*, 49.
20. Qutb, *Social Justice in Islam*, 52.
21. Qutb, *Social Justice in Islam*, 53.
22. Qutb, *Social Justice in Islam*, 55.
23. Qutb, *Social Justice in Islam*, 59.
24. Qutb, *Social Justice in Islam*, 60.
25. Qutb, *Social Justice in Islam*, 68.
26. The Prophet Muhammad, as recorded in al-Qudai, *Musnad al-Shihab*, I, 145.
27. Qutb, *Social Justice in Islam*, 79.
28. Qutb, *Social Justice in Islam*, 86.
29. Qutb, *Social Justice in Islam*, 90.
30. Qutb, *Social Justice in Islam*, 94–95.
31. Qutb, *Social Justice in Islam*, 99.
32. Qutb, *Social Justice in Islam*, 99–102.
33. Qutb, *Social Justice in Islam*, 119–120.
34. Qutb, *Social Justice in Islam*, 121.
35. Qutb, *Social Justice in Islam*, 124.
36. Iqbal, *Reconstruction of Religious Thought in Islam*; Rahman, "Principle of 'Shūrā' and Role of Umma"; El Fadl, *Islam and the Challenge of Democracy*; An-Náim, *Islam and the Secular State*.
37. An-Nawawi, *Forty Hadith of An-Nawawi*, 32.
38. Qutb, *Social Justice in Islam*, 134.
39. Qutb, *Social Justice in Islam*, 150–162.
40. Qutb, *Social Justice in Islam*, 162–164.
41. Qutb, *Social Justice in Islam*, 205.
42. Qutb, *Social Justice in Islam*, 215.
43. Qutb, *Social Justice in Islam*, 205–210.
44. Qutb, *Milestones*.
45. Abrahamian, "'Ali Shariati," 16.
46. Shariati, "Worldview of Tawhid."
47. Shariati, "Worldview of Tawhid," 87.
48. Shariati, "World Vision," sec. Kindle Locations, 586–588.
49. Shariati, "World Vision," sec. Kindle Locations, 608–618.
50. In *Religion vs Religion*, Shariati argues that most human history can be understood as a struggle between monotheist religion and polytheist religion rather than as a struggle between religion and nonreligion (Shariati, *Religion vs Religion*).
51. Shariati, "World Vision," secs. 608–618.
52. Shariati, "Man and Islam."
53. Similar to Qutbian equilibrium between spiritual and material, the *Shariatian* two-dimensionality in man creates a balance between worldliness and spiritual.
54. Shariati, "Man and Islam," sec. Kindle Locations, 391–393.
55. Shariati, "Modern Man and His Prisons."
56. Shariati, "Modern Man and His Prisons," sec. Kindle Locations, 1160.
57. This paragraph provides a general overview of Shariati's influential essay titled "Modern Man and His Prisons."
58. Shariati, "Modern Man and His Prisons," sec. Kindle Locations, 1379–1380.
59. Shariati, "Eslam-Shenasi (Islamology)," 79.

60. Danesh and Abniki, "Relation between Liberty and Justice," 1.
61. Shariati, "Modern Man and His Prisons."
62. Shariati, "Eslam-Shenasi (Islamology)"; Shariati, "Modern Man and His Prisons"; Shariati, "Man and Islam."
63. Shariati, "Eslam-Shenasi (Islamology)"; Shariati, "Modern Man and His Prisons"; Shariati, "Man and Islam"; Shariati, "Reflections of a Concerned Muslim."
64. Shariati, "Reflections of a Concerned Muslim."
65. Shariati, "Reflections of a Concerned Muslim."
66. Shariati, "And Once Again Abu-Dhar," pt. 5, accessed on May 28, 2018, available at http://www.shariati.com/kotob.html.
67. Shariati, "And Once Again Abu-Dhar," pt. 5, accessed on May 28, 2018, available at http://www.shariati.com/kotob.html.
68. Shariati, "Reflections of a Concerned Muslim," pt. 5, accessed on May 28, 2021, available at http://www.shariati.com/english/reflect/reflect2.html.
69. El-Affendi, *Who Needs an Islamic State?*, 171–183.
70. Qutb, *Social Justice in Islam*.
71. Shariati, *Man and Islam*; Shariati, *Religion vs Religion*; Shariati, "And Once Again Abu-Dhar."
72. Al-Mawdudi, "Islam in Transition."
73. Nasr, *Mawdudi and the Making of Islamic Revivalism*.
74. Al-Rikabi, "Bāqir al-Ṣadr and the Islamic State"; Jamalzadeh, "Sociopolitical Justice."
75. Tamimi, *Rachid Ghannouchi*; March, *Caliphate of Man*.
76. March, *Caliphate of Man*.
77. This brief overview hardly captures the sophisticated political philosophy of al-Ghannūshī. Two excellent and detailed accounts of al-Ghannūshī are Andrew March's *Caliphate of Man* and Azzam Tamimi's *Rachid Ghannouchi*.
78. Yavuz and Esposito, *Turkish Islam and the Secular State*; Yavuz, *Toward an Islamic Enlightenment*; Markham and Pirim, *Introduction to Said Nursi*.
79. Vahide, *Islam in Modern Turkey*.
80. Nursi, *Risale-i Nur Külliyatı*.
81. Yavuz, *Islamic Political Identity in Turkey*.
82. Lorenz, "Emergence of Social Justice"; Rawls, *Theory of Justice*; Smith, *Emergence of Liberation Theology*.

CHAPTER 5

1. Phillips and Hardy, "Understanding Discourse Analysis."
2. Hardy, Harley, and Phillips, "Discourse Analysis and Content Analysis," 20.
3. Weedon, *Feminist Practice and Post-Structuralist Theory*, 108.
4. Foucault, *Discipline and Punish*; Foucault, *Archaeology of Knowledge*.
5. Bartky, "Foucault, Femininity, and the Modernization," 61–86.
6. El-Affendi, *Who Needs an Islamic State?*
7. Khadduri, *Islamic Conception of Justice*.
8. Thompson, *Justice Interrupted*.
9. Ayoob, "Challenging Hegemony."
10. Türköne, *Siyasi Ideoloji Olarak Islamciligin Dogusu*.
11. Yavuz, "Turkey: Islam without Shariʻa?"

12. Tuğal, *Passive Revolution*.
13. The same label is used in the names of not only the Justice and Development Party (AKP) in Turkey but other Islamist parties: two examples are Justice and Development Party in Morocco (PJD) and Prosperous Justice Party in Indonesia (PKS).
14. Surprisingly, as the analysis presented here demonstrates, the debate about Islam and democracy is only marginally relevant for the Turkish Islamists since the 1960s.
15. Karpat, *Politicization of Islam*; Yavuz, "Turkey: Islam without Shari'a."
16. Kara, *Türkiye'de İslamcılık Düşüncesi (I–II)*, 27.
17. Karpat, *Politicization of Islam*; Yavuz, *Nostalgia for the Empire*.
18. Yavuz, "Nationalism and Islam"; Cetinsaya, "Rethinking Nationalism and Islam."
19. Yavuz, "Nationalism and Islam."
20. Yavuz, *Islamic Political Identity in Turkey*.
21. Kara, *Türkiye'de İslamcılık Düşüncesi (I–II)*; Özdalga, "Necip Fazıl Kısakürek"; Altun, "Alternatif Tarih Yazmak"; Duran, "Cumhuriyet Dönemi İslamcılığı."
22. Özdalga, "Necip Fazıl Kısakürek"; Altun, "Alternatif Tarih Yazmak"; Duran, "Cumhuriyet Dönemi İslamcılığı."
23. Yavuz, *Nostalgia for the Empire*.
24. Karpat, *Gecekondu*.
25. Karpat, *Gecekondu*.
26. Yavuz, *Secularism and Muslim Democracy in Turkey*; Madi-Sisman, *Muslims, Money, and Democracy in Turkey*.
27. The rise of the AKP since 2002 is the most significant development in the Islamist sociopolitical reality. The focus of this chapter is on the period of 1960–2010, and it only covers the first two terms of the AKP in power.
28. Cizre-Sakallioglu and Cinar, "Turkey 2002."
29. Işık, Köroğlu, and Sezgin, *1960–1980 Arası İslamcı Dergiler*; Kara, *Türkiye'de İslamcılık Düşüncesi (I–II)*.
30. Tuğal, *Passive Revolution*; Kara, *Türkiye'de İslamcılık Düşüncesi (I–II)*; Madi-Sisman, *Muslims, Money, and Democracy in Turkey*.
31. Gumuscu, "Class, Status, and Party."
32. Işık, Köroğlu, and Sezgin, *1960–1980 Arası İslamcı Dergiler*.
33. Ayoob, "Challenging Hegemony"; Ayoob, "Political Islam."
34. Kara, *Türkiye'de İslamcılık Düşüncesi (I–II)*, 17.
35. In Turkish, "İslâmcılık, XIX–XX. yüzyılda İslâmı bir bütün olarak (inanç, ibadet, ahlâk, felsefe, siyaset, hukuk, eğitim. . .) 'yeniden' hayata hâkim kılmak ve akılcı bir metotla Müslümanları, İslâm dünyasını batı sömürüsünden, zalim ve müstebit yöneticilerden, esaretten, taklitten, hurafelerden kurtarmak, medenileştirmek, birleştirmek ve kalkındırmak uğruna yapılan aktivist ve eklektik yönleri baskın siyasî, fikrî ve ilmî çalışmaların, arayışların bütününü ihtiva eden bir düşünce ve harekettir."
36. Bulaç, "Islamcilik Nedir?" para. 4. In Turkish: "İslâmcılık, İslâm'ın ana referans kaynaklarından hareketle 'yeni' bir insan, toplum, siyaset/devlet ve dünya tasavvurunu, buna bağlı yeni bir sosyal örgütlenme modelini ve evrensel anlamda İslâm Birliği'ni hedefleyen entelektüel, ahlaki, toplumsal, ekonomik, politik ve devletler arası harekettir. Başka bir deyişle İslâm'ın hayat bulması, hükümlerinin uygulanması, dünyanin her tarihsel ve toplumsal durumunda İslâm'a göre yeniden kurulması ideali ve çabasıdır."
37. Türköne, *Siyasi Ideoloji Olarak Islamciligin Dogusu*.
38. Kemal, "And Seek Their Council."
39. Ersoy, *Safahat*; Cetinsaya, "Rethinking Nationalism and Islam."
40. Türköne, *Siyasi Ideoloji Olarak Islamciligin Dogusu*.

41. Maydan, "Islam and Islamism in Turkey," sec. 7, para. 1.
42. Ayoob, "Challenging Hegemony."
43. Wallerstein, "Islam, the West, and the World"; Wallerstein, "Political Construction of Islam."
44. Madi-Sisman and Sisman, "Immanuel Wallerstein, Islam, Islamists." A similar view is proposed by Tuğal (*Passive Revolution*).
45. 'Ali Shariati's thought is inspired by the Shiite tradition that has developed a theology of justice against tyranny based on traumas related to the massacre of 'Ali's children and prosecution of Shia scholars or people throughout history. Ayatollah Khomeini, for example, used this framework to revoke historical traumas in the context of the shah's repressive regimes. He especially used the notion of ẓulm (tyranny) to invite people to rebellion in the wake of Islamic Revolution. Khomeini defines ẓulm in the broadest terms as "oppression or transgression against the self or other people." Ẓulm is the opposite of justice and its existence justifies rebellion against domestic tyrants (Khomeini, "Theory of Justice"). The same ideology was also put at the service of anti-Americanism as a rallying point in Iran.
46. Türköne, *Siyasi Ideoloji Olarak Islamciligin Dogusu*.
47. See Elizabeth Özdalga for a scholarly treatment of Kısakürek's work (Özdalga, "Necip Fazıl Kısakürek").
48. Ibn Taymiyya (2012, 230, 258–259), cited in Michot, "Mamlūks, Qalandars, Rāfiḍīs."
49. Köroğlu, "Türkiye'de İslamcılık Düşüncesinin Seyrini Dergiler Üzerinden Okumak." One of the first Islamist journals *Sırat-ı Müstakim/Sebilürreşad* was edited by Eşref Edip and the leading author of the journal was Mehmed Akif. The journal was published between 1908 and 1925 until it was banned by the government. The journal started its second period during 1948–1966, and it is acknowledged as the most influential Islamist journal.
50. Işık, Köroğlu, and Sezgin, *1960–1980 Arası İslamcı Dergiler*. The analysis utilizes some articles during the AKP period, but the bulk of the articles come from the journals published before 2002.
51. The digitizing effort is carried by the Islamist Journals Project, İDP, or İslamci Dergiler Projesi.
52. A research assistant helped with the collection of the archives and cross-checked the selection and elimination of articles.
53. The full list of journals in the İLEM Archives is presented in Table A5.1 in Appendix A.
54. Shariati, "Red Shi'ism"; Shariati, "Eslam-Shenasi (Islamology)"; Khomeini, "Theory of Justice"; Enayat, *Modern Islamic Political Thought*.
55. Ironically, the opposite of justice (adalet, adalah) is not zulüm, rather it is *jawr* (جور), which is only sporadically used to refer to injustice and transgression in the post-1980 Islamist writings (see Khadduri, *Islamic Conception of Justice*, for a discussion of the etymology of *adalah* and *jawr*).
56. Sevgili, "Allahın Adaleti," 14.
57. Pilavoğlu, "Dünya Medeniyetleri Arasında İslâm," 8.
58. Tosun, "Mağaralarımızın Tıkaçlarına İlahi Çözüm," 42.
59. Çağlak, "Ebedi Adalet," 35.
60. Yeniçeri, "İslâm'da Ölçü ve Tartı," 11.
61. Emiroğlu, "İnsanlık Âdil İdareye Muhtaçtır," 11.
62. Altunkaya, "Mevlid-i Şerif'inin 1480," 18.
63. Eliaçık, "Sivil Dönüşüm," 44.

64. Yazgan, "Adalet ve Zulüm," 20.
65. In a sophisticated account of 1960s Turkish intellectual landscape, Yavuz argues that the Ottoman Empire is presented as the golden age by Turkish Islamists (Yavuz, *Nostalgia for the Empire*).
66. Khadduri, *Islamic Conception of Justice*.
67. Eliaçık, "Adalet 'Kozmos'un Temelidir," 62.
68. Eliaçık, "İslam Uygarlığı Tarihten Mi Çekiliyor?" 44.
69. El Fadl, *Islam and the Challenge of Democracy*.
70. An-Náim, *Islam and the Secular State*.
71. Yıldırım, "Şura, Biat ve Adalet Temeldir."
72. Ayoob, "Challenging Hegemony."
73. Türköne, *Siyasi Ideoloji Olarak Islamciligin Dogusu*.
74. İkiz, "Tahkirciler," 62.
75. Editorial, "Adalet, Politikaya Alet Edilemez," 16.
76. Editorial, "İslam'ın Kayıp Savaşçıları ve Susturulan Adalet Çığlığı," 58.
77. Altunkaya, "Mevlid-i Şerif'inin 1480," 18.
78. Çakır, "Amerikan Adaleti ve Zenciler," 16.
79. Türkmen, "Toplumu Kuran Ekseninde Donusturmeyi Esas Almaliyiz."
80. Yavuz, *Nostalgia for the Empire*.
81. Kemal, "And Seek Their Council."
82. Sarfati, "Challenging Hegemony."
83. Yenigun, "New Antinomies of the Islamic Movement."
84. Emre, "'Müslümancılık' Ya Da Klan Siyaseti."

CHAPTER 6

1. Tarlabaşı is a neighborhood in the Beyoğlu district of Istanbul. In the 1990s, it was occupied by the Kurds migrating from the Southeastern provinces. Currently, it is a neighborhood hosting African immigrants, Kurds, the poor and homeless individuals, and a sizable transgender community.
2. Some of these groups include Labor and Justice Platform, Anticapitalist Muslims, and the Movement against the Violence toward Women. I discuss some activities of these groups in this chapter.
3. Sarfati, "Challenging Hegemony."
4. Melucci, *Challenging Codes*; Castells, *Networks of Outrage and Hope*.
5. Bayat, "Revolution without Movement."
6. I am indebted to one of my interviewees for inspiring this concept. He tirelessly explained to me how charity by government imposed hierarchical relations and structures of domination, whereas true Islamic activism was based on nonhierarchical, egalitarian helping.
7. Yenigun, "New Antinomies of the Islamic Movement."
8. Emek ve Adalet Platformu, "Emek ve Adalet'ten Gezi Parkı Bildirisi."
9. Hodgson, *Venture of Islam*; Yenigun, "New Antinomies of the Islamic Movement."
10. Eliaçık, *Adalet Devleti*.
11. Nurtsch, "Koran and Social Justice."
12. Emre, "'Müslümancılık' Ya Da Klan Siyaseti."
13. Yenigun, "New Antinomies of the Islamic Movement."
14. Hodgson, *Venture of Islam*.

15. Yenigun, "New Antinomies of the Islamic Movement," 239.
16. Yenigun, "New Antinomies of the Islamic Movement," 240.
17. The Uludere incident occurred on December 28, 2011, when two Turkish jet fighters bombed a convoy of civilian smugglers, judging them to be militants of the Kurdistan Workers' Party (PKK). Later, the government refused to apologize and compensate these victims, an episode that created much controversy in Turkish politics.
18. Haber7, "5 Yıldızlı Otel Karşısında Yerde Iftar."
19. This fieldwork is supported by the Global Religion Research Initiative at Notre Dame University (Award #BG5225). The University Research Compliance Office at Kansas State University has reviewed the field proposal and approved it (IRB approval #8776).
20. Demographic information about the interviewees and the core questions used in the interviews are presented in Appendixes A and B. I also had follow-up conversations with the participants, but these secondary meetings were not recorded. In addition to interviews, I also attended several events organized by these groups.
21. Throughout this chapter, I provide excerpts from the recorded interviews in text. In these citations, I use pseudonyms to protect the identity of the interviewees and to comply with the ethical guidelines of field research.
22. Lorenz, "Emergence of Social Justice."
23. Hodgson, *Venture of Islam*; El-Affendi, *Who Needs an Islamic State?*
24. Lapidus, "Separation of State and Religion."
25. Kuru, *Islam, Authoritarianism, and Underdevelopment*.
26. Moaddel, *Islamic Modernism, Nationalism, and Fundamentalism*; Ayoob, "Political Islam."
27. Shariati, *Man and Islam*; Qutb, *Social Justice in Islam*.
28. This notion is derived from the following verse in the Koran: "O you who have believed, be persistently standing firm for Allah, witnesses in justice, and do not let the hatred of a people prevent you from being just. Be just; that is nearer to righteousness. And fear Allah; indeed, Allah is acquainted with what you do." (Koran, 5:8).
29. El-Affendi, *Who Needs an Islamic State?* An-Náim, *Islam and the Secular State*.
30. Hale is referring to the adjectives in the name of the Justice and Development Party and presenting a criticism of their modernization approach neglecting justice.
31. An-Náim, *Islam and the Secular State*.
32. Norris, *Critical Citizens*.
33. Gellner, *Muslim Society*; Kedourie, *Democracy and Arab Political Culture*; Lewis, "Islam and Liberal Democracy: Historical Overview."

CHAPTER 7

1. Brannen, Haig, and Schmidt, "Age of Mass Protests."
2. Sim, "FIFA World Cup 2014."
3. Nurtsch, "Koran and Social Justice."
4. Licht, Goldschmidt, and Schwartz, "Culture Rules"; Gorodnichenko and Roland, "Culture, Institutions and Democratization."
5. Kyriacou, "Individualism–Collectivism, Governance and Economic Development"; Licht, Goldschmidt, and Schwartz, "Culture Rules"; Pitlik and Rode, "Individualistic Values, Institutional Trust."
6. Gellner, *Muslim Society*; Huntington, "Clash of Civilizations"; Kedourie, *Democracy and Arab Political Culture*; Lewis, "Islam and Liberal Democracy: Historical Overview."

7. Esposito and Voll, *Islam and Democracy*; Sachedina, *Islamic Roots of Democratic Pluralism*; Kemal, "And Seek Their Council"; El Fadl, *Islam and the Challenge of Democracy*; Ramadan, *Islam, the West and Challenges of Modernity*; March, *Caliphate of Man*; Hashemi, *Islam, Secularism, and Liberal Democracy*.

8. Tessler, "Islam and Democracy"; Tessler, *Islam and Politics*; Jamal, "Reassessing Support for Islam and Democracy"; Rizzo, Abdel-Latif, and Meyer, "Gender Equality and Democracy"; Ciftci, "Modernization, Islam, or Social Capital"; Fish, *Are Muslims Distinctive?* Spierings, "Influence of Islamic Orientations"; Driessen, "Sources of Muslim Democracy."

9. Rose, "Does Islam Make People Anti-Democratic?"; Tessler, "Islam and Democracy."

10. Karakoç and Başkan, "Religion in Politics"; Ciftci, "Secular-Islamist Cleavage, Values, and Support"; Driessen, "Sources of Muslim Democracy."

11. Fish, *Are Muslims Distinctive?* Spierings, "Influence of Islamic Orientations."

12. Ciftci, Wuthrich, and Shamaileh, "Islam, Religious Outlooks, and Support."

13. Hasan, "Social Justice in Islam."

14. Koran, 2:215.

15. Qutb, *Social Justice in Islam*.

16. Shariati, "And Once Again Abu-Dhar."

17. Kuran, *Islam and Mammon*.

18. Clark, *Islam, Charity, and Activism*; Cammett and Issar, "Bricks and Mortar Clientelism."

19. Davis and Robinson, "Egalitarian Face of Islamic Orthodoxy," 167.

20. Acemoglu and Robinson, *Economic Origins of Dictatorship and Democracy*.

21. Boix, *Democracy and Redistribution*; Acemoglu and Robinson, *Economic Origins of Dictatorship and Democracy*.

22. For example, the following verse is cited during Friday sermons in many parts of the Muslim world: "Verily, Allah commands *'Adl* (fairness, equity, justice) *'Iḥsān* (excellence in servitude to Allah, benevolence towards people, graciousness in dealings) and giving to those close to you, while He forbids *fahshā* (lewdness, indecency, licentiousness, immorality), *munkar* (bad actions, undesirable activities, generally unaccepted behavior, not fulfilling one's obligations), and *baghy* (rebellion, transgressing limits, exploiting or violating others' rights, abuse of authority or freedom). He admonishes you so that you heed the activity" (Koran 16:90). Explanations of the terms, in parentheses, are taken from several English translations of the Koran.

23. An-Nawawi n.d., 32.

24. An-Náim, *Islam and the Secular State*.

25. Putnam, *Bowling Alone*; Uslaner, "Democracy and Social Capital"; Newton, "Trust, Social Capital, Civil Society, and Democracy."

26. An-Náim, *Islam and the Secular State*.

27. Shariati, "Worldview of Tawhid."

28. Qutb, *Social Justice in Islam*, 99.

29. Greif and Laitin, "Theory of Endogenous Institutional Change"; Schwartz, *Values and Culture*.

30. Weber, *The Protestant Ethic and Spirit of Capitalism*; Kyriacou, "Individualism–Collectivism, Governance and Economic Development"; Pitlik and Rode, "Individualistic Values, Institutional Trust."

31. Gorodnichenko and Roland, "Culture, Institutions and Democratization"; Licht, Goldschmidt, and Schwartz, "Culture Rules."

32. Licht, Goldschmidt, and Schwartz, "Culture Rules."

33. Gorodnichenko and Roland, "Culture, Institutions and Democratization." Schwartz specified three value dimensions based on his survey about main issues facing human societies. These dimensions are embeddedness/autonomy, hierarchy/egalitarianism, and mastery/harmony. Embeddedness refers to values that constrain the individual within the social hierarchy and norms in favor of group solidarity and order. The autonomy cultures, in contrast, emphasize individual uniqueness, autonomy, and initiative. The hierarchy/egalitarianism dimension contrasts the cultural emphasis on obedience against voluntary behavior dedicated to the welfare of others. Finally, the mastery cultures promote personal action for success whereas harmony cultures value acceptance of existing conditions and assign priority to the group (Schwartz, *Values and Culture*; Licht, Goldschmidt, and Schwartz, "Culture Rules.")

34. Weber, *The Protestant Ethic and Spirit of Capitalism*.

35. La Porta et al., "Quality of Government."

36. Aggregated religiosity may conform to individualistic or collectivist orientations leading to cross-national variation in this metric. At the individual level, a robust test of this hypothesis requires a nuanced measurement strategy recognizing various religious outlooks conducive to individualistic or collectivist orientations. The statistical analyses in this chapter use the survey data to account for this nuance.

37. Iannaccone, "Sacrifice and Stigma"; Chen and Lind, "Political Economy of Beliefs"; Pepinsky and Welborne, "Piety and Redistributive Preferences."

38. Gellner, *Muslim Society*.

39. See Gorodnichenko and Roland, "Culture, Institutions and Democratization," for a similar argument derived from a formal model.

40. Muslim-only respondents are obtained according to the following method: Respondents who report their identity as "Muslim" (Question X051); those who choose their religious group to be either Sunni, Shia, or Muslim (Question F025); and all respondents in countries where these questions were not asked in some surveys (e.g., Turkey).

41. Although the majority status of Muslims is debated in Nigeria and Lebanon, I include these cases given the relatively large share of the Muslim population in these countries.

42. Factor analysis shows that all four items strongly load on a single factor. The scale reliability coefficient (Cronbach's alpha) is 0.49.

43. Pitlik and Rode, "Individualistic Values, Institutional Trust."

44. Pitlik and Rode, "Individualistic Values, Institutional Trust."

45. Schwartz, "Mapping and Interpreting Cultural Differences."

46. Bandura, "Self-Efficacy."

47. Rotter, "Generalized Expectancies."

48. S. Feldman, "Structure and Consistency in Public Opinion."

49. Pitlik and Rode, "Individualistic Values, Institutional Trust."

50. It should be noted that Equation 2 is run with two indicators of individualistic value orientations. Therefore, in some models four equations are estimated at the same time. The results of factor analysis and measures of scaling do not justify index construction for these two items.

51. Some examples from the Koran include 4:36, 6:151, 17:23–24, 31:14–15. In a famous hadith, it is reported that Muhammad said: Stay with her (your mother), for Paradise is beneath her feet (Sunan al-Nasā'ī 3104).

52. As for the control variables, no consistent or significant effects are detected for gender, age, income, and personal trust. However, at higher levels of education, individuals are more prodistribution, individualistic, and supportive of democracy. Women tend

to hold more collectivist attitudes than men. Egalitarian gender beliefs decrease support for democracy.

53. Johnson, "On Church and Sect"; Stark and Finke, *Acts of Faith*; Djupe and Gilbert, *Political Influence of Churches*.

54. Ciftci, Wuthrich, and Shamaileh, *Beyond Piety and Politics*; Ciftci, Wuthrich, and Shamaileh, "Islam, Religious Outlooks, and Support."

55. Davis and Robinson, "Egalitarian Face of Islamic Orthodoxy."

56. Davis and Robinson, "Egalitarian Face of Islamic Orthodoxy."

57. Davis and Robinson, "Egalitarian Face of Islamic Orthodoxy," 169–170.

58. Stark and Finke, *Acts of Faith*.

59. Davis and Robinson, "Egalitarian Face of Islamic Orthodoxy," 170.

60. Egypt and Saudi Arabia are dropped from the estimations reported here because some of the variables used in the seemingly unrelated regressions are not available for these countries.

61. These countries are Algeria, Azerbaijan, Iraq, Jordan, Kazakhstan, Kyrgyzstan, Lebanon, Malaysia, Morocco, Nigeria, Pakistan, Palestine, Tunisia, Turkey, Uzbekistan, and Yemen.

62. Davis and Robinson, "Egalitarian Face of Islamic Orthodoxy"; Pepinsky and Welborne, "Piety and Redistributive Preferences"; Ciftci, "Islam, Social Justice, and Democracy."

CHAPTER 8

1. Hendawi, "Sudan's 'Nubian Queen' Protester."
2. Stepan and Robertson, "An 'Arab' More Than a 'Muslim.'"
3. Esposito and Mogahed, "Battle for Muslims' Hearts and Minds"; Tessler, Jamal, and Robbins, "New Findings on Arabs and Democracy."
4. Khatib and Lust, *Taking to the Streets*.
5. Thompson, *Justice Interrupted*.
6. McAdam, Tarrow, and Tilly, "Comparative Perspectives on Contentious Politics."
7. Bayat, *Life as Politics*; Beinin and Vairel, *Social Movements, Mobilization, and Contestation*; Khatib and Lust, *Taking to the Streets*.
8. Jamal and Robbins, "State of Social Justice in the Arab World."
9. Moore, *Social Origins of Dictatorship and Democracy*; North, Wallis, and Weingast, *Violence and Social Orders*; Blaydes and Chaney, "Feudal Revolution and Europe's Rise."
10. Moore, *Social Origins of Dictatorship and Democracy*, 415–416.
11. Moore, *Social Origins of Dictatorship and Democracy*; North, Wallis, and Weingast, *Violence and Social Orders*; Blaydes and Chaney, "Feudal Revolution and Europe's Rise."
12. Beinin, *Workers and Peasants*; Darling, *Social Justice and Political Power*; Thompson, *Justice Interrupted*; Hashemi, *Islam, Secularism, and Liberal Democracy*.
13. Darling, *Social Justice and Political Power*.
14. Darling, *Social Justice and Political Power*; Thompson, *Justice Interrupted*.
15. Darling, *Social Justice and Political Power*.
16. Thompson, *Justice Interrupted*.
17. Thompson, *Justice Interrupted*, 3.
18. Lewis, "Why Turkey"; Lewis, *Shaping of the Modern Middle East*.
19. Mardin, *Genesis of Young Ottoman Thought*.
20. Lewis, *Emergence of Modern Turkey*; Mardin, *Genesis of Young Ottoman Thought*.
21. Thompson, *Justice Interrupted*.

22. Keddie, *Religion and Rebellion in Iran*.
23. Abrahamian, *Iran between Two Revolutions*; Thompson, *Justice Interrupted*.
24. Keddie, *Islamic Response to Imperialism*; Moaddel, *Islamic Modernism, Nationalism, and Fundamentalism*; Ayoob, "Political Islam."
25. Lapidus, "Islamic Revival and Modernity."
26. The basis for the argument presented by Kemal is a Koranic verse: Washawirhum fee al-amri (Koran, 3:159).
27. Kemal, "And Seek Their Council," 144.
28. Khadduri, *Islamic Conception of Justice*; Enayat, *Modern Islamic Political Thought*; March, *Caliphate of Man*.
29. Kemal, "And Seek Their Council," 147.
30. Kemal, "And Seek Their Council," 145–148.
31. Thompson, *Justice Interrupted*.
32. Darling, *Social Justice and Political Power*; Thompson, *Justice Interrupted*.
33. Brownlee, Masoud, and Reynolds, *Arab Spring*.
34. Korany, "Redefining Development for a New Generation."
35. Brownlee, Masoud, and Reynolds, *Arab Spring*; Gause, "Middle East Studies Missed"; Schwedler, "Comparative Politics." For exceptions, see Kuhn, "Role of Human Development"; Batniji et al., "Governance and Health"; Hoffman and Jamal, "Religion in the Arab Spring"; Robbins and Jamal, "The State of Social Justice in the Arab World."
36. "Methodology," Arab Barometer. Available at https://www.arabbarometer.org/survey-data/methodology/.
37. The difference of means test for protesters and nonprotesters in perceptions of political and social injustices show that protesters are more likely to hold critical views of government and economic conditions. The difference of means test did not reveal a statistical difference in average religiosity between the two groups.
38. Hoffman and Jamal, "Religion in the Arab Spring."
39. There are many studies examining the roots of Arab authoritarianism, explaining this phenomenon by distributive politics (Blaydes, *Elections and Distributive Politics*), external factors (Jamal, *Of Empires and Citizens*), personality cults (Wedeen, *Ambiguities of Domination*), and coercive institutions (Bellin, "Robustness of Authoritarianism"), among other factors.
40. Tessler, "Islam and Democracy"; Tessler, Jamal, and Robbins, "New Findings on Arabs and Democracy."
41. *Wasta*, or connections, refers to the common practice involving "a person (or person's action) who intercedes using influence to garner favor, often unmerited, for another person" (Gold and Naufal, "Wasta," 59).
42. These figures can be found at the Transparency International website in the snapshot report for MENA, "Middle East and North Africa," available at https://www.transparency.org/en/news/regional-analysis-mena.
43. Khawaja, "Fighting Corruption."
44. Jamal and Robbins, "Social Justice and the Arab Uprisings," 139–142.
45. Hoffman and Jamal, "Religion in the Arab Spring"; Kabbani, "Youth Unemployment."
46. Kemal, "And Seek Their Council."
47. Kuran, "Now Out of Never"; McAdam, Tarrow, and Tilly, "Comparative Perspectives on Contentious Politics."
48. Djupe and Gilbert, "Resourceful Believer"; Philpott, "Political Ambivalence of Religion"; Arikan and Bloom, "Religion and Political Protest."

49. Philpott, "Political Ambivalence of Religion"; Putnam, *Bowling Alone*; Hoffman and Jamal, "Religion in the Arab Spring."
50. Hoffman and Jamal, "Religion in the Arab Spring."
51. Thompson, *Justice Interrupted*; Beinin, *Workers and Peasants*.
52. Hoffman and Jamal, "Religion in the Arab Spring."
53. Hoffman and Jamal, "Religion in the Arab Spring"; Brownlee, Masoud, and Reynolds, *Arab Spring*.
54. In the third wave, the responses to these questions use a five-point scale. The scales are harmonized to obtain an index ranging from 2 to 10 (which is then recoded to range from 1 to 9).
55. The summary statistics for all variables used in the models and fixed effects are presented in Appendix A, Table A8.1 through Table A8.3.
56. Hoffman and Jamal, "Religion in the Arab Spring," 601.
57. None of the interaction effects are statistically significant except for distrust in government, which takes a negative sign. Full estimation results are presented in Appendix A, Table A8.4.
58. Hoffman and Jamal, "Religion in the Arab Spring."
59. The logistic regression results are presented in tabular format in Appendix A, Table A8.5. The reduced sample estimation is similar to the interaction effects of religiosity with all other variables in the model.
60. Bayat, "Revolution without Movement."
61. Filali-Ansary, "Muslims and Democracy"; Bayat, *Life as Politics*.

CHAPTER 9

1. El Fadl, *Islam and the Challenge of Democracy*; Abdelkader, *Social Justice in Islam*.
2. Kuru, *Islam, Authoritarianism, and Underdevelopment*.
3. Ahmed, *What Is Islam?*
4. Khadduri, *Islamic Conception of Justice*.
5. Abdelkader, *Social Justice in Islam*; Darling, *Social Justice and Political Power*; Thompson, *Justice Interrupted*.
6. An-Náim, *Islam and the Secular State*.
7. Chomsky, *Failed States*; Jamal, *Of Empires and Citizens*; Yom, *From Resilience to Revolution*; Thompson, *Justice Interrupted*.
8. See Mitchell (*Carbon Democracy*) for an elaborate account of this argument in the context of the Western powers' relations with oil-rich Gulf monarchies.
9. Khadduri, *Islamic Conception of Justice*.
10. Kuru, *Islam, Authoritarianism, and Underdevelopment*.
11. Grewal et al., "Poverty and Divine Rewards."
12. Ciftci, Wuthrich, and Shamaileh, *Beyond Piety and Politics*.
13. I am inspired by Nader Hashemi's terminology for this succinct expression (Hashemi, *Islam, Secularism, and Liberal Democracy*).

Bibliography

Abdelkader, Dina. *Social Justice in Islam*. Herndon, VI: International Institute of Islamic Thought, 2000.
Abrahamian, Ervand. "'Ali Shariati: Ideologue of the Iranian Revolution." *Merip Reports* 102 (1982): 24–28.
———. *Iran between Two Revolutions*. Princeton, NJ: Princeton University Press, 1982.
Acemoglu, Daron, and James A Robinson. *Economic Origins of Dictatorship and Democracy*. Cambridge: Cambridge University Press, 2005.
Ahmed, Shahab. *What Is Islam? The Importance of Being Islamic*. Princeton, NJ: Princeton University Press, 2016.
Al-Qadhi Muhammad bin Salama. *Musnad al-Shihab*. Lebanon: Dar al-Kutub al-Ilmiya, 1985.
Al-Rikabi, Jaffar. "Bāqir al-Ṣadr and the Islamic State: A Theory for 'Islamic Democracy.'" *Journal of Shi'a Islamic Studies* 5, no. 3 (2012): 249–275.
Al- Ṣadr, Ayatullah Bāqir. *Iqtisaduna (Our Economics)*. Beirut: Dir al-Ta'aruf, 1982.
Altun, Fahrettin. "Alternatif Tarih Yazmak: Necip Fazıl Kısakürek'in Hafıza Siyaseti." *Toplum ve Bilim* 123 (2012): 170–203.
Altunkaya, M. "Mevlid-i Şerif»in 1480. Yılında Adalet ve Özgürlük Peygamberi Muhammed (Sav)." *Özgün İrade* 5, no. 49 (2008): 17–19.
Amaeshi, Kenneth. "Decolonizing African Scholarship." Project Syndicate, November 27, 2019.
An-Náim, Abdullahi Ahmed. *Islam and the Secular State*. Cambridge, MA: Harvard University Press, 2008.
———. *Muslims and Global Justice*. Philadelphia: University of Pennsylvania Press, 2011.

An-Nawawi. *Forty Hadith of An-Nawawi*, accessed May25, 2021. Available at https://sunnah.com/nawawi40.
Arab Barometer. "Methodology." Available at https://www.arabbarometer.org/survey-data/methodology/.
Arat, Reşit Rahmeti. "Yusuf Has Hacip. Kutatgu Bilig Çeviri II." Ankara: Atatürk Kültür, Dil ve Tarih Yüksek Kurumu, Türk Tarihi Kurumu Yayınları, 1985.
Arikan, Gizem, and Pazit Ben-Nun Bloom. "Religion and Political Protest: A Cross-Country Analysis." *Comparative Political Studies* 52, no. 2 (2019): 246–276.
Ayoob, Mohammed. "Challenging Hegemony: Political Islam and the North–South Divide." *International Studies Review* 9, no. 4 (2007): 629–643.
———. *The Many Faces of Political Islam: Religion and Politics in the Muslim World*. Ann Arbor: University of Michigan Press, 2008.
———. "Political Islam: Image and Reality." *World Policy Journal* 21, no. 3 (2004): 1–14.
Balcı, İsrafil. "'Umar (r.a) : A Leader Crowned with Truth and Justice." *Life and Religion*. Istanbul: Turkish Diyanet Foundation, 2013. Available at https://www.lastprophet.info/umar-r-a-a-leader-crowned-with-truth-and-justice.
Bandura, Albert. "Self-Efficacy: Toward a Unifying Theory of Behavioral Change." *Psychological Review* 84, no. 2 (1977): 191–215.
Bartky, Sandra Lee. "Foucault, Femininity, and the Modernization of Patriarchal Power." In *Feminism and Foucault: Reflections on Resistance*, edited by Sandra Lee Bartky, Irene Diamond, and Lee Quinby, 61–86. Boston, MA: Northeastern University Press,1988.
Batniji, Rajaie, Lina Khatib, Melani Cammett, Jeffrey Sweet, Sanjay Basu, Amaney Jamal, Paul Wise, and Rita Giacaman. "Governance and Health in the Arab World." *The Lancet* 383, no. 9914 (2014): 343–355.
Bayat, Asef. *Life as Politics: How Ordinary People Change the Middle East*. Stanford, CA: Stanford University Press, 2013.
———. "Revolution without Movement, Movement without Revolution: Comparing Islamic Activism in Iran and Egypt." *Comparative Studies in Society and History* 40, no. 1 (1998): 136–169.
Beblawi, Hazem, and Giacomo Luciani. *The Rentier State*. New York: Routledge, 2016.
Beinin, Joel. *Workers and Peasants in the Modern Middle East*. Vol. 2. Cambridge: Cambridge University Press, 2001.
Beinin, Joel, and Frédéric Vairel. *Social Movements, Mobilization, and Contestation in the Middle East and North Africa*. Stanford, CA: Stanford University Press, 2013.
Bellin, Eva. "The Robustness of Authoritarianism in the Middle East: Exceptionalism in Comparative Perspective." *Comparative Politics* 36, no. 2 (2004): 139–157.
Berger, Lars. "Sharīʿa, Islamism and Arab Support for Democracy." *Democratization* 26, no. 2 (2019): 309–326.
Blaydes, Lisa. *Elections and Distributive Politics in Mubarak's Egypt*. Cambridge: Cambridge University Press, 2010.
Blaydes, Lisa, and Eric Chaney. "The Feudal Revolution and Europe's Rise: Political Divergence of the Christian West and the Muslim World before 1500 CE." *American Political Science Review* 107, no. 1 (2013): 16–34.
Bloom, Pazit Ben-Nun, Gizem Arikan, and Marie Courtemanche. "Religious Social Identity, Religious Belief, and Anti-Immigration Sentiment." *American Political Science Review* 109, no. 2 (2015): 203.

Boix, Carles. *Democracy and Redistribution*. Cambridge: Cambridge University Press, 2003.

Bourdeau, M. "Auguste Comte." *The Stanford Encyclopedia of Philosophy*. Stanford, CA: Stanford University Press, 2011.

Brannen, Samuel J., Christian S. Haig, and Katherine Schmidt. "The Age of Mass Protests: Understanding an Escalating Global Trend." Center for Strategic and International Studies. Washington, DC, March 2020. Available at https://csis-website-prod.s3.amazonaws.com/s3fs-public/publication/200303_MassProtests_V2.pdf?u L3KRAKjoHfmcnFENNWTXdUbf0Fk0Qke.

Braudel, Fernand. "Histoire et Sciences Sociales: La Longue Durée." *Annales: Histoire, Sciences Sociales*, 13, no. 4 (1958): 725–753.

Brownlee, Jason, Tarek Masoud, and Andrew Reynolds. *The Arab Spring: Pathways of Repression and Reform*. New York: Oxford University Press, 2015.

Bulaç, Ali. "Islamcilik Nedir?" *Zaman*, July 2012.

Çağlak, C. "Ebedi Adalet." *İktibas* 19, no. 274 (2001): 31.

Çakır, Y. "Amerikan Adaleti ve Zenciler." *Haksöz* 1, no. 14 (1992): 16.

Cammett, Melani, and Sukriti Issar. "Bricks and Mortar Clientelism: Sectarianism and the Logics of Welfare Allocation in Lebanon." *World Politics* 62, no. 3 (2010): 381–421.

Castells, Manuel. *Networks of Outrage and Hope: Social Movements in the Internet Age*. Malden, MA: Polity Press, 2015.

Cetinsaya, Gokhan. "Rethinking Nationalism and Islam: Some Preliminary Notes on the Roots of 'Turkish-Islamic Synthesis' in Modern Turkish Political Thought." *Muslim World* 89, nos. 3–4 (1999): 350–376.

Chakrabarty, Dipesh. *Provincializing Europe: Postcolonial Thought and Historical Difference*. Princeton, NJ: Princeton University Press, 2000.

Chen, Daniel L., and Jo Thori Lind. "The Political Economy of Beliefs: Why Fiscal and Social Conservatives/Liberals Come Hand-in-Hand." Unpub. paper, 2005.

Chomsky, Noam. *Failed States: The Abuse of Power and the Assault on Democracy*. New York: Metropolitan Books, 2007.

Ciftci, Sabri. "Islam, Social Justice, and Democracy." *Politics and Religion* 12, no. 4 (2019): 549–576.

———. "Modernden Postmoderne Iktidar Kavramındaki Değişim." Master thesis, Ankara Üniversitesi Sosyal Bilimler Enstitüsü Kamu Yönetimi ve Siyaset, 1997.

———. "Modernization, Islam, or Social Capital: What Explains Attitudes toward Democracy in the Muslim World?" *Comparative Political Studies* 43, no. 11 (2010): 1442–1470.

———. "Secular-Islamist Cleavage, Values, and Support for Democracy and Shari'a in the Arab World." *Political Research Quarterly* 66, no. 4 (2013): 781–793.

———. "Self-Expression Values, Loyalty Generation, and Support for Authoritarianism: Evidence from the Arab World." *Democratization* 25, no. 7 (2018): 1132–1152.

Ciftci, Sabri, Fred. M. Wuthrich, and Ammar Shamaileh. *Beyond Piety and Politics: Religion, Social Relations, and Public Preferences in MENA*, n.d.

Ciftci, Sabri, F. Michael Wuthrich, and Ammar Shamaileh. "Islam, Religious Outlooks, and Support for Democracy." *Political Research Quarterly* 72, no. 2 (2019): 435–449.

Cizre-Sakallioglu, Umit, and Menderes Cinar. "Turkey 2002: Kemalism, Islamism, and Politics in the Light of the February 28 Process." *South Atlantic Quarterly* 102, no. 2 (2003): 309–332.
Clark, Janine A. *Islam, Charity, and Activism: Middle-Class Networks and Social Welfare in Egypt, Jordan, and Yemen.* Bloomington: Indiana University Press, 2004.
Crone, Patricia. *God's Rule: Government and Islam.* New York: Columbia University Press, 2004.
Danesh, Maryam, and Hassan Abniki. "The Relation between Liberty and Justice in Ali Shariati' Political Thought." *International Journal of Political Science* 5, no. 9 (2015): 1–8.
Danışman, Zuhuri. *Koçi Bey Risalesi.* 1000 Temel Eser, vol. 609. Ankara: Kültür ve Turizm Bakanlığı Yayınları, 1985.
Darling, Linda T. *A History of Social Justice and Political Power in the Middle East: The Circle of Justice from Mesopotamia to Globalization.* New York: Routledge, 2013.
Davis, Nancy J., and Robert V. Robinson. "The Egalitarian Face of Islamic Orthodoxy: Support for Islamic Law and Economic Justice in Seven Muslim-Majority Nations." *American Sociological Review* 71, no. 2 (2006): 167–190.
Djupe, Paul A., and Ryan L. Claassen. *The Evangelical Crackup? The Future of the Evangelical-Republican Coalition.* Philedelphia: Temple University Press, 2018.
Djupe, Paul A., and Christopher P. Gilbert. *The Political Influence of Churches.* Cambridge: Cambridge University Press, 2008.
———. "The Resourceful Believer: Generating Civic Skills in Church." *Journal of Politics* 68, no. 1 (2006): 116–127.
Driessen, Michael D. "Sources of Muslim Democracy: The Supply and Demand of Religious Policies in the Muslim World." *Democratization* 25, no. 1 (2018): 115–135.
Duran, Burhanettin. "Cumhuriyet Dönemi İslamcılığı: İdeolojik Konumları, Dönüşümü ve Evreleri." *Modern Türkiye'de Siyasi Düşünce* 6 (2005): 129–156.
Editorial. "Adalet, Politikaya Alet Edilemez." *Yeniden Milli Mücadele* 10, no. 516 (1979): 16.
———. "İslam'ın Kayıp Savaşçıları ve Susturulan Adalet Çığlığı." *İktibas* 20, no. 277 (2002): 58.
El-Affendi, Abdelwahab. *Who Needs an Islamic State?* London: Malaysia Think Tank, 2008.
Eliaçık, İhsan. "Adalet 'Kozmos'un Temelidir." *Bilgi Ve Düşünce* 9 (2003): 58–63.
———. "İslam Uygarlığı Tarihten mi Çekiliyor?" *Bilgi Ve Düşünce* 8 (2003): 37–46.
———. "Sivil Dönüşüm." *Değişim* 5, no. 44 (1997): 44.
Eliaçık, R. İhsan. *Adalet Devleti: Ortak İyinin İktidarı.* İnşa Yayınları, 2015.
Emek ve Adalet Platformu. "Emek ve Adalet'ten Gezi Parkı Bildirisi." Accessed July 10, 2017. Available at http://platformhaber.net/?p=19298.
Emiroğlu, T. "İnsanlık âdil İdareye Muhtaçtır." *Sebil* 4, no. 167 (1979): 11.
Emre, Akif. "'Müslümancılık' Ya Da Klan Siyaseti." *Yeni Şafak*, August 26, 2008. Available at https://www.yenisafak.com/yazarlar/akif-emre/muslumancilik-ya-da-klan-siyaseti-12487.
Enayat, Hamid. *Modern Islamic Political Thought: The Response of the Shi 'i and Sunni Muslims to the Twentieth Century.* New York: I. B. Taurus, 2005.
Ersoy, Mehmed Âkif. *Safahat.* Istanbul: Bilgeoğuz Yayınları, 1989.

Esposito, John L., and Dalia Mogahed. "Battle for Muslims' Hearts and Minds: The Road Not (yet) Taken." *Middle East Policy* 14, no. 1 (2007): 27–41.

Esposito, John, and John L. Voll. *Islam and Democracy*. New York: Oxford University Press, 1996.

Fadl, Khaled Abou El. *Islam and the Challenge of Democracy: A Boston Review Book*. Princeton, NJ: Princeton University Press, 2004.

Fakhry, Majid. *A History of Islamic Philosophy*. New York: Columbia University Press, 2004.

Feldman, Noah. *The Fall and Rise of the Islamic State*. Princeton, NJ: Princeton University Press, 2012.

Feldman, Stanley. "Structure and Consistency in Public Opinion: The Role of Core Beliefs and Values." *American Journal of Political Science* 32, no. 2 (1988): 416–440.

Filali-Ansary, Abdou. "Muslims and Democracy." *Journal of Democracy* 10, no. 3 (1999): 18–32.

Fish, M. Steven. *Are Muslims Distinctive? A Look at the Evidence*. New York: Oxford University Press, 2011.

Foucault, Michel. *Archaeology of Knowledge*. Translated by A. Sheridan. New York: Routledge, 2013.

———. *Discipline and Punish: The Birth of the Prison*. Translated by A. Sheridan. New York: Vintage, 1991.

Gause, F. Gregory, III. "Why Middle East Studies Missed the Arab Spring: The Myth of Authoritarian Stability." *Foreign Affairs* 90, no. 4 (2011): 81–90.

Gellner, Ernest. "Islam and Marxism: Some Comparisons." *International Affairs* 67, no. 1 (1991): 1–6.

———. *Muslim Society*. Cambridge: Cambridge University Press, 1983.

Goizueta, Roberto S. "Liberation Theology 1: Gustavo Gutierrez." In *Wiley Blackwell Companion to Political Theology*, edited by William T. Cavanaugh and Peter Manley Scott, 280–292. New York: John Wiley and Sons, 2019.

Gold, Gary D., and George S. Naufal. "Wasta: The Other Invisible Hand—A Case Study of University Students in the Gulf." *Journal of Arabian Studies* 2, no. 1 (2012): 59–73.

Gorodnichenko, Yuriy, and Gerard Roland. "Culture, Institutions and Democratization." *Public Choice* 187 (2020): 1–31.

Greif, Avner, and David D. Laitin. "A Theory of Endogenous Institutional Change." *American Political Science Review* 98, no. 4 (2004): 633–652.

Grewal, Sharan, Amaney A. Jamal, Tarek Masoud, and Elizabeth R. Nugent. "Poverty and Divine Rewards: The Electoral Advantage of Islamist Political Parties." *American Journal of Political Science* 63, no. 4 (2019): 859–874.

Grzymała-Busse, Anna. *Nations under God: How Churches Use Moral Authority to Influence Policy*. Princeton, NJ: Princeton University Press, 2015.

Gumuscu, Sebnem. "Class, Status, and Party: The Changing Face of Political Islam in Turkey and Egypt." *Comparative Political Studies* 43, no. 7 (2010): 835–861.

Haber7. "5 Yıldızlı Otel Karşısında Yerde Iftar." Available at https://ramazan.haber7.com/tarihi-mekanlar/haber/771822-5-yildizli-otel-karsisinda-yerde-iftar.

Hardy, Cynthia, Bill Harley, and Nelson Phillips. "Discourse Analysis and Content Analysis: Two Solitudes." *Qualitative Methods* 2, no. 1 (2004): 19–22.

Harris, Kevan. "A Martyrs' Welfare State and Its Contradictions: Regime Resilience and Limits through the Lens of Social Policy in Iran." In *Middle East Authoritarianisms: Governance, Contestation, and Regime Resilience in Syria and Iran*, edited by Steven Heydemann and Reinoud Leenders, 61–80. Stanford: Stanford University Press, 2013.

Harvey, Ramon. *The Qur'an and the Just Society*. Edinburgh: Edinburgh University Press, 2018.

Hasan, Ahmad. "Social Justice in Islam." *Islamic Studies* 10, no. 3 (1971): 209–219.

Hashemi, Nader. *Islam, Secularism, and Liberal Democracy: Toward a Democratic Theory for Muslim Societies*. New York: Oxford University Press, 2009.

Hendawi, Hamza. "Sudan's 'Nubian Queen' Protester Becomes Iconic Image of Anti-Government Demonstrations." *National News*, April 10, 2019. Available at https://www.thenational.ae/world/africa/sudan-s-nubian-queen-protester-becomes-iconic-image-of-anti-government-demonstrations-1.847419.

Hodgson, Marshall G. S. *The Venture of Islam, Volume 1: The Classical Age of Islam*. Chicago: University of Chicago Press, 1974.

Hoffman, Michael, and Amaney Jamal. "Religion in the Arab Spring: Between Two Competing Narratives." *Journal of Politics* 76, no. 3 (2014): 593–606.

Horkheimer, Max. *Critical Theory: Selected Essays*. Translated by Matthew J. O'Connell and Others. New York: Continuum, 2002.

Huntington, Samuel. "The Clash of Civilizations." *Foreign Affairs* 72, no. 3 (1993): 22–49.

Iannaccone, Laurence R. "Sacrifice and Stigma: Reducing Free-Riding in Cults, Communes, and Other Collectives." *Journal of Political Economy* 100, no. 2 (1992): 271–291.

İkiz, M. L. "Tahkirciler." *İslamın İlk Emri Oku* 5, no. 49 (1965): 12.

Iqbal, Muhammad. *The Reconstruction of Religious Thought in Islam*. Lahore: Sh. Muhammad Ashraf, 1968.

Işık, Vahdettin, Ahmet Köroğlu, and Yusuf Enes Sezgin. *1960–1980 Arası İslamcı Dergiler: Toparlanma ve Çeşitlenme*. Ankara: İlem Kitaplığı, 2016.

Israel, Jonathan Irvine. *Radical Enlightenment: Philosophy and the Making of Modernity, 1650–1750*. New York: Oxford University Press, 2001.

Izutsu, Toshihiko. *Ethico-Religious Concepts in the Qur'an*. Vol. 1. Montreal and Kingston: McGill-Queen's University Press, 2002.

Jafri, Askari, trans. *Peak of Eloquence, Nahjul Balagha Sermons and Letters of Imam*, 11th rev. ed. Islamic Seminary Publications, n.d.

Jamal, Amaney A. *Of Empires and Citizens: Pro-American Democracy or No Democracy at All?* Princeton, NJ: Princeton University Press, 2012.

———. "Reassessing Support for Islam and Democracy in the Arab World? Evidence from Egypt and Jordan." *World Affairs* 169, no. 2 (2006): 51–63.

Jamalzadeh, Naser. "Sociopolitical Justice in Three Jurisprudential, Philosophical and Sociological Approaches." *Islamic Political Thought* 2, no. 1 (2015): 7–42.

Johnson, Benton. "On Church and Sect." *American Sociological Review* 28, no. 4 (1963): 539–549.

Kabbani, Nader. "Youth Unemployment in the Middle East and North Africa: Revisiting and Reframing the Challenge," February 26, 2019. Available at https://

www.brookings.edu/research/youth-employment-in-the-middle-east-and-north-africa-revisiting-and-reframing-the-challenge/.

Kara, İsmail. *Türkiye'de İslamcılık Düşüncesi (I–II)*. İstanbul: Dergah Yayinlari, 2013.

Karagiannis, Emmanuel. *The New Political Islam: Human Rights, Democracy, and Justice*. Philadelphia: University of Pennsylvania Press, 2018.

Karakoç, Ekrem, and Birol Başkan. "Religion in Politics: How Does Inequality Affect Public Secularization?" *Comparative Political Studies* 45, no. 12 (2012): 1510–1541.

Karpat, Kemal. *The Gecekondu: Rural Migration and Urbanization*. Cambridge: Cambridge University Press, 1976.

Karpat, Kemal H. *The Politicization of Islam: Reconstructing Identity, State, Faith, and Community in the Late Ottoman State*. New York: Oxford University Press, 2001.

Keddie, Nikki R. *An Islamic Response to Imperialism: Political and Religious Writings of Sayyid Jamāl Al-Dīn Al-Afghānī*. Vol. 586. Berkeley: University of California Press, 1983.

———. *Religion and Rebellion in Iran: The Tobacco Protest of 1891–1892*. London: Frank Cass, 1966.

Kedourie, Elie. *Democracy and Arab Political Culture*. Portland: Frank Cass, 1994.

Kemal, Namık. "And Seek Their Council in the Matter." In *Modernist Islam 1840–1940: A Source Book*, edited by Charles Kurzman, 144–148. New York: Oxford University Press, 2002.

———. "Renan Müdafaanamesi." In *Külliyat-ı Kemal*, 1st ed., edited by Ali Ekrem Bulayir, 58. Istanbul: Selanik Matbaasi, n.d.

Khadduri, Majid. *The Islamic Conception of Justice*. Baltimore: Johns Hopkins University Press, 1984.

Khan, M. A. Muqtedar. *Islam and Good Governance: A Political Philosophy of Ihsan*. New York: Palgrave MacMillan, 2019.

Khanani, Ahmed. "Contemporary Islamism and the Sacralization of Democracy." Political Theology, 2013. Avialable at https://politicaltheology.com/political-theology-and-islamic-studies-symposium-contemporary-islamism-and-the-sacralization-of-democracy/.

Khatib, Lina, and Ellen Lust. *Taking to the Streets: The Transformation of Arab Activism*. Baltimore: Johns Hopkins University Press, 2014.

Khawaja, Mustafa. "Fighting Corruption: From the Missing Link to Development Priority." In *Arab Human Development in the 21st Century: The Primacy of Empowerment*, edited by Bahgat Korany, 105–130. Cairo: American University in Cairo Press, 2014.

Khomeini, Sayyid R. M. *Theory of Justice*. Translated by Hussein Karamyar. Available at https://www.al-islam.org/theory-justice-sayyid-ruhullah-musawi-khomeini.

Korany, Bahgat. "Redefining Development for a New Generation: A Political Economy Analysis." In *Arab Human Development in the Twenty-First Century: The Primacy of Empowerment*, edited by Bahgat Korany, 3–19. Cairo: American University in Cairo Press, 2014.

Köroğlu, Ahmet. "Türkiye'de İslamcılık Düşüncesinin Seyrini Dergiler Üzerinden Okumak." In *1960–1980 Arasi Islamci Dergiler: Toparlanma ve Cesitlenme*, edited by Vahdettin Işık, Ahmet Köroğlu, and Yusuf Enes Sezgin, 5–41. Ankara: İlem Kitaplığı, 2016.

Kuhn, Randall. "On the Role of Human Development in the Arab Spring." *Population and Development Review* 38, no. 4 (2012): 649–683.

Kuran, Timur. *Islam and Mammon*. Princeton, NJ: Princeton University Press, 2010.

———. "Now Out of Never: The Element of Surprise in the East European Revolution of 1989." *World Politics: A Quarterly Journal of International Relations* 44, no. 1 (1991): 7–48.

Kuru, Ahmet T. *Islam, Authoritarianism, and Underdevelopment: A Global and Historical Comparison*. Cambridge: Cambridge University Press, 2019.

———. "Passive and Assertive Secularism: Historical Conditions, Ideological Struggles, and State Policies toward Religion." *World Politics* 59, no. 4 (2007): 568–594.

Kurzman, Charles. *Liberal Islam: A Source Book*. New York: Oxford University Press, 1998.

Kyriacou, Andreas P. "Individualism–Collectivism, Governance and Economic Development." *European Journal of Political Economy* 42 (2016): 91–104.

Lapidus, Ira. "Islamic Revival and Modernity: The Contemporary Movements and the Historical Paradigms." *Journal of the Economic and Social History of the Orient* 40, no. 4 (1997): 444–460.

Lapidus, Ira M. *A History of Islamic Societies*. Cambridge: Cambridge University Press, 2002.

———. "The Separation of State and Religion in the Development of Early Islamic Society." *International Journal of Middle East Studies* 6, no. 4 (1975): 363–385.

Levitsky, Steven, and Daniel Ziblatt. *How Democracies Die*. New York: Broadway Books, 2018.

Lewis, Bernard. *The Emergence of Modern Turkey*. New York: Oxford University Press, 1961.

———. "Freedom and Justice in the Modern Middle East." *Foreign Affairs* 84 (2005): 36.

———. "Islam and Liberal Democracy." *Atlantic Monthly* 271, no. 2 (1993): 89–97.

———. "Islam and Liberal Democracy: A Historical Overview." *Journal of Democracy* 7, no. 2 (1996): 52–63.

———. *The Shaping of the Modern Middle East*. New York: Oxford University Press, 1994.

———. "Why Turkey Is the Only Muslim Democracy."*Middle East Quarterly*, March (1994): 41–49.

Licht, Amir N., Chanan Goldschmidt, and Shalom H. Schwartz. "Culture Rules: The Foundations of the Rule of Law and Other Norms of Governance." *Journal of Comparative Economics* 35, no. 4 (2007): 659–688.

———. "The Emergence of Social Justice in the West." In *Routledge International Handbook of Social Justice*, edited by Michael Reisch, 14–26. New York: Routledge, 2014.

Lyotard, Jean-Francois. *The Postmodern Condition: A Report on Knowledge*. Translated by G. Bennington and B. Massumi. Minneapolis: University of Minnesota Press, 1979.

Madi-Sisman, Özlem. *Muslims, Money, and Democracy in Turkey: Reluctant Capitalists*. New York: Palgrave MacMillan, 2017.

Madi-Sisman, Özlem, and Sisman, Cengiz. "Immanuel Wallerstein, Islam, Islamists, and the World-System Theory." *The Maydan*, November 2018. Available at https://themaydan.com/2018/11/immanuel-wallerstein-islam-islamists-world-system-theory/.

Maguire, Daniel C. "Religious Influences on Justice Theory." In *Routledge International Handbook of Social Justice*, edited by Michael Reisch, 53–64. New York: Routledge, 2014.

March, Andrew F. *The Caliphate of Man: Popular Sovereignty in Modern Islamic Thought*. Cambridge, MA: Belknap Press of Harvard University Press, 2019.

———. "Genealogies of Sovereignty in Islamic Political Theology." *Social Research: An International Quarterly* 80, no. 1 (2013): 293–320.

———. "Taking People as They Are: Islam as a 'Realistic Utopia' in the Political Theory of Sayyid Qutb." *American Political Science Review* 104, no. 1 (2010): 189–207.

Mardin, Serif. *The Genesis of Young Ottoman Thought: A Study in the Modernization of Turkish Political Ideas*. Syracuse, NY: Syracuse University Press, 2000.

Markham, Ian S., and Suendam Birinci Pirim. *An Introduction to Said Nursi: Life, Thought and Writings*. New York: Ashgate, 2011.

Marx, Karl. "Theses on Feuerbach (1845)." In *Karl Marx and Frederick Engels, Selected Works*, translated by W. Lough, 13–15. Moscow, USSR: Progress Publishers, 1969.

Masoud, Tarek. *Counting Islam: Religion, Class, and Elections in Egypt*. Cambridge: Cambridge University Press, 2014.

Mawdudi, Abu al-A'la. "Nationalism and Islam." In *Islam in Transition: Muslim Perspectives*, edited by John Donahue and John L. Esposito, 94–97. New York: Oxford University Press, 1982.

Maydan. "Islam and Islamism in Turkey: A Conversation with İsmail Kara." *The Maydan*, 2017. Available at https://themaydan.com/2017/10/islam-islamism-turkey-conversation-ismail-kara/.

McAdam, Doug, Sidney Tarrow, and Charles Tilly. "Comparative Perspectives on Contentious Politics." In *Comparative Politics: Rationality, Culture, and Structure*, edited by Mark Irving Lichbach and Alan S. Zuckerman, 260–290. Cambridge: Cambridge University Press, 2009.

Melucci, Alberto. *Challenging Codes: Collective Action in the Information Age*. Cambridge: Cambridge University Press, 1996.

Menchik, Jeremy. *Islam and Democracy in Indonesia: Tolerance without Liberalism*. Cambridge: Cambridge University Press, 2016.

Mesquita, Bruce Bueno De, Alastair Smith, Randolph M. Siverson, and James D. Morrow. *The Logic of Political Survival*. Cambridge, MA: MIT Press, 2005.

Michot, Yahya. "Mamlūks, Qalandars, Rāfidīs, and the 'Other' Ibn Taymiyya." Public Lecture at Hartford Seminary, CT, 2015. Avialable at https://www.academia.edu/32096818/Yahya_Michot_Mamlūks_Qalandars_Rāfidīs_and_the_Other_Ibn_Taymiyya_.

Mirakhor, Abbas, and Hossein Askari. *Conceptions of Justice from Islam to the Present*. Cham, Switzerland: Palgrave MacMillan, 2020.

Mitchell, Timothy. *Carbon Democracy: Political Power in the Age of Oil*. London: Verso Books, 2011.

Moaddel, Mansoor. *Islamic Modernism, Nationalism, and Fundamentalism: Episode and Discourse*. Chicago: University of Chicago Press, 2005.

Moore, Barrington, Jr. *Social Origins of Dictatorship and Democracy: Lord and Peasant in the Making of the Modern World*. Boston: Beacon, 1993.
Murphy, Caryle. "Saudi King Unveils Massive Spending Package." *National News* (Abu Dhabi), March 19, 2011. Available at https://www.thenational.ae/news/world/saudi-king-unveils-massive-spending-package#page2.
Nasr, Seyyed Vali Reza. *Mawdudi and the Making of Islamic Revivalism*. New York: Oxford University Press on Demand, 1996.
Newton, Kenneth. "Trust, Social Capital, Civil Society, and Democracy." *International Political Science Review* 22, no. 2 (2001): 201–214.
The Noble Quran. Quran.com. Saheeh International translation. Available at https://www.quran.com.
Norris, Pippa. *Critical Citizens: Global Support for Democratic Government*. Oxford: Oxford University Press, 1999.
North, Douglass C., John Joseph Wallis, and Barry R. Weingast. *Violence and Social Orders: A Conceptual Framework for Interpreting Recorded Human History*. Cambridge: Cambridge University Press, 2009.
Nursi, Said. *Risale-i Nur Külliyatı*, 2 Vols. Istanbul: Nesil, 1996.
Nurtsch, Ceyda. "The Koran and Social Justice: Interview with Turkish Theologian İhsan Eliaçık," January 15, 2014. Qantara. Accessed August 13, 2014. Available at http://en.qantara.de/content/interview-with-turkish-theologian-ihsan-eliacik-the-koran-and-social-justice.
Özdalga, E. "Necip Fazıl Kısakürek: Heroic Nationalist in the Garden of Mysticism." *Meddelanden: Swedish Research Institute in Istanbul, Stockholm* 19 (1994): 5–27.
Pepinsky, Thomas B., R. William Liddle, and Saiful Mujani. "Testing Islam's Political Advantage: Evidence from Indonesia." *American Journal of Political Science* 56, no. 3 (2012): 584–600.
Pepinsky, Thomas B., and Bozena C. Welborne. "Piety and Redistributive Preferences in the Muslim World." *Political Research Quarterly* 64, no. 3 (2011): 491–505.
Phillips, Nelson, and Cynthia Hardy. *Understanding Discourse Analysis*. Thousand Oaks, CA: Sage, 2002.
Philpott, Daniel. "Explaining the Political Ambivalence of Religion." *American Political Science Review* 101, no. 3 (2007): 505–525.
Pilavoğlu, M. K. "Dünya Medeniyetleri Arasında İslâm Medeniyeti İslâm Medeniyetinin Temeli Adâlettir İslâmiyetin Adalet Anlayışı." *İlahi Işık* 5, no. 104 (1971): 8.
Pitlik, Hans, and Martin Rode. "Individualistic Values, Institutional Trust, and Interventionist Attitudes." *Journal of Institutional Economics* 13, no. 3 (2017): 575–598.
Porta, Rafael La, Florencio Lopez-de-Silanes, Andrei Shleifer, and Robert Vishny. "The Quality of Government." *Journal of Law, Economics, and Organization* 15, no. 1 (1999): 222–279.
Putnam, Robert D. *Bowling Alone: The Collapse and Revival of American Community*. New York: Simon and Schuster, 2000.
Quisay, Walaa, and Thomas Parker. "Thought, On the Theology of Obedience: An Analysis of Shaykh Bin Bayyah and Shaykh Hamza Yusuf's Political." *The Maydan*, 2019.
Qutb, Sayyid. *Milestones*. International Islamic, 1981.
———. *Social Justice in Islam*. Translated by John B. Hardie. Oneonta, NY: Islamic Publications International, 2000.

Rahman, Fazlur. "The Principle of 'Shūrā' and the Role of the Umma in Islam." *American Journal of Islamic Social Sciences* 1, no. 1 (1984): 1.

Ramadan, Tariq. *Islam, the West and the Challenges of Modernity.* Leicester, UK: The Islamic Foundation, 2001.

———. *Western Muslims and the Future of Islam.* Oxford: Oxford University Press, 2003.

Rawls, John. *A Theory of Justice.* Cambridge, MA: Harvard University Press, 2009.

Renan, Ernest. "Islamism and Science." In *The Poetry of the Celtic Races and Other Studies*, translated by William G. Hutchison, 84–108. Port Washington, NY: Kennikat Press, 1970.

Rizzo, Helen, Abdel-Hamid Abdel-Latif, and Katherine Meyer. "The Relationship between Gender Equality and Democracy: A Comparison of Arab versus Non-Arab Muslim Societies." *Sociology* 41, no. 6 (2007): 1151–1170.

Robbins, Michael, and Amaney Jamal. "The State of Social Justice in the Arab World: The Arab Uprisings of 2011 and Beyond." *Contemporary Readings in Law & Social Justice* 8, no. 1 (2016): 127–157.

Rose, Richard. "Does Islam Make People Anti-Democratic? A Central Asian Perspective." *Journal of Democracy* 13, no. 4 (2002): 8–37.

Rotter, Julian B. "Generalized Expectancies for Internal versus External Control of Reinforcement." *Psychological Monographs: General and Applied* 80, no. 1 (1966): 1.

Sachedina, Abdulaziz. *The Islamic Roots of Democratic Pluralism.* New York: Oxford University Press, 2001.

Said, Edward W. *Orientalism.* New York: Pantheon Books, 1978.

Sarfati, Yusuf. "Challenging Hegemony: Voices of Dissent from the Islamic Left in Turkey." In *Political Muslims: Understanding Youth Resistance in the Global Context*, edited by Tahir Abbas and Sadek Hamid, 149–172. Syracuse, NY: Syracuse University Press, 2019.

Schmitter, Philippe C., and Terry Lynn Karl. "What Democracy Is . . . and Is Not." *Journal of Democracy* 2, no. 3 (1991): 75–88.

Schwartz, Shalom H. "Mapping and Interpreting Cultural Differences around the World." In *Comparing Cultures, Dimensions of Culture in a Comparative Perspective*, edited by H. Vinken, J. Soeters, and P. Ester. Boston, MA: Brill, 2004.

———. *Values and Culture.* New York: Routledge, 1997.

Schwedler, Jillian. "Comparative Politics and the Arab Uprisings." *Middle East Law and Governance* 7, no. 1 (2015): 141–152.

Sedgwick, Mark. *Muhammad Abduh.* London: Oneworld, 2014.

Sen, Amartya Kumar. *The Idea of Justice.* Cambridge, MA: Harvard University Press, 2009.

Sevgili, M. "Allahın Adaleti." *İslamın İlk Emri Oku* 15, no. 177 (1977): 14.

Shariati, 'Ali . "And Once Again Abu-Dhar." n.d.

———. "Eslam-Shenasi (Islamology)." *Tehran: Ershad*, 1971.

———. "Man and Islam." In *Man and Islam*, edited by Fatollah Marjani. New Jersey: IPI, 1981. Kindle.

———. *Man and Islam.* Edited by Fatollah Marjani. New Jersey: IPI, 1981. Kindle.

———. "Modern Man and His Prisons." In *Man and Islam*, edited by Fatollah Marjani. New Jersey: IPI, 1981. Kindle.

———. "Red Shi'ism (the Religion of Martyrdom) vs. Black Shi'ism (the Religion of Mourning)." Accessed May 20, 2021. Avialable at https://www.iranchamber.com/personalities/ashariati/works/red_black_shiism.php.

———. "Reflections of a Concerned Muslim on the Plight of Oppressed People." 2 Pts. Accessed May 5, 2018. Available at http://www.shariati.com/kotob.html.

———. *Religion vs Religion*. Chicago: ABC International, 2003.

———. "Worldview of Tawhid." In *On the Sociology of Islam*. Translated by Hamid Algar. Berkeley, CA: Mizan Press, 1979.

———. "World Vision." In *Man and Islam*, edited by Fatollah Marjani. New Jersey: IPI, 1981. Kindle.

Sim, David. "FIFA World Cup 2014: Brazilian Batman Crusades for Justice in Rio Protests." June 13, 2014. Available at https://www.ibtimes.co.uk/fifa-world-cup-2014-brazilian-batman-crusades-justice-rio-protests-1452546.

Smith, Christian. *The Emergence of Liberation Theology: Radical Religion and Social Movement Theory*. Chicago: University of Chicago Press, 1991.

Spierings, Niels. "The Influence of Islamic Orientations on Democratic Support and Tolerance in Five Arab Countries." *Politics and Religion* 7, no. 4 (2014): 706–733.

Stark, Rodney, and Roger Finke. *Acts of Faith: Explaining the Human Side of Religion*. Berkeley: University of California Press, 2000.

Stepan, Alfred C., and Graeme B. Robertson. "An 'Arab' More Than a 'Muslim' Democracy Gap." *Journal of Democracy* 14, no. 3 (2003): 30–44.

Svolik, Milan W. *The Politics of Authoritarian Rule*. Cambridge: Cambridge University Press, 2012.

Tamimi, Azzam. *Rachid Ghannouchi: A Democrat within Islamism*. Oxford: Oxford University Press, 2001.

Tessler, Mark. "Islam and Democracy in the Middle East: The Impact of Religious Orientations on Attitudes toward Democracy in Four Arab Countries." *Comparative Politics* 34, no. 3 (2002): 337–354.

———. *Islam and Politics in the Middle East: Explaining the Views of Ordinary Citizens*. Bloomington: Indiana University Press, 2015.

Tessler, Mark, Amaney Jamal, and Michael Robbins. "New Findings on Arabs and Democracy." *Journal of Democracy* 23, no. 4 (2012): 89–103.

Thompson, Elizabeth F. *Justice Interrupted: The Struggle for Constitutional Government in the Middle East*. Cambridge, MA: Harvard University Press, 2013.

Tilly, Charles. *Contention and Democracy in Europe, 1650–2000*. Cambridge: Cambridge University Press, 2004.

Tosun, M. H. "Mağaralarımızın Tıkaçlarına İlahi Çözüm Saygı İffet ve Adaleti Kuşanmak." *Özgün İrade* 6, no. 65 (2009): 40–42.

Transparency International. "Middle East and North Africa: Corruption Continues as Institutions and Political Rights Weaken." January 29, 2019. Available at https://www.transparency.org/en/news/regional-analysis-mena.

Tuğal, Cihan. *Passive Revolution: Absorbing the Islamic Challenge to Capitalism*. Stanford, CA: Stanford University Press, 2009.

Türkmen, Hamza. "Toplumu Kuran Ekseninde Donusturmeyi Esas Almaliyiz." *Yeni Yeryüzü* 1 no. 9 (1994): 7.

Türköne, Mümtazer. *Siyasi Ideoloji Olarak Islamciligin Dogusu*. Istanbul: Iletisim, 1991.

Tusi, Nasir Al-Din Muḥammad Ibn Muḥammad. Akhlāq-i Nāṣirī. [18th Century] Manuscript/Mixed Material. Avialable at https://www.loc.gov/item/2016404676/.
Uslaner, Eric M. "Democracy and Social Capital." In *Democracy and Trust*, edited by Mark Warren, 121–150. Cambridge: Cambridge University Press, 1999.
Vahide, Sukran. *Islam in Modern Turkey: An Intellectual Biography of Bediuzzaman Said Nursi*. Albany: State University of New York Press, 2012.
Wallerstein, Immanuel. "Islam, the West, and the World." *Journal of Islamic Studies* 10, no. 2 (1999): 109–125.
———. "The Political Construction of Islam in the Modern World-System." In *Islam and the Orientalist World-System*, edited by Khaldoun Samman and Mazhar Al-Zo'by, 33–44. London and New york: Routledge, 2015.
Walzer, Richard. *Abū Naṣr Al-Fārābī's Mabādi' Ārā' Ahl Al-Madīna Al-Fāḍila: A Revised Text with Introduction, Translation, and Commentary*. New York: Oxford University Press, 1985.
Weber, Max. *The Protestant Ethic and the Spirit of Capitalism*. London: Allen and Unwin, 1930.
Wedeen, Lisa. *Ambiguities of Domination: Politics, Rhetoric, and Symbols in Contemporary Syria*. Chicago: University of Chicago Press, 2015.
Weedon, C. *Feminist Practice and Post-Structuralist Theory*. Oxford: Basil Blackwell, 1987.
Yavuz, M. Hakan. *Islamic Political Identity in Turkey*. New York: Oxford University Press, 2003.
———. "Nationalism and Islam: Yusuf Akçura and 'Üç Tarz-ı Siyaset.'" *Journal of Islamic Studies* 4, no. 2 (1993): 175–207.
———. *Nostalgia for the Empire: The Politics of Neo-Ottomanism*. New York: Oxford University Press, 2020.
———. *Secularism and Muslim Democracy in Turkey*. Vol. 28. Cambridge: Cambridge University Press, 2009.
———. *Toward an Islamic Enlightenment: The Gülen Movement*. New York: Oxford University Press, 2013.
———. "Turkey: Islam without Shari'a?" In *Shari'a Politics: Islamic Law and Society in the Modern World*, edited by Robert W. Hefner, 146–178. Bloomington: Indiana University Press, 2011.
Yavuz, M. Hakan, and John L. Esposito. *Turkish Islam and the Secular State: The Gülen Movement*. Syracuse, NY: Syracuse University Press, 2003.
Yazgan, M. "Adalet ve Zulüm." *Büyük Doğu* 13, no. 20 (1967): 20.
Yeniçeri, C. "İslâm'da Ölçü ve Tartı." *İslam Medeniyeti* 2, no. 13 (1968): 11.
Yenigun, Halil Ibrahim. "The New Antinomies of the Islamic Movement in Post-Gezi Turkey: Islamism vs. Muslimism." *Turkish Studies* 18, no. 2 (2017): 229–250.
Yıldırım, E. "Şura, Biat ve Adalet Temeldir." *Yeni Zemin* 1, no. 5 (1993): 20–21.
Yom, Sean L. *From Resilience to Revolution: How Foreign Interventions Destabilize the Middle East*. New York: Columbia University Press, 2015.

Index

Page numbers followed by the letter t *refer to tables. Page numbers followed by the letter* f *refer to figures.*

Abdelkader, Dina, 4, 39
Abduh, Muhammad, 42, 133
Abrahamian, Ervand, 55
Abū Bakr, 54–55, 60
Abu-Dhar al-Ghifārīy, 59, 61
Acemoglu, Daron, 43
Affendi, Abdelwahab El-, 36
Afghānī, Jamāl al-Dīn al-, 17, 31, 42
Ahmed, Shahab, 31, 37–38, 47
Akif, Mehmed, 70–71, 76–77
AKP (Justice and Development Party), 74, 89–92, 94–95, 151, 156
'Ali, 34–35, 54–55, 59–61, 154
Al-Ṣadr, Muhammad Bāqir, 48, 63, 65
altruism, 8f, 9. *See also* benevolence; charity; zakat
Amaeshi, Kenneth, 15
American hegemony, 68, 74, 86–87
And Once Again Abu-Dhar (Shariati), 59
"And Seek Their Council in the Matter" (Kemal), 134
An-Náim, Abdullahi Ahmed, 3, 22–26, 28, 48, 102, 109

antiausterity movement, 105
Anticapitalist Muslims movement, 91, 93–95
anti-imperialism, 76, 85–87, 157
Arab Barometer surveys, 14, 131, 137–141, 143–148, 150
Arab Spring: Arab Barometer surveys, 14, 131, 137–141, 143–148, 150; authoritarianism and, 138; conception of justice and, 132, 135–141, 156–157, 158; constitutionalism and, 130–132; economic injustice and, 137–138, 140–141, 140f; as evidence for desire for democracy, 2; outcomes of, 135–136, 150, 159; as part of history of democratic revolt, 5, 13–14; Revolution of Smiles in Algeria, 129; rulers response to, 38; Saleh in Egypt, 129; in Tunisia, 130; "You Stink" movement in Lebanon, 129. *See also individual movements*; protest behaviors
Association for Human Rights and Solidarity for the Oppressed (Mazlumder), 94–95

autocratic regimes: Arab Spring and, 138; benevolent, 10, 37–38, 42–43; collectivist orientations and, 111f, 112–113; distributive preferences and, 111f, 112–113; exploitation of charity value of, 43; obedience value and, 44; political justice trajectory and, 42–43; political preferences revealed in interviews and, 99–104; WVS data on support for, 113–114
Ayoob, Mohammed, 77

Baqir al-Sadr, Muhammad, 12
benevolence: Islamist justice theories and, 46, 62, 66; Qutb and, 66, 109; Shariati on, 58, 62–63, 66, 109; support for democracy and, 108–109; tendency toward democratic preference and, 9; as underpinning of social justice trajectory, 7, 43. See also charity; public interest
Boix, Carles, 43
Bouazizi, Mohamed, 2, 130, 136
Bulaç, Ali, 73, 75–76

capitalism, 54, 69, 86–87
charity, 8f, 9, 43, 46, 52–53, 62, 108. See also benevolence; public interest
Christianity, 6, 50, 110
circle of justice, 5, 38
civil war (first, A.D. 657). See succession crisis
Cold War, 68, 70. See also communism
colonialism, 17, 69, 130, 157
communism, 12, 50, 54–55, 72, 82, 85–87
Comte, Auguste, 16–17
constitutionalist movements: Arab Spring and, 130; encounters with West and, 130; ideas of Kemal and, 134–135; in Istanbul, 131; justice discourse and, 42, 132–136; in Ottoman Empire, 131–135; in Qajar Empire, 131; Urabi Revolt, 131, 133, 135
corruption, 93, 138–140, 139f, 142, 144, 145t, 147t, 148t, 150
counteressentialist scholarship, 11, 16–17, 20–21, 106, 134
Crone, Patricia, 34

Darling, Linda, 4–5, 132, 135
Davis, Nancy J., 108, 123–124
democracy: Arab-majority country support for, 2, 138; association with the West and, 102; collectivism and, 111f, 112–113; counteressentialist theories and, 11, 16–17, 20–21, 106, 134; cultural compatibility theory and, 15–16; dignity (*karama*) and, 3; distributive processes and, 126, 127t; early modernist Islamic scholars and, 20; essentialist approach to, 2, 11, 16–20, 23, 106; El Fadl and, 25–28; forbearance norms and, 10, 26, 31; free will/predestination dichotomy and support for, 110–111; Islamic values orientation and support for, 26, 106–107; justice discourse analysis and, 88–90; path to in West, 131; political justice trajectory and support for, 107, 109–112, 111f; political preferences revealed in interviews and, 99–104; rebellion against tyranny theme and, 131; religion vs. science data and, 124–126; religiosity and, 120, 123–124, 126, 153, 158–159; role of enlightenment values in, 16–17; scholarship of paths to democracy in Muslim majority countries, 22–25, 28; self-determinism and support for, 126, 127t, 128, 158; self-direction and, support for, 126, 127t, 128, 158; sharia and, 3, 126; source of government and, 25–27; WVS data on support for, 113–114, 118, 119t, 120–121, 122t
desert, 78, 96–97, 104
dignity (*karama*), 3
Directorate of Religious Affairs (Diyanet), 70
Durkheim, Émile, 17

economic distribution: Arab Spring and, 137–138; democracy and resolution of, 22; Industrial Revolution and, 6; Qutb's social justice theory and, 50; social justice trajectory and, 43; support for democracy and, 108–109. See also benevolence; public interest; welfare provision
Edip, Halide, 135
egalitarian policies, 43, 108–109, 121
Egypt, 5, 42, 48, 133, 135
Eliaçık, İhsan, 73, 83–84, 90, 93–94, 105
Emek ve Adalet, 90
Emre, Akif, 90, 94
Ennahda movement, 150
equality of men, 50–51, 96, 99

equality of opportunity, 96
Esposito, John, 21
essentialist scholarship, 2, 11, 16–20, 23, 106

El Fadl, Khaled Abou, 3–4, 25–28
Fanon, Frantz, 55
Farabi, Abu Nasr al-, 39–40
Filali-Ansary, Abdou, 8, 20
Finke, Roger, 124
fitna. See succession crisis
forbearance norms, 10, 26, 31, 40
freedom of conscience, 48, 50–51, 62–63, 66
free will: collectivist/individualistic cultural framework and, 109–110, 111f; contemporary Islamist movement activists and, 13; Islamic justice theories and, 48, 62, 66; as philosophical underpinning of political justice, 8f, 35–36, 154; political preferences and, 9, 41, 107, 110–111; succession crisis and historical discourse around, 9, 33–37, 48, 54, 58–61, 60, 69, 153–154; support for democracy and, 159; WVS and individualism data, 123

Gellner, Ernest, 17–18
Gezi Park protests (2013), 66, 90, 93–94, 105, 151
Ghannūshī, Rāshid al-, 12, 48, 63–64, 102, 150
globalization, 12, 68, 74, 82–83
Gülen Community, 64

Hamdi, Elmalılı, 70
Hashemi, Nader, 3, 23–25, 28
Hayreddin Pasha, 133
History of Social Justice and Political Power in the Middle East, A (Darling), 4–5
Hodgson, Marshall, 36, 94
Hoffman, Michael, 142, 146
human agency, 48, 50–53, 57–58, 62, 152. *See also* free will
Huntington, Samuel, 17, 19–20

Ibn Khaldun, 18, 40
Ibn Taymiyya, 7, 39–40, 77, 83
"institutional forbearance", 10. *See also* forbearance norms
interviews: association of democracy with the West and, 102; conceptions of justice revealed by, 96–99, 104; justice and Islam in, 98; methodology, 4, 6, 12–13, 95–99, 153; political preferences and justice conceptions in, 99–104; skepticism about systems of governance, 99–104; themes of, 95–96, 104; and WVS data, 123

In the Shade of the Quran (Qutb), 49
Iqbal, Muhammad, 20–21
Iran, 37, 44, 100, 131–133
Iranian Revolution, 7, 37, 72, 132
Islam: autocratic tendencies and values of, 3, 8f; democratic tendencies and values of, 2–3, 8f; essentialist approach to democracy and, 2; Gellner's high and low, 18; Islamist justice theory's approach to, 46–47; Kedourie's enlightened absolutism theory, 18; Lewis's historical approach, 19; native democratic theories and, 2; positivist philosophy and, 16–17; Shariati's understanding of, 55; views on antithesis to progress and, 16–17
Islamic scholarship: essentialist, 2, 11, 16–20; El Fadl's focus on justice, 25–27on paths to democracy in Muslim-majority countries, 22–25
Islamic scripture, 25–26, 39, 48. *See also* Muhammad
Islamism: anti-imperialism and, 76–77; defining, 75–78; as nonreactive, 76–77. *See also* Islamist journals; Islamist justice theories; Turkish Islamism
Islamist journals: American hegemony and, 12, 68, 74; book's use of, 4, 6, 87; definitions of justice and, 67; discourse analysis method and, 12, 68–70; during Cold War, 12, 67; globalization and, 12, 68, 74; neoliberalism and, 12, 68, 85; political justice trajectory and, 11–12; social justice trajectory and, 11–12; Turkish Islamism's use of, 73–74. *See also* justice discourse analysis
Islamist justice theories: An-Náim and, 48; comparisons of, 64–65; freedom of conscience and, 63; free will and, 46, 63; private property and, 61; schism of early prophetic community and, 60–61; social justice as praxis and, 48, 52–55, 63; tawhid and, 63. *See also* Qutb, Sayyid; Shariati, 'Ali
Islam, Secularism, and Liberal Democracy (Hashemi), 23
Istanbul Think House, 95

Jabrī school, 35, 110
Jamal, Amaney, 142, 146
jawr (tyranny), 33
just government, 83–84, 87
justice (*al-'adl*): Abdelkader's work and, 4; Arab Spring and conceptions of, 132, 135–141, 151; concept of divine justice, 33; contemporary Islamist movement activists and, 13; counteressentialist scholarship and role of, 11, 20; El Fadl's treatment of, 3–4, 25–27; and foundation of democratic ideal, 3; historical origins of conception of, 5, 9, 33–37, 48, 54, 58–61, 60, 69, 153–154; interviews and themes of, 81–82, 95–99, 104; political justice dimension, 6–7, 8f; political preference and, 8f; primacy of shaping Muslim political attitudes, 3, 32, 152, 157; religious roots of, 5; role of in Islamic faith, 1; semantics of, 33; social activism and, 92; social justice dimension, 7–8, 8f; trajectories of, 6, 8f; Western development of concept of, 6. *See also* political justice trajectory; social justice trajectory
justice discourse analysis: advantages of with regard to Turkish Islamism, 69–70; American hegemony and, 68, 86–88; anti-imperialism in, 85–87, 157; communism and, 82, 85–87; democracy in, 88–90; equality and rights and, 82; globalization and, 82–83, 88; just government/just state theme in, 83–84, 87; methodology, 78, 79f, 80; myriad of voices in Turkish Islamism, 74–75; political reform theme in, 83–85; schematic of analysis, 80f; social order theme and, 63, 83–85, 87; sociopolitical context for Turkish Islamism, 69–74, 82, 88; sources of, 67–68; Turkish journals and sources for, 78, 79f, 80; *zulüm/zulm* (oppression) in, 81–82
Justice Interrupted (Thompson), 5
justice state theory (Eliaçık), 84
just testimony, 99

Kara, İsmail, 70, 75–77
Karakoç, Sezai, 71–72
Karl, Terry Lynn, 22
Kedourie, Elie, 17–18
Kemal, Namık, 17, 31, 76, 134–135, 141
Khadduri, Majid, 7, 37–38

khalifa (men as God's viceregent): al-Ṣadr and, 63; connection to concept of justice and, 32; democracy and, 20, 25, 159; Ghannūshī and, 63–64; Islamist justice theory and, 46–47, 54; Kemal's ideas and, 134; political preferences, 42; succession crisis, 110; themes of in interviews, 99
Khanani, Ahmed, 3
Kharijites, 31, 34–35, 98
Kısakürek, Necip Fazıl, 71–72, 77
Koçi Bey, 39
Kuru, Ahmet, 8, 39

Labor and Justice Platform, 91, 93
law: in Cold War-era Turkey, 70; equality under, 96; Islamic jurisprudential theory, 8, 39; medieval, 43; pluralistic framework and, 3; Qutb and, 52, 54, 61; Shariati's approach to, 61; social justice trajectory and, 40
Levitsky, Steven, 10
Lewis, Bernard, 18–19, 132
liberation theology, 6, 55

March, Andrew, 3
Marwani caliphs, 36
Marx, Karl, 17, 55
Mawdudi, Abu al-A'la, 31, 48, 63, 65, 72, 102
mazalim courts, 30
Menchik, Jeremy, 3
Meşrutiyet, 133
methodology: Arab Barometer surveys, 14, 131, 137–141, 143–148, 150, 153; interviews, 4, 6, 12–13, 95–99, 153; Islamist journal survey, 4, 6, 12, 153; public-opinion surveys, 4, 6, 12, 153; World Values Surveys (WVS), 13, 113–118, 119t, 120–121, 122t, 153
Milestones (Qutb), 48
Mongol invasion, 7, 38, 41, 69, 155
Moore, Barrington, Jr., 131
Mu'āwiya, 34, 54–55, 59–60, 154
Muhammad: benevolence and, 109; on equality of men, 51; on justice, 157; political struggle with al-Ma'mūn, 22; Shariati's depiction of, 59; succession of, 6–7, 33–37, 60–61, 154; zakat and, 108
Murad IV (Sultan of Ottoman Empire), 39
Muslim Brothers (Egypt), 48
Muslims: development of justice conceptions for, 32–34; interpretations of Muslim values by, 2; obedience of

the ruled and, 53; political preferences of devout, 101; skepticism of modernity from colonizing West, 20, 22; "way of life" (din) approach to, 47. See also interviews; protest behavior
Muslims' Initiative against the Violence toward Women, 94

National Order Party, 89
neoliberalism, 12, 68, 73, 85–87
Nursi, Said, 12, 48, 63–65, 70, 84

On the Perfect State (Farabi), 39
Orientalism, 17, 47
Ottoman Empire, 39, 69, 76, 131–133
Ottomanism, 71

Pitlik, Hans, 115–116
political accountability, 25, 31, 41
political justice trajectory: Arab Spring and, 140–141; collectivist/individualistic cultural framework and, 109–110, 111f; early Islamic political struggle and, 107; *ethicalist* vs. *realist* vision of power and, 36; free will/predestination dichotomy, 110–111; historical nature of focus of, 32; historical roots of, 33–37, 107; Islamist justice theory and, 48; political preferences and, 11–12, 41–43, 107, 109–112, 111f, 152–153, 155–156; rebellion vs. obedience dichotomies and, 36–37
political struggle: circle of justice concept and, 5, 38; democracy and resolution of, 22; political Islamists of twentieth century and, 24; role of religion in, 22–24; succession of Muhammed and, 5–7, 9, 32, 33–37, 48, 54, 58–61, 60, 69, 153–154
popular sovereignty, 25, 35, 41–42, 64, 110
power relations, 96–97
predestination: collectivist/individualistic cultural framework and, 110; contemporary Islamist movement activists and, 13; legitimization of authoritarianism and, 42; as philosophical underpinning of political justice, 8f, 154; political preferences and, 9, 41, 110–111; succession crisis and historical discourse around, 9, 33–37, 48, 54, 58–61, 60, 69, 153–154
private property, 19, 61, 65
protest behavior: antiausterity movement and, 105; Arab Spring and, 13–14, 31, 129–130; Batman protestor, 105; corruption and, 138–140, 139f, 142, 144, 145t, 147t, 148t, 150; distributive preferences, 146; economic pessimism and, 140, 144, 147f, 148f, 150; Gezi Park protests (2013), 66, 90, 93–94, 105, 151; Kharijites, 31; Koran readership, 145t, 146; Ottoman constitutionalists and, 31; outcomes of, 135–136, 150, 159; political access and, 144, 145t, 147–148, 147f, 148f; political justice concerns and, 42, 141–142, 147, 150; political trust and, 138, 139f, 142, 144, 147f, 148f, 150; religiosity and, 31, 141–142, 144, 145t, 146–149, 147f, 148f, 149, 150–151, 153; social justice concerns and, 141–142, 144, 145t, 147, 147f, 150; support for democracy and, 105–106; unemployment and, 142, 144, 145t, 147t, 148f; Urabi Revolt, 131, 133, 135. See also Arab Spring
public interest (maṣlaḥa): circle of justice concept and, 38; as early manifestation of the social justice trajectory, 7–8, 37; forbearance norms and, 10, 31; goals of Islamic law and, 31; medieval era and, 43, 155; obedience to rulers and, 9; as philosophical underpinning of social justice, 8f; political preference and, 107; and support for authoritarian rule, 38; support for democracy and, 108. See also benevolence; charity
public-opinion surveys. See Arab Barometer surveys; World Values Surveys (WVS)

Qadarī School, 35, 98
Qutb, Sayyid: avoidance of religious/secular dichotomy and, 47; benevolence and, 66, 109; charitable acts and, 12; criticism of Western societies and, 49; economic distribution and, 50, 53–54; focus of just political order, 12; golden age early prophetic community as model, 48, 54, 60; grounding of political justice in doctrine and, 31, 48; human agency and, 48, 50–52; influence of Islamist thought, 63; Muslim Brothers and, 48; private property and, 61; response to communist/capitalist systems of Cold War and, 49; social justice as praxis and, 48, 52–55; tawhid (unity) principle and social justice theory of, 48–50, 54; translation into Turkish and, 71–72; works of, 48–49

Ramadan, Tariq, 28
Reflections of a Concerned Muslim on the Plight of Oppressed People, The (Shariati), 59
religion: collectivist/individualistic cultural framework and, 110; political norms and, 25; political preferences and, 114–115, 118, 120, 123–124, 128; reform movements and, 23–24; role of in democratic state, 22–23
Renan, Ernest, 17
rizq (provision), 51
Robinson, James A., 43
Robinson, Robert V., 108, 123–124
Rode, Martin, 115–116
rule of law, 5, 25–26
rulers: ʿaqd (contract) with people and, 26; aspirations to justice, 30; benevolent dictators, 10, 37–38, 42–43, 112, 156; circle of justice concept and, 38; constraint of by religious norms, 10; Farabi on, 39–40; forbearance norms and maṣlaḥa, 10; goals of Islamic law and, 30–31; mirrors for princes and, 40; principle of rebellion against unjust, 36; Qutb on, 53; response to Arab Spring of, 38; social justice and just, 37, 83; social justice and obedience to, 9; succession crisis and obedience to, 110

Sachedina, Abdulaziz, 28
Saleh, Alaa, 129, 136
Saudi Arabia, 100
Schmitter, Philippe C., 22
science, 16, 58, 76, 124–126
sectarianism. *See* succession crisis
secularism, 22–24
secular state model, 22–24
servitude (*kulluk*), 98
sharia: benevolence and, 108; communitarian outlook and, 123–124; El Fadl's treatment of, 26; independent body of legislation (*qānūn*) and, 32; Qutb's justice theory and, 62; secular state model and, 23; WVS data and, 123–126
Shariati, ʿAli: avoidance of religious/secular dichotomy and, 47; benevolence and, 58, 62–63, 66, 109; Cain and Abel story and, 56, 61; charity and, 108; dialectical approach of, 55–56, 59, 77; *ensan* vs. *bashar*, 57, 60; four prisons and, 57–58, 66; golden age early prophetic community as model, 48, 58–61; grounding of political justice in doctrine and, 31, 37, 48; human agency/free will focus and, 12, 48, 57–58, 60; influence of Islamist thought, 63; influences of, 55; private property and, 61; social justice as praxis and, 48, 58–60; tawhid (unity) principle and, 48, 55–57, 59–60; translation into Turkish of, 72
Shia political theory, 7, 36, 81
Shia-Sunni schism. *See* succession crisis
shirk (polytheism), 55–56, 59, 61, 103
shūrā (consultation), 20–21, 26–27
social activism, 91–95, 101
socialism, 51, 55, 69
Social Justice in Islam (Abdelkader), 4
Social Justice in Islam (Qutb), 48–49
social justice paradigm, 39, 155
social justice trajectory: Arab Spring and, 140–141; during medieval period, 7, 32; forbearance norms and, 40; historical nature of focus of, 32; historical roots of, 37–41; implications for how rulers are viewed, 37–38; Islamist justice theory and, 48; Koran readership and, 145t, 146; modern prodemocracy movements and, 31; political preferences and, 11, 41, 43–44, 107–109, 152–153, 155–156; public interest and, 7–8, 8f; renewal of religion in contact with West, 32; social justice paradigm, 39; social order theme in justice discourse analysis, 83; support for democracy and, 107–109; theory of Ibn Taymiyya and, 39
social order, 68, 83–85, 87, 89
Social Origins of Dictatorship and Democracy (Moore), 131
Soviet Union, 85–86
Stark, Rodney, 124
succession crisis (of Muhammad), 5, 9, 33–37, 48, 54, 58–61, 60, 69, 110, 153–154
Sufi orders, 70, 72–73
Sunni political theory, 36, 81

Tabatabaʾi, Muhammad Husayn, 133
Tanzimat reforms, 39, 133
tawhid (unity principle), 20–21; connection to concept of justice and, 32; justice

discourse analysis and, 82; justice state theory (Eliaçık) and, 84; Qutb's Islamic justice theory and, 48–51, 54, 62, 84; Shariati's Islamic justice theory and, 48, 55–57, 59–62, 84

Thompson, Elizabeth, 5, 132, 135

Tobacco Protest (1890–1891), 37, 133

Topçu, Nurettin, 71–72

Transparency International, 139

True Path Party, 73

Turkey: Committee on Union and Progress, 64; Democratic Party, 71; Directorate of Religious Affairs (Diyanet), 70; February 28 intervention (1997), 73; Gezi Park protests (2013), 66, 90, 93–94, 105, 151; Kemalist project, 70; military coup of 1980, 72; Ottomanism, 71; shifts in rebellion-obedience dichotomies in Islamist movements, 37; sociopolitical evolution of Islamism in, 69–74; transition to democracy of, 71; Turkism, 71. *See also* Islamist journals; Turkish Islamism

Turkish Islamism: AKP (Justice and Development Party), 74, 85, 89–92, 151, 156; Anticapitalist Muslims, 91, 93–95; Association for Human Rights and Solidarity for the Oppressed (Mazlumder), 94–95; constitution of 1961! and, 71; defining, 75–76; degeneration of youth and, 72; emerging groups opposed to AKP and, 90, 93–95; global Islamism vs., 77; historical changes in, 69; Istanbul Think House, 95; journal publishing sources and, 78; Labor and Justice Platform, 91, 93–95; Muslimism vs., 90, 94; Muslims' Initiative against the Violence toward Women, 94; myriad voices in, 74–75; nationalism and, 70–72; National Order Party, 89; Ottoman state and, 71; reemergence of in 1960s, 71; social activism and, 91–93; sociopolitical context of, 69–74; True Path Party, 73; Welfare Party, 73–74, 89. *See also* Islamism

Türköne, Mümtazer, 76

'Umar, Caliph, 30, 54–55, 59–60, 83

Umayyad Empire: *ethicalist* vs. *realist* vision of power and, 36; Islamist justice theory and, 60; *jamā'a* model and, 36; justice discourses and, 69; Shariati and, 60–61

Umayyad family, 54, 59

United Arab Emirates, 38

Urabi, Ahmad, 135

Urabi Revolt (Egypt, 1879–1882), 5, 42, 131, 133, 135

'Uthmān, 54–55, 60–61

Voll, John L., 21

Wahhabi scholars, 38

Wallerstein, Immanuel, 77

"way of life" (*din*), 47

Weber, Max, 17, 110

Weedon, C., 68

Welfare Party, 73–74, 89

welfare provision, 38, 43, 109, 155. *See also* benevolence; public interest

World Values Surveys (WVS): distributive preferences data and, 114–115, 117f; individualistic value orientation data and, 114–117, 123; religion vs. science data, 124–126; religiosity data and, 114–115, 124–126, 127t; self-determination data, 126, 127t, 128; self-direction data, 126, 127t, 128; sharia and, 123–126; statistical analysis and, 118, 119t, 120–121, 122t; support for democracy and, 13, 106, 114

Worldview of Tawhid (Shariati), 55

Yavuz, M. Hakan, 71

zakat, 52, 85, 108. *See also* charity

Ziblatt, Daniel, 10

zulüm/zulm (oppression), 81–82, 97–98, 104

Sabri Ciftci is a Professor of Political Science and Michael W. Suleiman Chair at Kansas State University.

www.ingramcontent.com/pod-product-compliance
Lightning Source LLC
Chambersburg PA
CBHW030135240426
43672CB00005B/142